THE GOOD LIFE

Truths That Last
in Times of Need

PETER J. GOMES

HarperSanFrancisco
A Division of HarperCollinsPublishers

Permissions credits appear on page 374 and constitute a continuation of this copyright page.

Grateful acknowledgment is made for the following permissions:

Excerpt from "Little Gidding" in *Four Quartets*. Copyright © 1942 by T.S. Eliot and renewed in 1970 by Esme Valerie Eliot, reprinted with the permission of Harcourt, Inc. and Faber and Faber Ltd.

Excerpt from *The Book of Virtues* by William J. Bennett. Copyright © 1995 by William J. Bennett, reprinted with the permission of Simon & Schuster, Inc.

Excerpt from *Letters and Papers From Prison, Revised, Enlarged Edition* by Dietrich Bonhoeffer. Copyright © 1953, 1967, 1971 by SCM Press Ltd., reprinted with the permission of Simon & Schuster, Inc.

Excerpt from "Obituary for The Reverend Ernest Gordon." Copyright © 2002 by the New York Times Co., reprinted with permission.

Scripture quotations marked "NKJV" are taken from the New King James Version. Copyright © 1982 by Thomas Nelson, Inc, used with permission. All rights reserved.

All biblical quotations, unless otherwise noted, are taken from the Revised Standard Version, © 1952, by the Division of Christian Education of the National Council of the Churches of Christ in the United States of America.

HarperCollins Web site: http://www.harpercollins.com
HarperCollins®, ■®, and HarperSanFrancisco™ are trademarks of HarperCollins Publishers, Inc.

FIRST HarperCollins PAPERBACK EDITION
PUBLISHED IN 2003
Designed by Joseph Rutt

Library of Congress Cataloging-in-Publication Data has been ordered
ISBN 0–06–000076–7 (paperback)

04 05 06 RRD(H) 10 9 8 7 6 5 4 3 2

To
Nathan Marsh Pusey, A.B., 1928
(1907–2001)
Twenty-fourth President of Harvard University
(1953–1971)

and to

Robert Alexander Kennedy Runcie, D.D.
(1921–2000)
102nd Archbishop of Canterbury and Primate of All England
(1980–1991)

From generation to generation, passing into holy souls,
wisdom maketh men friends of God and prophets.
THE WISDOM OF SOLOMON 7:27 (KJV),
Apocrypha

CONTENTS

ACKNOWLEDGMENTS

In the writing of a book there are many obligations. The proper attribution of sources, of which I have consulted many, I have endeavored to make in the notes at the end of the book. Those I have directly quoted I have cited as thoroughly as possible, and where I have appropriated ideas or paraphrased the original thoughts of others I have also sought to give appropriate citation. Where I have misquoted or misattributed I make profound apologies and will make necessary corrections and acknowledgments in subsequent printings and editions: in every instance I have tried to give full credit where credit is due. I will be grateful for any corrections in quotations or attributions that readers may care to direct to me.

Among the many to whom personal thanks are extended I include my colleagues on the staff of The Memorial Church, with particular reference to my executive assistant, Janetta Cothran Randolph, who protected me from the ravages of my own schedule in order that I might complete the manuscript, and Daniel Ayers Sanks, my senior colleague, whose wise counsel and support in this effort I greatly appreciate. I wish to thank my literary agent, John Taylor "Ike" Williams, who always knew when to speak and when to keep silent; Stephen W. Hanselman, my editor and publisher at Harper San Francisco, whose faith in this work and patience with me heartened me in many a bleak hour; and Fred Hills, whose encouragement of this project in an earlier incarnation was a significant incentive to complete the book in this form.

My thanks go also to the many who wished me well over the long tenure of this project, and to my students Seth Wilbur Moulton and James Joseph Meeks, who helped far more than they knew. I thank all of those who refrained from asking awkward questions at inopportune times, and all of those who wished me well in silence and prayed that I would be delivered from the burden of great expectations. This book was written in the full throttle of Term, and not on the benefit of a sabbatical leave of absence or on the grant of any foundation or eleemosynary institution, and so I thank all of those who endured my spasms of writing, reading, and research: I could not have completed this task without their sympathetic understanding.

Finally, as in all of my books and other writings, I wish to thank my superb editor, Cynthia Wight Rossano, a true professional in the literary arts, whose competence and devotion have brought this manuscript to pass. Without her there would be no book.

Such errors, infelicities, and misinterpretations as may appear herein are entirely my responsibility. I have attempted much, and in my ambition my reach may have exceeded my grasp. For what I have failed to do, or have done badly, I ask the reader's forgiveness and indulgence. For what has worked, thanks be to God.

For growth in virtue the important thing is
to be silent and work.
ST. JOHN OF THE CROSS

Peter J. Gomes
Sparks House
Cambridge, Massachusetts
February 2002

INTRODUCTION

We shall not cease from exploration
And the end of all our exploring
Will be to arrive where we started
And know the place for the first time.
T. S. ELIOT, "LITTLE GIDDING"

A book about the good life in these early years of the twenty-first century can easily be obsessed with the American sense of material success that is tantamount to excess. On January 20, 2002, the *New York Times* carried a story in its Sunday Styles section under the titillating headline "Can a Kid Squeeze by on $320,000 a Month?" The story, under the byline of Alex Kuczynski, began:

> The tale of Lisa Bonder Kerkorian, the 36-year-old former tennis pro who is demanding $320,000 a month in child support from her former husband, the 84-year-old billionaire Kirk Kerkorian, has caused a stir among hard-working Americans.

As well it might. Among the things desired for the three-year-old child of their union is $14,000 per month for parties and play dates, and:

> $5,900 for eating out; $4,300 for eating in; $2,500 for movies and other outings; $7,000 for charitable donations; $1,400 for laundry

and cleaning; $1,000 for toys, books, and videos; $436 for the care of Kira's bunny rabbit and other pets; and $144,000 for travel on private jets.[1]

This was just the opening paragraph in a feature on child-rearing excess in California, where money appears to be no object, or at least not to the father of the child in question. In her court papers, Mrs. Kerkorian said of her former husband: "Money was never a limitation, or even a consideration, when Kirk wanted to either construct, acquire, own, charter, hire, or pay for such desires as homes, airplanes, yachts, hotels, cars, staff, or entertainment. . . . Essentially, whatever Kirk wanted, Kirk got."

On reconsideration of the size of her demands, Mrs. Kerkorian determined that she hadn't asked for enough; her lawyer said, "We forgot the category for major yacht charters." This story apparently generated a hefty correspondence in the local press, including some not infrequent comparisons to Marie Antoinette, whose ideas of the good life cost both herself and her unfortunate husband, Louis XVI, their heads.

That was then, however, and this is now, and no such drastic action is likely to be taken in the land where excess has come to be seen as normal. The fact that one such story was regarded as news, though, eliciting a sense of moral outrage and social indignation, suggests that most people are still able to distinguish between the quality and the quantity of what appears to make life good. This story, and so many thousands of others like it, provides the contemporary context for a discussion not only about greed and envy, but also about what it takes to make modern people happy. The search for the good life, which so often is defined in terms of "things" and the means to get as many "things" as possible, has turned into a dead end as more and more people have more and more. Not just Californian culture but American culture in general has produced the richest, most indulged society in history, putting ancient Rome and prerevolutionary eighteenth-century France to shame.

The Midas culture, however, has not produced the happiness or joy that it would have appeared to have promised. Most of the enormous wealth seems to end up in the hands of lawyers designed to protect it or, increasingly, in the hands of the pharmaceutical companies whose drugs monitor the anxieties, paranoias, and neuroses of those who thought that money was the only medicine they needed. Meanwhile we live in a land of fractured families, poisoned personal relationships, unfulfilling work, disloyal corporations, fragile self-esteem, and social distrust. Our public life seems riven by one scandal after another, from O. J. to Monica to Enron, and our private lives punctuated by a sense of fragility and drift. In the land that invented the "talk show," we seem to have less and less worth saying to say to one another. In the land whose Constitution guarantees the pursuit of happiness, we seem terribly unhappy. In the land whose founding metaphor was the mutuality of John Winthrop's seventeenth-century vision of a "city set on a hill," we live more and more in estranged, hostile, exclusive enclaves, linked only by the anonymity of the Internet and the destructive, dumbed-down medium of television, a "vast and vacuous wasteland" that Newton Minnow, who coined the phrase in the medium's infancy, could never in his worst nightmare have imagined.

Yet, in the midst of this bleak, lunar-like landscape where, in the words of George Bernard Shaw nearly a century ago, "All our progress is but improved means to unimproved ends," there has been a small chorus of people—many of them, surprisingly enough, young people—which suggests that there must be a better way. Surely the whole history of the world has not led to this moment when we can regard as an entitlement for the good life $320,000 per month for the care, feeding, and diversion of a three-year-old girl in California?

This book could easily have been just another jeremiad on the moral poverty of our times, and such books are easy to write, for all one needs to do for data is to read the newspapers, watch television, and listen to "talk radio." I have been moved to a different course of action, however, inspired largely by my daily exposure to college students in a great university during the course of a preaching and teaching ministry that has now extended over thirty years. Often we are tempted to write off college students as simply people-in-waiting for what we presume to call "real life"; and it has long been an important spectator sport to denigrate the colleges and universities of the land, where such students are found, as places of privilege, indolence, and irrelevance to that "real world" against which they stand in conspicuous comparison. What has impressed me, however, about these young people during several generations, but most particularly in this most recent one, is not their intellectual ability, despite the fact that on balance they are probably smarter than their parents were at the same age; nor their boundless energy and the varying zeals, which still manage to confound their elders, who, although they may not be as smart, do by dint of time and experience know more than they do. No, what has impressed me is their moral curiosity, their desire to know, to be, and to do good.

This is all the more intriguing to me because in so many ways, purposely and inadvertently, this generation of young people has been cut off from its own moral tradition, deprived of a tradition of virtue, leaving it both stranded and unsatisfied in a cultural environment that has neither limits nor ends, nor center. What is impressive about these young people is that for the most part they know this. They sense their own drift. They know that the traditional sources of guidance—family, church, school, and state—are all themselves in some disarray, and they are intelligent enough not to believe that true happiness is to be found in the culture of materialism and sensual diversion that is ceaselessly thrust upon them in their role as passionate consumers.

Some time ago, in those generational revolts that periodically roil the culture, young people determined that they wanted neither their father's Oldsmobile nor their mother's career. Certainly, they wanted the advantages of the freedoms won for them by the labors and struggles of earlier generations, for they do not intend to flock back to settle in Mayberry RFD; June and Ward Cleaver are not countercultural icons. Young people want and deserve something better: they want a good life, true happiness, and a chance to do something worth doing. They want to be able to live their lives and to offer them, if necessary, for something worthy of sacrifice and service; and they want to live so as to leave the world a better place than the mess that they have inherited. Despite the poverty of our educational system and our almost suicidal deprecation of anything that has preceded our small moment on the stage, these young people have a hint and a suspicion that, somewhere in the reaches of human history, other people may well have asked the same questions that animate them, questions of value, meaning, and worth. It is for such as these that I have written this book.

Were I alone in this enterprise, I would take consolation in the preacherly conceit of the "voice crying in the wilderness," of those grim parsons and mordant cynics of another age such as William Ralph Inge, the so-called gloomy dean of St. Paul's, who saw the moral poverty of 1920s London and named it for what it was; H. L. Mencken, whose scabrous commentary defrocked middle-class American values in the 1920s; and Reinhold Niebuhr, whose hard-headed neo-orthodox theology punctured the self-satisfied American piety of prosperity in the 1940s and 1950s. I share neither their anger nor their pessimism. They knew all about what philosopher Martha Nussbaum, in quite another connection, calls the "fragility of goodness," and many of the young people with whom I work and to whom I speak know the same thing.

There is more to goodness than this, however. I began my ministry at Harvard in 1970, when it seemed that the generations were no longer on speaking terms with one another, and that anything that had been received was by definition suspect and even complicit in the well-documented breakdown of social and civil discourse. Colleges no longer dared to think *in loco parentis* (on behalf of the parents); and although the subsequently liberated individuals were free to do as they pleased, institutions were now expected to behave morally and to "do the right thing" without impinging in any way upon the rights and liberties of individuals. I watched the development of the fields of moral reasoning and values clarification and the development of the case method for the discussion of ethics in professional schools; and all the while I watched the young people who were subject to these new endeavors ask, "What's in it for me?" It was an increasingly loud *cri de coeur*: "What do I need to be good? How can I be truly happy? To whom or to what dare I give my ultimate loyalty, my deepest love, my full and total service? Out of all of this moral discourse and analysis, what can I find and use to make a life, and not just a living?"

Once upon a time it was the perceived purpose of colleges not simply to secure jobs for their graduates, but, rather, in the now antique-sounding 1901 words of Harvard's President Charles William Eliot, "to cultivate within each of you young men and women the durable values and satisfactions of life." It seems that just as institutions withdrew from preaching and teaching those values—under the self-serving rubric of noninterference in anything other than the purely academic life of the young—students increasingly seemed to demand and expect that very thing from them.

Two recent books have given me encouragement in my own book. The first, *Moral Freedom: The Search for Virtue in a World of Choice*, by Alan Wolfe, of Boston University, emerged in 2001 to very good reviews. "Once upon a time," he writes, "Americans raised families without being able to know whether their children would turn out to be good or bad. Now they raise children uncertain about what good and bad actually are." Wolfe, a sociologist and not a preacher, is addicted to data, not to doctrine. Yet in his rather extensive research, conducted with a variety of respondents throughout an equally diverse range of American population centers, he concluded that Americans are not running away from morality and virtue, but are exercising what he calls their "moral freedom" to adapt what could easily be seen as fixed abstractions to the ever changing demands and experiences of modern life. Character is an issue for many of the moderns Wolfe interviewed. In his chapter "The Moral Philosophy of Americans," he notes:

> Many of our respondents find themselves more comfortable with the language of psychology than they do with the language of sin. But this hardly means that character is dead. . . . Our respondents are not so much rejecting character as they are asking for new ways to form it that are compatible with a generally positive view of human potential.[2]

The very phrase "moral freedom" sounds a bit anarchic and dispensing with order, tradition, and discipline, but that is not so, says Wolfe:

> None of this means that our respondents tend to be opposed to discipline or think that there is something wrong with upholding absolute standards of right and wrong. It is more about the way messages ought to be delivered than it is about the messages themselves.[3]

What twenty-first century Americans want is the right to make up their own moral minds, and this means freedom to take seriously both the sacred and the profane theories of value, virtue, and the moral good. It can even be argued, as Wolfe does argue it, that moral freedom, as he has observed and defined it, takes more moral work than simple blind obedience to a fixed and absolute code. He writes:

> Moral freedom involves the sacred as well as the profane; it is freedom over the things that matter most. The ultimate implication of the idea of moral freedom is not that people are created in the image of a higher authority. It is instead that any form of higher authority has to tailor its commandments to the needs of real people.[4]

I have not yet read the second book, but the two reviews that have just crossed my desk whet my appetite: one in the *Spectator* of January 2002, and the other in the *New Statesman* of January 28, 2002. Written by Andre Comté-Sponville, translated by Catherine Temerson, and published by William Heinemann, the book was a runaway best-seller in France; in English it goes by the title *A Short Treatise on the Great Virtues: The Uses of Philosophy in Everyday Life*. In his review in the *New Statesman*, Edward Skidelsky notes that one no longer expects from the formal discipline of philosophy anything either readable or useful to the general public. I can testify to this, not out of the old enmity between theology and philosophy, but out of the sad anecdotal experiences of students who have said that they came to study philosophy—which in their naiveté they thought would teach them about the true, the good, and the beautiful—only to discover that most philosophers, both in small liberal arts colleges and in great research universities, spend most of their time talking to one another in a language nobody understands about subjects in which nobody is interested. Just as the public seems to be continually more interested in the great questions of life, meaning, being, and doing, the academic philosophers seem less interested and even less capable of helping with the answers. Few professionals in the field seem to want to speak to those whom they perceive to be the "great unwashed," lest their credentials as experts be compromised; and so it is left to popularizers, clergy, and laity to fill in the gaps, to the horror of the professionals. Thus, in his review, Skidelsky calls *A Short Treatise on the Great Virtues* "that rare thing, a work of philosophy that is both readable and good." Of its fourteen-month stay on the French best-seller list Skidelsky says:

A long time, even in a country famous for celebrating its philosophers. Its popularity is easy to understand. Andre Comté-Sponville writes clean, lapidary prose, very much in the manner of the classical French *moralistes*. He manages to be precise, scholastic even, yet also passionate—a combination unfamiliar in England, where precision is associated with aridity, and passion with vagueness. This is the way French philosophy used to be written before it was corrupted by Derrida and the rest.

Contrary to the views of much of modern philosophy, *A Short Treatise* understands virtue as the pursuit of wisdom. It discusses eighteen virtues beginning with politeness and including fidelity, prudence, temperance, courage, justice, generosity, compassion, mercy, gratitude, humility, simplicity, tolerance, purity, gentleness, good faith, humor, and love. Reflections on these virtues are not organized around some grand unifying theory, but concern what these qualities are and how they contribute to the wisdom, goodness, and happiness of a good everyday life. Systematic thinkers and so-called virtue mavens will hate it, and professional philosophers "will wince," says Skidelsky; but ordinary people, mystified by philosophy and theology and suspicious of street-corner gurus, yet desperate to find some guide to life in the midst of their moral perplexity, will love it. This is the sort of instruction in moral philosophy that was once routinely given by the presidents of American colleges to students in their senior year as the required course to cap the liberal arts career. Comté-Sponville recognizes the intellectual conflict in the tradition between Christian self-abnegation and classical self-assertion, and yet does not seem eager to provide the great synthesis. This is probably the key to the book's success: people want moral help and, happily, he has given it to them.

The Good Life: Truths That Last in Times of Need is an effort to do in English at least part of what Comté-Sponville has done so well in French. I do it, however, as a Christian, and I rely upon the great tradition of moral instruction that the West has received from Aristotle through that Christian tradition. The book is organized into three parts.

Part I addresses what I call "the search for noble purpose," and here I was inspired by the student address given by my friend and former pupil Seth Wilbur Moulton at the 2001 Harvard Commencement. I felt he spoke for the generations of young men and women whom I have come to know as moral pilgrims in search of a great purpose. In Part II I speak of the considerations that must be given to the elements of failure and success, freedom and discipline, in the construction of one's moral life in search of goodness; and in Part III I offer a discussion of the four cardinal virtues of prudence, justice, temperance, and fortitude, and the three great theological virtues of faith, hope, and love. My sources are drawn from the Bible, from the classical tradition, and from Christian theology. In every case I have tried to relate the traditional discussions of the virtues, inspired more often than not by Roman Catholic moral philosophy, to the contemporary moment, honoring, while aiding, I hope, the "moral freedom" of my readers to construct for themselves a good life with truths that last in times of need. For the fact that these conversations are often episodic, homiletic, eclectic, and even preachy, I do not apologize; and if my own personal story intrudes too much, it is only because I believe that both teaching and preaching are fundamentally autobiographical, not in the sense that it is "my" story that counts, but in the sense that "my" story may be a useful footnote to "the" story, and even of some relevance to "your" story.

I dedicate this book to two men whose lives have been to me shining examples of how to live the good life. Nathan Marsh Pusey was the twenty-fourth president of Harvard and the man who gave me my diploma in 1968 and, in 1970, my first appointment in The Memorial Church. For the thirty-one years of his life that coincided with my ministry in the church and university that he loved, he was to me the example of the Christian scholar and gentleman. As the first Pusey Minister in The Memorial Church, I proudly bear his name as if it were my own. His steadfast friendship, counsel, and example over these many years has placed me forever in his debt; and it was from him that

I learned the most important of all lessons: "If you would learn virtue, study the lives of virtuous men."

Robert Alexander Kennedy Runcie was the 102nd Archbishop of Canterbury and Primate of All England. At his funeral in the abbey and cathedral church of St. Albans in July 2000, it was said that the Church of England would never see his like again. I do not doubt it, and I know that I shall never again have such a good and faithful friend as he. We met when I invited him to deliver some lectures at Harvard in 1986, when he was at the full zenith of his powers, and a friendship formed that lasted and flourished until his death. Frequently he was my house guest in Cambridge, Massachusetts, when he came to preach at Harvard, and I visited him often in England. It is said that he had the gift of making everybody and anybody feel as though they were his best and most intimate friend; and so he did with me, and for it I will ever be grateful. I regard our friendship as one of the greatest blessings of my life. In a demanding and unforgiving time, Lord Runcie made an art of living with integrity and style the difficult Christian life, and he made it look easy, and certainly desirable. My last conversation with him was within a few weeks of his death, when I went to ask him if I might dedicate this long-contemplated book to him. "I'm not sure it will do you any good, my name in your book," he said, "but for what it is worth, it is all yours, and gladly." It was, and it remains, worth everything. *Laus Deo*.

PART I

THE GOOD LIFE

IN SEARCH OF
NOBLE PURPOSE

CHAPTER I

A MORE
EXCELLENT WAY

But earnestly desire the higher gifts. And I will show you a
still more excellent way.

I CORINTHIANS 12:31

Harvard Yard is never more grand than it is on Commencement Day. Beneath its shading elms, thirty thousand proud parents, friends, and pumped-up, soon-to-be graduates sit in the glow of unmitigated mutual self-congratulation. On the platform in front of the towering portico of the University's Memorial Church, dedicated to the Harvard dead of America's twentieth-century wars, sit the great and the good, which includes faculty from all over the world, resplendent in academic regalia; candidates for honorary degrees and the University's most favored guests of the day; and the vaguely familiar faces of those who actually run the place, the members of the governing boards, the deans, and the administrators. Harvard Commencement is arguably America's oldest continuing public ceremony, doing business since 1642 in essentially the same form.

In June 2001, in the midst of this heady mix of pomp and circumstance, the undergraduate speaker, Seth Moulton,[1] rose and, doffing his cap, making his ceremonial bow to the president, and squaring his feet at the microphone, began his five-minute oration. Unlike most American colleges, Harvard does not have to endure a major address at the time it gives out its degrees, and thus the only speeches are those given by three students, one speech of which is in Latin and thus mercifully inaccessible to all but the seniors and faculty who have been provided a translation. Our young orator could be expected to touch upon the usual pieties: students helping one another through the trials of college life, the sense of joy and relief at going out into the "real world," and the greatness of Harvard and, by implication, its newest graduates. It became clear early on, however, that this young orator was not proposing to rest content with the conventional wisdom of Commencement Day.

After invoking a litany of Harvard greats: John Adams and John Quincy Adams, Theodore Roosevelt and Franklin Delano Roosevelt, W. E. B. Du Bois, Helen Keller, and John Fitzgerald Kennedy, he asked what they all had in common, and then answered his own question. "Dead," he said. "They are all dead. The University now belongs to us, as do the times. What will we do with them?" Earlier generations had been summoned from the Commencement platform to lives of conflict and responsibility. The grandparents of many seniors—the much-celebrated "Greatest Generation"—had grown up in the Great Depression and responded to the demands of World War II and Korea. The parents of many present on this day had found themselves engaged in the war in or about Vietnam, and for many others of that era there had been struggles for civil rights and women's rights and the peace movement. Our orator essentially asked his classmates: What will be our call to greatness, our summons to nobility? In this season of endless prosperity and self-interest, is there anything that will require the best of what we have to offer? Is there any cause great or good enough to provoke goodness and greatness in us?

As with much discourse, the questions were better than the answers, and our young speaker received a polite but not enthusiastic response to his eloquence. The alumni magazine, in fact, took so little notice of the speech that neither it nor the speaker was mentioned in its major news and feature accounts of Commencement. The question of a call to nobility, however, touched a nerve among many of the young present that morning.

My own observation had long been that students were becoming increasingly restive about the moral dimension of their education. Certainly they appreciated the opportunity provided by study at a great university, and most of them had done reasonably well at their tasks and had had some fun into the bargain. Nearly all of them had interesting futures upon which to embark as soon as they left Cambridge, which included going on to graduate and professional schools, taking up foreign fellowships and travel or coveted entry-level positions with New York consultancy or financial houses, or even a little unprogrammed R and R; as one student pointed out to me, "My parents have had me on this college track since I was in day care, and now, after twenty-two years, I'd like a little time to myself."

Noble thoughts would appear to be far away from the minds of this indulged and indulgent generation, yet many conversations over recent years have told me otherwise. More and more students are asking questions about the moral use of their lives and their education, and about their value, when value questions about education used to be rigorously utilitarian. "How much is my degree worth," the students used to ask, "and how much will it get me of this world's goods?" It is not because of the intrinsic intellectual merit of the field of economics that most undergraduates have chosen to major in that subject over the past decade. The primacy of economics, the so-called dismal science, is acute everywhere, and particularly so at Harvard, where the last three Commencement speakers have included such economic superstars as Amartya Sen, Alan Greenspan, and Robert Rubin and where the new president, Lawrence H. Summers, who served briefly as Secretary of the Treasury in the Clinton administration, is an economist by profession. The value questions now, however, which were once tied to potential net worth, increasingly have to do with matters of moral value, public and private virtue, and a sense of a fit vocation for making a good life and not just a good living.

Our student orator that Commencement Day was my student and is now my friend, and over the course of his college career we had many conversations about the large questions of value, virtue, worth, and vocation and what, if anything, his college education had to do with any of them. He and many of his classmates had recognized a disconnect between the ideas and moments of which they had heard and read in their studies and the sense of what they might be called upon to do in life beyond simply satisfying a set of course requirements.

Except for the occasional deferential nod to the notion of public service, American higher education in the last decades of the twentieth century has seemed to go out of its way to avoid any kind of moral claims upon the minds, hearts, and lives of its young constituents. It almost seems as though, with the death of the concept *in loco parentis* and the demise of parietal rules and dress codes, any claims for public good on behalf of the highly educated young were considered, if at all, either in the baccalaureate sermon or in the Commencement address, where they were offered too late to do much harm or to be of much good. In 1701, for instance, Yale was founded to fit the best and the brightest for "service in church and state," which fairly well summed up eighteenth-century Connecticut's public sector; and nearly every other American college since has stored among its founding documents a notion having to do with the noble civic and virtuous ends for the public good toward which the educational product of the institution was directed.

Excellence and Fairness

At Sunday lunch following a preachment at Cornell University a few years ago, I found myself engaged in a lively conversation with the new president of the university, Dr. Hunter Rawlings. We spoke of many things, and in particular of his transition from the classroom to the top academic job. The conversation turned to the subject of university values and what the university holds most dear, without which it would not be possible to be the university, or to be recognizable as such. Earlier generations had been pleased to place their moral ambitions in florid Latin inscriptions over the doors of libraries, on coats of arms emblazoned over the fronts of administration buildings, and in speeches given at the ceremonial conferrals of degrees. When Harvard's Memorial Hall, for example, was erected as a memorial to the Union dead of the Civil War, it was the largest academic building then standing in North America, and it was dedicated to *Humanitas*, *Virtus*, and *Pietas*. The very words "humanity," "virtue," and "piety" now have a somewhat antique, quaint sound; and if there were to be a contest to find a suitable inscription for a university building today, it would be impossible to find a consensus for any sentiment worthy of perpetuation in stone. That is, unless Hunter Rawlings is right in his discovery that the values the modern university most espouses are not those of truth, virtue, and service, or even of learning, teaching, and wisdom, but rather those of excellence and fairness.

Every university, and every aspect of every university, President Rawlings noted, aspires to excellence. It is no good to be number two, and it is upon that ambition that national magazine surveys of American colleges and universities depend in order to keep up their circulation. Who can be against excellence? Surely, in the modern university, no one would make the argument that Richard Nixon made when one of his nominees for a seat on the Supreme Court was deemed less than excellently learned in law. In fact, the judge was described as mediocre. Nixon's response, not at all ironic, was that the mediocre deserved as much to be represented on the high Court as did the excellent.

Every year our colleges tell their entering freshmen that they form "the most excellent class of people ever to be admitted to old 'Siwash

University.'" Proud parents are prepared to believe that statement, for they are paying enough for it to be true, and the students believe it, up to a point, as an innocent, even a useful fiction, although most of them really know better. They know the truth about themselves, or at least they suspect of themselves that there is less there than meets the admissions committee eye, but they are determined to prove themselves against the high expectations of the admissions process. So, to that end they spend the best years of their lives in attempting to achieve an impossible goal: the justification of their own merit. One bright young pupil observed to me many years ago, "My parents think I'm excellent, and so does the school. I'm the only one who knows better, and the tension between reality and expectation is killing me."

Excellence, of course, presupposes merit, and meritocracy is one of the hallmarks of a modern university education. If everyone is excellent, however, not only is the term meaningless, but it requires a cohort of the less than excellent by which excellence can be measured. For it all to work as well as it can, as one admissions officer once suggested to me, the trick is to choose the bottom half of the class with the same care as the top half, while mindful of the fact that excellence comes in many forms and is measured in many ways.

Excellence seems a rather abstract and cold virtue, for simply to be the best at what one does without reference to what one does empties the term of any moral content. Al Capone was an excellent gangster, very good at what he did and perhaps even the best; but surely, even in the age of the nearly universal appeal of *The Sopranos*, we would not hold him as an example to be emulated or as a person to be rewarded simply because he was the very best at what he did.

The other virtue identified by Dr. Rawlings, that of fairness, is designed to ensure that whatever is done is done properly and in a way that is transparently equal to all concerned. As a trustee of a small liberal arts college, I once served on the Committee on Promotion, Review, and Tenure. There I learned that academic fairness, essential in the granting of a job for life, could be compromised in the tenure process only by the consideration of inappropriate things in the candidate's case, such as a handicap, a protected disability, or gender or sexual issues, or by a failure to abide by the agreed-upon process, otherwise known as improper consideration. Fairness in admissions and promotion, indeed in the conduct of all of the affairs of the institution, is essential to the well-being of the institution and in the interests of all who would benefit from the institution.

Well, our institutions abound in excellence and fairness, but is that good enough? Is ambition and process enough for those who seek what St. Paul once called "a more excellent way"?

Among the many groups of students with which I have worked over the years, none has given me more pleasure or moral encouragement than the groups of very secular students engaged in what is loosely called "public service." Harvard has Phillips Brooks House, the largest extracurricular activity in the College, which engages nearly a third of the student population in some form of good works. Many other colleges have similar organizations, most of which began out of the religious motivations of the old YMCAs and YWCAs of nearly a century ago and the sense of *noblesse oblige* and social service that embraced the fundamental moral principle of giving back. These institutions generally had long slipped from their old religious moorings and gained a new life in the post-Watergate environment of the 1970s. Harvard's then president, Derek Bok, and other university and college leaders of the day were horrified that Watergate might engender a cynicism in the young that would make them suspicious of government, indifferent to service, and generally incapable of civic virtue. So, along with academic efforts of "values clarification" and "moral reasoning"—secular efforts designed anew to help teach students how to be and to do good—public service and volunteerism reemerged as a central priority of extracurricular life, even producing in some enthusiastic institutions the oxymoron of "compulsory volunteerism."

Early in September 2001, during the week before September 11, I attended what was called a "Public Service Summit." Dozens of Harvard's most active student public-service leaders held a two-day conference in which they discussed their aims and objectives for the year and, at a deeper level, good and bad motivations for public service. The bad reasons for it included resumé building, bossing people around, playing out a private agenda on those unable to resist it, power-tripping, and social condescension. The good reasons included a desire for social reform and not merely the palliatives of social service; a learning experience that not only transcended the classroom, but transformed the participant; and a sense that it was worthwhile to participate in something that was truly good and truly great.

In the question period, after a few stabs at particular situations, one of the students, not by any means a bomb thrower, asked why it was that his University, which was teaching about virtue and presumably encouraging him in the pursuit of it, stood as an institution squarely in the way of every virtuous and humane civic, social, and political change that he and his fellow social activists were trying to achieve. "Why, in these matters," he asked, "is our College nearly always our enemy?"

Clearly, pieties about the need of the University to protect its assets from partisan attacks by keeping out of public-policy matters would cut little ice here. Students had been demonstrating in the late spring for a cause known as "A Living Wage" for Harvard's lowest-paid workers, and part of what drove that argument and fueled a long and loud occupation of a University building in the first such occupation in many years, was a sense of economic justice. There was also the distinct sense of embarrassment that the very University that purported to be interested in the values and moral life of its students was not prepared, as a corporation, to exercise any moral judgment that would compromise its own security and well-documented wealth.

The moral embarrassment was not dissimilar to that felt by the parental generation of the 1960s, which, although its members resented any implication that their university should interfere in their own private moral lives, nonetheless wanted it to live up to their public moral ideals, and were ashamed when it could not or would not practice those standards. In this 2001 demonstration, one of the most vociferous of the student leaders confronting the University's policies was the daughter of a man who had played the same role thirty years before and had been disciplined for it. One student asked me at the summit meeting, more in sadness than in anger, "Why can't Harvard be both great and good at the same time?"

The question is neither peculiar to Cambridge nor to this generation, but in this generation the search for goodness, both institutional and personal, has reappeared as a defining characteristic in young people's renewed search for the good life. Their colleges and universities have much to say about excellence and fairness, yet somehow are reluctant to speak about goodness; and in their silence on that topic they seem unable to hear that the fundamental question of the young committed to their care today is, simply, "What will it take for me to make a good life, and not merely a good living?"

The academy does not know how to respond to such a reactionary perception of the role of goodness in education. "We are in the knowledge business," one of my colleagues is quick to remind me, "not in the virtue business." Another reacts with the well-worn aphorism of Mae West. When questioned by an admirer, "My goodness, where did you get those pearls?" the famous actress replied, "Goodness had nothing to do with it."

Who Are These People?

Images of drugged-out, body-pierced, estranged black-clad Gothic youth capable of Columbine and anarchic apostles of the white hip-hop rappers Eminem compete with pictures of hapless teenage loners whose cries for help include shooting anybody who gets in the way of their rage. Not since the early movies portraying "angry young men" such as James Dean and Marlon Brando have America's young people been seen as such a cultural threat, and yet, if we can believe a new study on what is called the "millennial generation"—those born in or after 1982—that image is both inaccurate and about to be superseded. In their book *Millennials Rising: The Next Great Generation*, Neil Howe and William Strauss write:

> As a group, Millennials are unlike any other youth generation in living memory. They are more numerous, more affluent, better educated, and more ethnically diverse. More important, they are beginning to manifest a wide array of positive social habits that older Americans no longer associate with youth, including a new focus on teamwork, achievement, modesty, and good conduct. Only a few years from now, this can-do youth revolution will overwhelm the cynics and pessimists. Over the next decade, the Millennial Generation will entirely recast the image of youth from downbeat and alienated to upbeat and engaged—with potentially seismic consequences for America.[2]

Howe and Strauss compare their findings with the cynical sentiments of a *Newsweek* column that said: "Kids today, they're just no good. No hardships + no cause = boredom, anger, and idiocy"; and they could not disagree more with the conventional wisdom of the punditry. Rather than just another alphabet-labeled lost generation, the Millennials are described as a "found" generation who are characterized as essentially optimistic, cooperative, respectful of authority, rule-following, bright, progressive, and engaged. One young person interviewed gave this self-description of her generation, "We're the kids who are going to change things."

To those generations which have given up expecting good news from their young, this account of the new Millennials could not be coming at a better time, and not a day too soon. What is remarkable about all of this is that much of it could have been anticipated by the changing college culture of the last decade. Stimulated by Howe and Strauss's observations of high-school youth, I began to ask their questions and apply their conclusions to my experience of college young people, and I must confess that my experience of the fundamental ambitions of college youth confirms their findings. Seth Moulton's Commencement speech on the search for noble purpose and useful service was, in part, a result of the kind of college community in which he had lived for four years. That community, taking its cue from the altruism behind its founding, is characterized by a combination of aggressive self-interest and idealism that continues to appeal to a diverse student community, which must struggle to have its values defined and affirmed against the prevailing culture. Ironically, it is the ancient mission of the modern university and the moral energy of its newest members that may well renew both college and society in the image of what Strauss and Howe call "the next great generation."

If that is so, they will have accomplished a revolution far more significant than all of the student protests of the 1960s and the curricular "reforms" of the 1970s and 1980s; but without these earlier, often inchoate spasms of reformation, the present moment of potential transformation would not be possible. While colleges are still easy to criticize as elitist, "out of the mainstream," and "ivory towers," and their relation to the "real world" seen as marginal, one must conclude that after a generation of diversity building in the American college—the self-conscious determination to change the demographics of higher education—most institutions bear a greater resemblance to the "real world" than to the communities from which young people come and are more likely to reflect the world into which they will graduate. To stand at a campus intersection at the changeover between classes in any American college or university, in these early days of the twenty-first century, is to see not simply a spectrum of America, but increasingly a spectrum of the world. If the saying is true that students learn more from other students than from their teachers, and more in the dining hall and dormitory than in the lecture hall or library, then we can expect that our young people will emerge from these institutions more cosmopolitan, more urbane, more capable of dealing with differences, more willing to find their places in a world that looks less and less like the homes from which they came, and less intimidated by change.

When on Sunday mornings I look out at my congregation, I see something of that same diversity, and a generational mix punctuated by a genuine spiritual hunger, an intellectual acuity, and a desire—I will even say a passion—for goodness. Excellence and fairness are assumed, and it is good that they can be assumed, but most people would argue that as good as that is, it is not good enough. What has moved and stimulated me over the years is the ever growing sense that young people, as self-aware a group as could be imagined, are eager to translate what they know and feel into something useful and good that they can do and be. Howe and Strauss calls this a "capacity for greatness."

Seth Moulton entitled his Commencement oration "Achieving Greatness," and it delivered not the usual invitation to go out and make a success of oneself. Describing the Western world of most of his listening contemporaries as "dominated by contentment and threatened by mediocrity," he invited his classmates to become the kind of people who are "bold and courageous . . . who are willing to take extraordinary steps to an uncertain future." Then, as if in contemplation of some summons to an as yet unidentified difficult challenge on some future day, he cited a favorite aphorism: "When you're damned if you do and damned if you don't; always do." Within three short months, and before the start of the next academic year, that challenge would present itself on the morning of September 11, 2001.

After the Fall

In the *Boston Globe* of Monday, September 10, 2001, in a column entitled "Don't Sell Teens Short—They Are the Future," Lily Rayman-Read, a senior at Lexington High School in that historic Massachusetts town famous for the opening skirmishes of the American Revolution, described her summer job as part of a Boston inner-city garden project:

> Garden Futures is an organization that connects people in different communities and neighborhoods by cultivating and developing a garden, and through these community gardens many bonds are formed, and a sense of community is strengthened. . . . By meeting so many different people, I learned a great deal about the significance of diversity for gardens and for people.

She also learned a greater lesson that she wished to share. Acknowledging that "teenagers have a reputation for apathy and not caring about the world around us," Lily went on to note: "The truth is, we do care; we often just don't know what to do or how to make a difference." I doubt very much that young Lily had read Howe and Strauss's new book, *Millennials Rising: The Next Great Generation*, or that she could have anticipated the calamitous events that within twenty-four hours of the appearance of her article in the newspaper would destabilize her world forever, but in the final paragraph of her article, which was prominently sited on the op-ed page, she wrote:

> Thanks to my experiences throughout the summer, I realize that all teenagers have the power to make a difference for ourselves and for our communities. If people gave us the chance to help out, I think the world would be surprised at just how committed teens can be in improving the world around us, because we are, after all, the future.

Lily's homily was lost in the terror of the next day and the epidemic of anxiety that has since been stylized simply as "9/11," but in her appeal to allow the realization of the potential goodness and greatness of her much-maligned generation, she has placed herself and her peers in the face of the greatest challenge to face our nation since the Civil War, the last time American blood was spilled on American soil.

The question for each rising generation since World War II has always been this: In the absence of a crisis, would the young know one when they saw one, and would they be capable of rising to meet it, indulged and diverted as they had been for nearly all of their young lives? The story is yet to be told about the young's capacity to respond to the events of September 11, but it certainly seems as if they have been in preparation for a long while for such a claim on their sense of identity and purpose. The Seths, the Lilys, and the thousands described as the "next great generation" seem to have anticipated the character-forming sense of crisis as a moment of moral opportunity, a proving ground for what the Bible calls, in St. Paul's words, "a more excellent way." In the aftermath of September 11 we have seen the young willingly respond to the call of their country for both military and social service. We have seen heroic youthful volunteer efforts in light of the horrific needs at Ground Zero. We have seen a revival of youthful patriotism, not simply of the flag-waving "U.S.A., U.S.A." sporting events sort, but of a desire to—in the famous and at once antique phrase of John F. Kennedy's inaugural address—"Ask not what your country can do for you; ask what you can do for your country." This youthful new patriotism, as I will call it, manifests itself within the new realities of our pluralistic culture and world.

Among the many urgent concerns I heard in the College Yard on the afternoon of September 11 was the desire for the well-being of Muslim students, and especially of those from Arab lands. In the Christian prayer groups that sprang into action within hours of the terrible news from New York, prayers for "our Muslim brothers and sisters" were uttered with a sincerity and passion that described the new patriotism as American, Christian, and compassionate. In many places, including at Harvard, young Jews, Christians, and Muslims gathered together by instinct for prayer and encouragement.

While I do not know this, I cannot imagine that on Sunday afternoon, December 7, 1941, many prayers were offered for our Japanese brothers and sisters. What I do know is that when The Reverend Charles Joy, minister of the First Parish Church in Portland, Maine, declared in a sermon preached just as we entered World War I, in April 1917, "If I remain your minister, prayers shall ascend for Germany and America alike," on the very next day he was burned in effigy on the iron railings in front of his church.[3]

Somehow, and often with little help from their elders, our young people, particularly in our schools, colleges, and universities, have begun to discover those truths that last in times of need. Unbeknownst to much of the profit-driven mavens of a corrosively materialistic popular culture that preys on the susceptibilities and anxieties of youth, these very same youth, shrewd critics of that culture and of those who run it, have been on a search for greatness, for goodness, and even for nobility, that "more excellent way" of which St. Paul speaks. They have been looking for that time, their time, in which to transform and be transformed. That time, I suggest, has now come, and the truths for making the most of that time will always expose the lies.

CHAPTER 2

THE SMART AND
THE GOOD

The multitude of the wise is the welfare of the world.
THE WISDOM OF SOLOMON 6:24 (KJV),
Apocrypha

The orations delivered at the induction of new members into Phi Beta Kappa, America's elite intellectual fraternity, have been eminently forgettable since the society was established in 1766 at the College of William and Mary. Only Ralph Waldo Emerson's address, given at Harvard in 1837 and first entitled "Man Thinking," but since 1856 known to the world as "The American Scholar," retains a place in American letters. When I was an undergraduate at Bates College, I did not have the grades to be elected to Phi Beta Kappa, which thus delivered, I think, the first significant disappointment of my academic career to my expectant and charitable parents. When many years later I was elected an honorary member of Alpha of Massachusetts, Harvard's chapter, founded in 1779, for my services as chaplain at the literary exercises, my mother simply said, "At last." To an older generation, Phi Beta Kappa was a universally acknowledged symbol of academic excellence and intellectual distinction, but in recent years the glitter of the key has grown tarnished. Perhaps it is the combination of elitism and obscurantism associated with the fraternal rituals, the insignia, and the rigorous rankings, but whatever it is, Phi Beta Kappa risks becoming the university equivalent of the Masons—stoutly defended by those who know and care and routinely ignored by everybody else.

Thus, it is a matter of some note when a contemporary Phi Beta Kappa address makes the feature pages of a major American daily paper, which is what happened in spring 2001, when Professor Sheldon Krimsky's address, cited by the newspaper as "Becoming Moral by Degrees," was published on the Focus pages of the *Boston Globe* at the height of the spring commencement season. Subtitled "Education Neither Implies, Includes, nor Promises Virtue," Krimsky's talk was given to the newly elected members of Phi Beta Kappa at Tufts University, where Krimsky teaches, provoking considerable discussion by posing the following questions:

> Are more educated people likely to lie less? to express more humanitarian values? to be more beneficent to others? to show more empathy? to make complex moral decisions? I don't think so.[1]

Knowledge and Right Action

The questions struck a cultural nerve. We have always placed significant value on the notion that knowledge and virtue are connected, and that the point of a college education—for as many as possible in a democracy—is to provide the connection between virtue and knowledge. We want to believe that smart people should be good people, and that the smarter we are, the more virtuous we are, or at least ought to be.

The question of the proper relationship between what we know and how we act—that is, between knowledge and virtue—is as old as Aristotle and Plato, but the tension between expectation and experience is as acute as the most recent scandal or morally dubious behavior committed by those persons dubbed the "great" and the "good." For this we have three vivid examples from late-twentieth-century American public life.

It was David Halberstam who coined the phrase "the best and the brightest" in referring to the American cultural elite who, accustomed to leadership and civic deference, led the country into the moral and political quagmire of Vietnam. No one would have ever mistaken Dwight D. Eisenhower for an intellectual, despite the fact that he went to the White House not from the army, but from the presidency of Columbia University. There are still many who insist that the trustees of Columbia thought they had elected Ike's brother Milton, the distinguished president of Johns Hopkins, but it was Ike who turned up at Morningside Heights to report for duty. The intellectual public-policy mavens would swarm about President John F. Kennedy, who, if not certifiably an intellectual himself, had the good taste to be married to a woman who most certainly was. After Inauguration Day 1961, the ranks of the Harvard faculty were depleted by the loss of its most glamorous members, including John Kenneth Galbraith and Arthur M. Schlesinger, to the inner circles of the Kennedy White House.

Perhaps the most conspicuously intellectual of those who went to the White House was McGeorge Bundy, who was often referred to at Harvard as the "boy wonder," not only for his legendary precocity during his school days at Groton, but because of the tender age at which he became Dean of the Faculty of Arts and Sciences and hence the most powerful academic figure in the University, including the president. Rumor had it that when "SuperMac," as he was also known, accepted Kennedy's offer of a post at cabinet rank in the White House, the president of Harvard, Nathan Marsh Pusey, breathed a great sigh of relief. Older rumors had it that Bundy himself had been a candidate for the Harvard presidency, but was passed over for the older, and some would say safer, Pusey, which led one Cambridge wag of a classical bent to say, upon hearing the news, *"Sic transit gloria Bundy."* Of Bundy's brains and talent there was no doubt, and even more than the possession of his own natural gifts, he had the ability to attract similarly talented colleagues, many of whom were often younger than himself and thrilled to be in his service. I remember the testimonials of many of his colleagues at his memorial service, who recalled the exhilaration of a Bundy-led analysis session. One of them said, "It was a wondrous thing to see his brain in action, like watching the engine of a magnificently tuned Mercedes at full throttle."

Lyndon Johnson inherited Bundy, his policies, and his colleagues, and the rest, as we know, is a sad story. The question always asked is how bright and good people could have become so badly enmeshed in the wrong place at the wrong time and for the wrong reasons. Unlike Henry Kissinger, another Harvard academic drawn to the candle of policy and power, Bundy never attempted to explain his Vietnam policy, and woe betide the person who asked him about it. He took to his grave many of his views on that period of his life; and both his friends and detractors, knowing him to have been a man of intellectual acuity and moral probity, were never able to reconcile those two qualities in him as expressed in his most conspicuous public-policy failure.

The second instance of good people of high intelligence doing stupid, even venial, things is found in the capers of Watergate, the infamous "two-bit burglary." Here the light does not shine on the principals in the drama, President Nixon, Secretary of State Kissinger, and Attorney General Mitchell, or on the operatives of the Republican National Committee, or on the aptly named CREEP, the Committee to Re-elect the President. Here, very much as in a Shakespearean tragedy, the moral burden of the action is carried by what the playbill might describe as the minor characters, who in this case were not Rosencrantz and Guildenstern, but John Dean and Jeb Magruder. They were bright young men, good Americans, good Christians, well-educated, conscientious, and even, up to a point, morally ambitious. They were fast-trackers on what they believed to be a good, and even a noble, cause. We must remember that while Richard Nixon may never have had a charisma that would have made him easily likable, still he was able to compel people to believe in what he believed, which included restoring balance and order to a national culture dangerously out of control. One did not have to believe in everything about Nixon, for he had enough faults for anyone to find at least one, but for that large company of people between the elite coasts whom Nixon himself had styled "the silent majority," who worried that the country was about to career into anarchy, with an unwinnable war abroad and an imploding cultural fabric at home, he was the only strong man available to save the day. It was out of a combination of cynicism and idealism that so many of the brightest and the best were drawn into his service, and ultimately ensnared in his pathetic downfall.

Because of the televised Watergate hearings, the major public civic entertainment between the army and McCarthy hearings of the 1950s and the O. J. Simpson trial of the 1990s, we know perhaps more than we might wish to know of the moral agonizings of such people as Macgruder and Dean. We realize that it was the moral self-scrutiny of Dean, heroic to many and traitorous to others, that contributed to the inevitable resignation of Nixon. To the general public the question was a relatively simple one, uncomplicated by lawyerly nuances or neat, philosophical distinctions, and it was this: How could such bright and intelligent young men of such obvious capacity and filled with good intentions have gone so badly wrong? After all, as talking head after talking head freely observed, they had the best education that money could buy. Implicit in that moral indictment of the Watergate men is a questioning of the fundamental assumptions about the virtue of education in a free and democratic society. A quarter of a century after Watergate, that question would be posed by Sheldon Krimsky in his Phi Beta Kappa address:

If there is no correlation between education and virtue, this has implications for public decision-making. There is no reason to embrace a moral meritocracy on the basis of academic achievements.[2]

In other words, what is the point of a costly college education, available on the basis of academic merit for the public good, if the education itself generates no sense of private probity or public good? Isn't it all rather an indulgent waste?

Profile in Virtue

I remember very well the determination of the then president of Harvard, Derek Bok, to answer that question by reaffirming the intentional relationship in a democracy between meritocratic education and the service of the public good. He did this in the name of another not so minor figure in the Watergate crisis, his old mentor and colleague in the Harvard Law School, Archibald Cox. Writing in 1984, at the time of Cox's mandatory retirement at age seventy from the Law School, Derek Bok said:

> No one at Harvard has meant more to me or had a greater influence on how I have thought and acted. If that strikes you as small praise, it is because you do not know what sort of unformed, wayward creature I was when I sat in your Labor Law class in 1953 — or started teaching five years later, for that matter.[3]

On Saturday night, October 20, 1973, an embattled President Nixon fired Special Prosecutor Archibald Cox, dissolved the office of the Watergate Special Prosecution Force, and remanded the investigation back to the cozy confines of the Justice Department, where, in presidential press secretary Ron Ziegler's immortal words, "It will be carried out with thoroughness and vigor." Thus began the greatest constitutional crisis in American history since the Civil War. Cox and his fellow Yankee Harvard man, Attorney General Elliot Richardson, became the national symbols of probity and citizenship, and Cox would be apotheosized as the "conscience of a nation." The "Saturday Night Massacre," as it soon came to be called, had an enormous national impact, with political ramifications that virtually changed the national climate for a generation.

The moral impact of the saga, with its cast of heroes, villains, and victims, also had a part to play in the nation's colleges and universities, which heretofore had been obsessed with their own parochial political intrigues. On Monday morning, October 29, 1973, President Bok, in office only since 1971, took the pulpit of the College chapel at a service of daily Morning Prayers. Bok was not a churchy man in any sense, and to my knowledge had never set foot in the chapel other than to attend funerals and deliver the annual baccalaureate address. The service of daily Morning Prayers at eight forty-five was definitely not a part of his morning routine, but extraordinary times call for extraordinary measures, and Bok asked me if he could come to speak about Harvard and the virtues of citizenship. I bumped the scheduled speaker of the day, an understanding colleague, and Bok appeared before a capacity—and very curious—congregation.

President Bok took as his text Exodus 23:2, "Thou shalt not follow a multitude to do evil . . ." and through it asked the question of the day: "When the occasion demands, can we summon the courage to stand alone and refuse to do what we know is wrong?" He was of course speaking of Cox, and he described him as having had to choose between remaining at his post in order to have a chance to influence a just outcome, and refusing to compromise a principle and obey what he regarded as a wrong order, which would thus invite his inevitable dismissal. "In the end," he said of his old professor, "he perceived a principle that could not be compromised even to placate the uncertain demands of international security and domestic harmony. It was a principle worth defending, even by refusing to obey a presidential order, in order to press its importance vividly on the mind of the nation." This was of added significance, Mr. Bok went on to say, "within the University community from whence he came, for the University must be sensitive to everything that bears upon the moral education of its members." Part of this responsibility can be discharged through the work of the classroom, and in anticipation of the curricular reforms in moral education he would soon spearhead at Harvard, he observed, "and there is more to be accomplished here than we have achieved thus far."

Apparently Cox and Bok had discussed Cox's reluctance to accept the post of Special Prosecutor, as Cox was concerned that it would set a bad example for his younger colleagues, suggesting as it did that vivid government service was more alluring than the mundane work of teaching. "In retrospect," Bok noted, "it appears that he [Cox] has taught us more in government service than he could have hoped to achieve in those Harvard classrooms where we welcome him back with admiration." Bok began his talk with the Bible, but he ended it on the highest note of Aristotle's *Ethics:* "If you would understand virtue, observe the conduct of virtuous men."*

To this day I am convinced that in this five-minute chapel talk, inspired by the loyalty of a pupil to his teacher, lay the foundations of Derek Bok's twenty-year campaign for the moral education, civil discourse, and public service by which his presidency and Harvard were reformed. The brightest and the best were now again to be virtuous.

Few, however, who read Krimsky's May 2001 talk, "Becoming Moral by Degrees," had in mind McGeorge Bundy, Archibald Cox, or even Richard Nixon. The most conspicuous gap between brains and virtue was to be found in the person of William Jefferson Clinton, whose poll ratings for his performance as president were through the roof, much to the annoyance of those who criticized his moral judgment and called him, among other hateful things, "Philanderer-in-Chief." In him the protean conflict between appetites and abilities took on Sophoclean dimensions.

In an era of so many polls that one could find favorable poll figures for almost any position—rather like looking for a Bible verse to proof-text your own opinion—one bit of public opinion remained consistent throughout the eight years of the Clinton scandals: people thought that Bill Clinton was a good president, but not a good person. Variously interpreted, that opinion suggested that in an era of peace and prosperity people approved of Clinton's performance as president and generally gave him credit for creating and sustaining the public policies by which more and more Americans saw themselves as benefiting; and though more people than not were willing to acknowledge as private his private behavior, they nevertheless did not approve of such behavior and saw him as a bad moral example to the young. Those most opposed to him used their moral revulsion to attack him on political grounds, their partisan Puritanism transparent to a country quite capable of distinguishing between appetites and abilities. Competence, not character, was the issue that allowed most Americans to give the president extraordinarily high job ratings while deploring his private conduct. Had Clinton not been so fortunate in his enemies, compared to whose zeal his own roguish indiscretions seemed forgivable, the gap between public and personal approval might have been more evenly resolved, and not in Clinton's favor. Only Hollywood could come up with a better cast of presidential enemies than that of Newt Gingrich, Linda Tripp, Bob Barr, and Ken Starr.

Clinton himself, however, remains the great moral enigma. How is it, so many would ask again and again, that this man, arguably the brightest incumbent of the White House since Thomas Jefferson, and a lot more fun than the "Sage of Monticello," could be so capable a master of public policy, so persuasive an advocate for the best in America, and yet be so stupidly ungovernable in his own private life? This man went to Georgetown, to Yale, and to Oxford. As a friend of mine, and no friend of Clinton, once remarked, "He gives higher education a bad name."

Part of the reason people have such a strong negative reaction to the misbehavior of the well-educated is the assumption, challenged by Krimsky among others, that knowledge and learning lead to virtue, and that virtue itself is the subject of sound learning. This is almost an article of faith on the part of those who, while not necessarily involved in the life of the academy, believe that the true and authentic subject of the academy is not simply the talking about virtue or the study of it in others, but actually virtue itself and its inculcation in the minds and hearts of the young.

The University's Job

In 1986, in a *New York Times* article, Norman Lamm, then president of New York's Yeshiva University, put the historic case for moral formation as a mission of the university:

> Until about fifty years ago, it was commonly accepted that the university was responsible for offering its students moral guidance. Professors regarded themselves as not only the teachers of knowledge and skills, but also as educational stewards of a special kind of wisdom: the nature of the good life; truth and goodness and beauty; and the value of thought and reflection.[5]

By 1986, however, the year in which Yeshiva celebrated its 100th anniversary and Harvard its 350th anniversary, that notion of the moral mission of American higher education had long been in eclipse. Lamm cites George Bernard Shaw's famously contemptuous view of what he called American value-agnosticism: "I doubt if there has been a country in the world's history where men were ashamed of being decent, of being sober, of being well-spoken, of being educated, of being gentle, of being conscientious, as in America."

Lamm does not simply rely on Shaw's condemnation of the American situation to make his point, writing: "An educational system that is amoral in the name of 'scientific objectivity' thus devours its own young. They fall prey to a variety of predators that rob them of their confidence in the life of the mind, the significance of culture, the intrinsic worth of knowledge." This tendency in American higher education permits an entire generation of students "to grow up as ethical illiterates and moral idiots, unprepared to cope with ordinary life experiences." It is a declaration, he says, of "education bankruptcy." Anticipating the claim that moral education is the province of church and synagogue, he continues: "It is no excuse to say that for moral instruction people ought to look to their churches and synagogues. Most of them never show up in churches and synagogues, and too many religious institutions, affected by the prevailing secularism, are afraid to use the words 'right' and 'wrong.'"

The university ought to allow "academic values and social-moral principles to come out of the closet and into the lecture hall; we must reassert the existence and value of the spirit." Reminding his readers that "Man is a spiritual as well as a biochemical, psychological, political, social, legal and economic animal," Lamm argues for an openness to what he calls "spiritual dignity." Again anticipating the howls of secular academic protest, he argues:

An openness to spiritual dignity does not imply denominationalism. It does mean that the prevalent dogmas of scientific materialism and philosophical despair are not the only points of view worthy of scholarly attention; that belief in the reality of the mind and the existence of the soul does not condemn one as intellectually inferior and scientifically backward; that faith and hope have equal claim on the heart and minds of educated people and deserve to be presented without coercion on the one side or derision on the other; that not all authority is authoritarian, not all morality is moralizing, not all religion is Khomeinism, not all spirituality is illusory.

The reference to "Khomeinism" is to the radical form of Islamic fundamentalism that drove the Shah of Iran from his throne and became the first fruits of a movement that has reached a horrific worldwide visibility in the concept of Islamic *jihad* and the works of Osama bin Laden in the opening years of the twenty-first century. In 1986, many academic secularists pointed to Islamic fundamentalism as proof positive of the clear and present danger of religion of any kind. To this canard, Lamm responds in conclusion:

A modern university should not be "spooked" by the specter of sectarianism. It should encourage a moral climate that elicits respect for the human spirit, for honor, or law, for the pursuit of knowledge and love of learning, for the human capacity for self-transcendence.

Few leaders of higher education in America would dare to be as forthright in asserting the right to "spiritual dignity" in the academy. Few would acknowledge that the young have need of such moral education, that the nation deserves such morally and spiritually informed young people, and that the nation and its youth have been deprived of this cultural necessity by the very academic communities that have continued to claim their place of subsidized privilege through the public purse and through ever increasing tuitions.

A generation earlier, Nathan Marsh Pusey, president of Harvard, made a similar case in his baccalaureate address to the Class of 1959. Calling his sermon "College Education and Moral Character," he reminded his listeners that moral education, once regarded as the capstone of a college education at Harvard and elsewhere, had long ceased to be that. Conceding that perhaps the times were against the recovery of this central moral mission, he nevertheless went on to suggest that "the finest fruit of serious learning should be the ability to speak the word 'God' without reserve or embarrassment, certainly without adolescent resentment; rather with some sense of communion, with reverence and with joy."

Himself a student of the history of moral education in American colleges and universities, Pusey reminded his young and perhaps indifferent audience that the purpose of such education, in the words of one of his nineteenth-century predecessors, was:

> to instill into the minds of youth . . . the principles of morality and rectitude which will give them a true and happy direction in the pursuit of all public and private virtues, and by the exercise of which they may become useful to themselves, good members of society, and ornaments to their country.[6]

Many students who have endured now nearly twenty years of post-Watergate instruction in values clarification, moral reasoning, and moral education, complain that the subjects seem antiseptic and irrelevant. Since much of this instruction is taken up in the vaunted case method used in law and business schools, which has a pronounced aversion to any hint of prescriptive or normative behavior, the students complain that they learn all about the problems of morality, but nothing of how to be good. Goodness, they say, has become just another intellectual abstraction, and most of them do not see what is in it for them.

In a recent conversation among some of my most able and articulate undergraduate students, one of them, complaining of the poor quality of community life at Harvard, observed at least half paradoxically, "The very qualities that I recognize as essential in getting me in here are those qualities I least like in others; and since we are all alike, at least at the level of ambitious self-achievement, we do not know how to like one another or to live with one another. This place is too intensively selfish." That is a harsh but not unjust assessment of the quality of life in college today. What is heartening about this verdict is that at least the young people in question, because they are as clever and able as they are, recognize what is wrong. They did not create the problem, for their academic elders did that, but they must now live with it and, with little institutional help or encouragement, manage to turn themselves into good people. Virtue is not something you were meant to lose in college. The old college population, and many members of the present population, continue to believe that they are meant to find virtue in college and to use it as an essential ingredient for life after college. This is how Krimsky, in his Phi Beta Kappa address, speaks of virtue:

> Virtue means that you have to consider your contributions beyond yourself. It starts with respect for the dignity of other people and the appraisal of your action on others. It is also something you can cultivate over many years of honest work and integrity and lose in an instant.[7]

There appears to be a general cultural consensus, developed now over the past twenty-five years or so, that what is missing in our civilization is a sense of private and civic virtue. In America, having waged two wars for freedom and democracy, in the postwar period we put our considerable faith and energy into glorious concepts designed to preserve and enhance what had been won at so great a cost: education and personal liberty. Nearly every college and university revised its curriculum after World War II to provide for what the Harvard "Red Book" on curricular reform called "education in a free society." At the same time, after fighting a war to liberate the world from Nazi and Japanese totalitarianism, the Western cultures could hardly ignore the struggles for liberation within their own boundaries, although in the case of France and

Britain and their colonies, and the United States, with its racial and other minorities, they certainly resisted those movements. In theory, by the start of the twenty-first century, with more educated and free people than at any other time in the history of the planet, something seemed strangely wrong and unsatisfying. Many would argue that this was the inevitable price of progress, and others would argue that it was too high a price to pay and that the only way to resolve the problem was to return to a simpler and clearer concept of what it means to be virtuous. Political, cultural, and religious conservatives seized the general state of discontent to urge a restoration of the *status quo ante*, the most outrageous of those appeals resulting in the various forms of religious fundamentalism in Islam and Christianity and the repudiation in politics of much of liberal culture. Margaret Thatcher in Great Britain and Ronald Reagan in America, in distinct but complimentary ways, represented the political face of this sense of cultural discontent.

In higher education, diversity and meritocracy became the buzzwords, together with the notion that to be educated was to be liberated from whatever cultural, spiritual, and religious values one may have managed to bring from home to college. Having produced the most diverse, achieving, and ambitious college generation in the history of American education, it was discovered that not only were these amazingly able young people neither happy nor good, but that they longed to be both, and aspired to a moral education that the institutions to which they had mortgaged their family's worldly goods were no longer willing to supply. Not only were many of these students frustrated and disappointed, but the general public, whose confidence in the redemptive powers of college remained amazingly high, began to be suspicious of the disconnect between their expectations of the benefits of education for the public good, and their experience of an educational system designed to produce either the pursuit of private pleasure or clones for the corporate state. At the very least, some private virtue and public good ought to be the result of the best education that money can buy.

One of the many books critical of the failure of contemporary education to produce good people is social critic Philip K. Howard's *The Lost Art of Drawing the Line: How Fairness Went Too Far.* In this modest jeremiad, Howard cites with approval an early-twentieth-century British jurist, Lord Moulton, who observed:

> The success of every culture hinges not on big points of morality—there will always be issues like abortion or school prayer over which people differ—but on smaller values, like being considerate of others and pulling your weight. These values are neither legally enforceable nor purely private, but constitute the connective tissue of people interacting in a healthy society.[8]

Lord Moulton called this "the world of manners": "Between 'can do' and 'may do' ought to exist the whole realm which recognizes the sway of duty, fairness, sympathy, taste and all the other things that make life beautiful and society possible."[9]

Lord Moulton may well have been a contemporary of that English Catholic lay theologian Gilbert Keith Chesterton, whose moral aphorisms challenged the smug self-confidence of the British upper classes in the opening decades of the twentieth century. In one of his most famous lines he argued that virtue, a concept hijacked by theologians and philosophers from the common realm, where Plato and Aristotle and Paul meant it to be, consisted of the little things that could and must be taught:

> We do not need the learned man to teach us the important things. We all know the important things, though we all violate and neglect them. Gigantic industry, abysmal knowledge, are needed for the discovery of the tiny things—the things that hardly seem worth the trouble.[10]

It is the challenge of life to find out what these "things that hardly seem worth the trouble"—these virtues or rules for living the good life—are all about. What are the truths that last in times of need and upon which we call in times of crisis?

Before we can consider any list of qualities or virtues that may make up the good life, we must confront one apparent problem. The moral life has always been understood to require some form of discipline. Discipline is seen as the opposite of freedom, and freedom is understood to be the essence of modernity. Before the events of September 2001, I would have agreed that a resolution of this tension was impossible, and that in any context between freedom and discipline, between autonomy and restraint, the cultural votes will always prevail on the side of freedom and autonomy. Since September 11, however, we have been in a period of significant reappraisal. What may have been settled wisdom before is now subject to a rethink, and by this I do not mean simply that our sense of political and geographical invulnerability has been violated. It is a fact that, despite the isolating factors of two oceans, the very technology that we have used to celebrate our freedom from the rest of the world has now brought the rest of the world to us, and we can never again be the isolationists that we once were. It is that larger geopolitical fact, and the reassessments it requires, that has required the more personal reassessments under way in the hearts and minds of most Americans since that fateful day.

A Teachable Moment

In my pastoral encounters with students and others, I hear over and over again the reconsideration of what, for lack of a better term, I will call "value" questions. At first, these questions were directed to the country: What did we do wrong? Why do they hate us? What ought we to do as a country, domestically, internationally? Should we reinvest in a world from which periodically we are tempted to withdraw? Should we reevaluate our policy in the Middle East? Should we seek better ways to maintain "fortress America" against future violations? Those questions have provoked endless chatter from the talking heads and the editorialists; and in a world-class university such as Harvard, they are questions that concern many.

The reassessment questions of which I hear more now, however, have to do with personal reassessment. People tell me that they do not want to postpone any longer than necessary the things that are important, and for many those things are not the things about which they obsessed before September 11. Realizing how frighteningly unpredictable and short life can be, many are asking how best to use the time they may have. How may I learn to cherish, and express what I cherish, before it's too late? How do I properly rationalize my fears and move from paralysis? How do I calculate quality beyond the old values of mere quantity? How do I nourish my spiritual side? How do I reconnect with a religious tradition from which I have been estranged or that I never knew in the first place? On the evening news of December 10, 2001, Dan Rather reported that the sale of Bibles is up 40 percent since September. Clearly that, together with the reported significant increase in religious practice and attendance from September to December 2001, as measured by church and synagogue, suggests that people are eager, indeed desperate, to place the fragility and vulnerability of their personal lives in some larger, more secure context.

For many whose sense of security was connected to all that those twin towers stood for in the modern world—technology, power, economic security, and all of the things that the most prosperous country in the world has taught us to value—the destruction of the towers placed those values in serious jeopardy. Nor to be discounted is this thought expressed to me by one thirty-something overachiever: "I hate those Muslims, but they were willing to die for what they believed in. I am not sure even of what I am living for."

All of this makes for what Pope John Paul II once called a "teachable moment." People are prepared to hear things they have heard before, but to hear them now for the first time, as it were. One woman asked me after church, a few weeks following the September 11 disaster, whether we had changed the translation of the psalms that we read responsively in church every Sunday morning. No, I assured her, we read the same old psalms in the same old translations. "Well," she said, "they certainly sound different, up-to-date, and suited to my condition." The psalms haven't changed, but we and the world have, and that means we may be willing and ready to hear old things anew.

Another of the things I have sensed among the people with whom I work and to whom I minister—and I know of no better way of putting it—is a desire for discipline. To hear old things anew may help us to reconstitute meaning from those old classical lists of virtues that Aristotle, Plato, Augustine, Aquinas, and any other number of moralists have constructed. Helping us to live the good life, in terms relevant to our modern situation as people in search of goodness, is the business of life now before us.

The good life may well be the life lived in constant search of the good life, but perhaps it will help us to know that such virtues exist, can be taught and learned, and must be practiced. What follows is an effort to discuss these virtues, these fantastic truths, against the backdrop of the plausible lies they are meant to confute and overcome. The good life is the one that is lived in pursuit of those fantastic truths that endure in times such as these.

CHAPTER 3

LIVING FOR GOODNESS' SAKE

For this reason it has correctly been proclaimed
that good is what all desire.

ARISTOTLE

One of the first books to cross my desk in the millennial year of 2001 was also one of the smallest. Beautifully printed and of just over one hundred pages, it bore the modest title *A Book of Courtesy: The Art of Living with Yourself and Others*, and it was written in 1910 by a literary unknown, Sister Mary Mercedes, O.P., a Dominican nun who had devoted her life to teaching girls at two convent schools in California. The *Book of Courtesy* was her guide to the good life for the girls committed to her charge. Within the limited circle of the schools where she taught, the book had attained over its long life something so much like legendary status that, on the occasion of the fiftieth reunion of the Class of 1950 and the sesquicentennial of the Dominican sisters in California where the schools were located, alumnae determined to bring out a revised edition of the book as a gift to the rising generation of the twenty-first century.

This is a work of neither profound scholarship nor social commentary, but not unlike Lord Chesterton's classic eighteenth-century volume of letters of advice to his son, it was intended to provide a practical guide to the good life through the vehicle of courtesy, which Sister Mary

Mercedes defines simply as "the art of living with yourself and others." Her former students never forgot her instruction and in this revised edition were determined to pass on, as they said, "its wisdom to their grandchildren, who inherit a world sorely in need of her message."

What a fundamental message it is: "Be gentle and kind. Be simple in your tastes and sincere in your actions and let everything you do and say be governed by this timeless rule: 'Love your neighbor as yourself, and do unto others as you would have them do unto you'" (Galatians 5:14). As a nun providing a Catholic education in a Catholic school, Sister Mercedes is never far from the biblical principles of the "fruit of the Spirit," St. Paul's list of virtues (Galatians 5:22–23). In this regard she writes: "Keep in mind that every person on earth carries the Spirit of God in his soul. The fruits of His presence are love, joy, peace, patience, kindness, generosity, faithfulness, gentleness, and self-control."[1]

When, in 1910, Sister Mercedes first produced her little book, it would not have been an exceptional thing to engage in a discussion of manners, morals, and the good life as an essential part of a secondary-school education. The question of what constituted the good life, and of how one might achieve it, was as old as civilization itself. Certainly Sister Mercedes, coming as she did from a European order of nuns founded in France in 1207, understood such a conversation to be a part of her Christian mission to the young of a still very young country. In 1850, when the Roman Catholic bishop of California had called for volunteers to open a convent and school in the fledgling state, the only one to answer the call was a Dominican nun. That history aside, what makes the re-publication of this book interesting in the opening days of the twenty-first century is the fact that the questions it seeks to answer are still being asked, and that people, and most particularly young people, continue to stand in great need of guidance in the nature of the good life and in "the art of living with yourself and others."

On the Opposite Shore

On the opposite coast, and not long before the reissuing of Sister Mercedes' book, I discovered an advertisement in the *New York Times* for a program called "Sponsor a Boy" at LaSalle Academy. The school had been started in 1848 in a church basement on Canal Street near the Bowery, with four teaching brothers, ninety boys, and the ambition to teach all poor boys who sought an education. The school's population now, as then, consists largely of the sons of immigrants. In 1848 they were mostly Irish. Today, 54 percent of them are Latin American, 24 percent African American, 17 percent European American, and 5 percent Asian American. More than sixty countries are represented in the school population. It is a Catholic school, and 70 percent of the students are of that faith, but no one is turned away because of religious affiliation. Building character is what the school is about, tailoring teaching to a boy's needs and aptitudes, and 92 percent of its graduates go on to college.

What caught my attention was a set of five rules that the school imposed on all of its students. The rules were understood to develop good personal habits for "future success in life" through a program that could be described as guidance in living the good life, or the life that is good.

1. Respect yourself. Respect others. Show this respect in your attitude, your daily actions, and speech.

2. Study hard. Concentrate. Devote enough time every day to your assigned work.

3. Do your homework. You are expected to do two hours of homework every night. Do more if necessary.

4. Be punctual. Be in school every day, on time. Get to class on time, with all your homework done.

5. Dress for success. Be clean and neat. Dress so LaSalle will be proud of you, and you will be proud of yourself.

What the brothers on the East Coast and the sisters on the West Coast have in common is the conviction that the habit of good conduct is an indispensable element in the construction of a good life. There is nothing new about that in the life of a school, and such rules have been in place since the invention of schools, as an efficient way to form the young. Nor is it odd that schools that deal either with new places, such as California at the turn of the century, or with new Americans as in the immigrant population of the Bowery in New York, should place confidence in what has long been called at Harvard Law School "those wise restraints that make us free."

Social liberals and social conservatives would each argue that the age in which those "wise restraints" would be celebrated is long past. The liberals applaud, and the conservatives deplore. They are like the optimist who says, "This is the best of all possible worlds," and the pessimist who responds, "I agree."

Rules such as these seem old-fashioned, out of step with the conventional wisdom that suggests that "progress" and "contemporary times" call for the lessening of restraints and the celebration of liberation. What once might have worked in civilizing the natural inclination to hedonistic anarchy now simply represses the natural instincts to self-discovery, affirmation, and esteem and, at the very least, imposes a classicist, bourgeois, conformist ethic upon otherwise blithe spirits. Indeed, invitations to civility, polite discourse, and the courtesies essential to living the good life for oneself and for others seem so fragile and so inadequate that, in despair, Americans at the start of the twenty-first century survey the scene and utter that all-purpose slogan, "There oughta be a law!"

The redoubtable Miss Manners, who, through her tart-tongued columns and books, has devoted her life to the rediscovery of etiquette, wants to keep the law out of the business of manners. Two legal efforts attempting to legislate good public behavior of the sort that our two schools take for granted set her off. The first was the case of a man who was hauled into court for the use of profanity when he lost control of his boat on a public waterway in Michigan. The second was the passing of legislation in Louisiana requiring public-school pupils to address their teachers as "Sir" or "Ma'am" or to employ courtesy titles such as Mr., Mrs., Miss, or Ms. when using their surnames.

Since on the subject of etiquette Miss Manners is perceived to function like an old Russian cultural commissar, she noted that most people would assume she would be in favor of such restraints on bad behavior. As she enjoys doing, however, she turned the tables by arguing that the long arm of the law is no substitute for the voluntary society of the well-mannered, and she asked her readers if they remembered her warning in 1979, twenty years earlier, that "tossing aside the ancient and noble practice of etiquette would ultimately result in less freedom, not more." By tossing out the rules we have made ourselves subject to more law, and that, in Miss Manners's opinion, was a backward rather than a forward step:

> Schools should be able to promulgate deportment rules without the law either ensuring enforcement or mounting challenges. Profanity should be banned from public spaces, not by law, but by society's ceasing to glamorize it, instead of treating it as a deplorable lapse, saved for exactly such occasions as tumbling in a lake, for which apologies are necessary.[2]

Unlike many in the contemporary secular value system, Miss Manners is unashamed to declare that self-discipline is essential to personal freedom, and hence to the good life, which is good for all. She concludes: "Etiquette is better at handling such matters than the mighty and clumsy legal system, but it does expect people to restrict their own freedom. That should be the method of choice for all freedom-loving people."[3]

It is not the preponderance of freedom, but rather the lack of discipline that contributes to the sense of both public and personal chaos. The popularity of home schooling and the revival of interest in Catholic parochial education even for non-Catholics suggest a desire for discipline that would impose some order upon the greatest culture of freedom the world has ever known. For many, and not simply for the conservative cultural critics of the last decade of the last century, our freedoms have been bought at a price that may be too high for us to pay. Very few cultural restraints remain; for instance, Madonna is free to be as vulgar and as profane as she wishes to be on television, and network censors cower at the exercise of her power to offend—although there are fewer and fewer people who appear to be offended. *Freedom from* restraint is a part of the liberty we celebrate, but what pleasure is there in the absence of restraint if one has no *freedom for* anything? Freedom, despite the rhetoric of the Fourth of July and in times of patriotic bravado such as we saw in the days immediately following September 11, is fundamentally a means, not an end. We do not fight to be free: we fight for freedom in order to exercise it in the pursuit of something else.

In every culture, freedom has been the essential prerequisite for the pursuit and preservation of something else. In America, we call it the pursuit of happiness. Moral philosophers have called it the search for the good life, that which allows us each and all to fulfill our ultimate destiny, and such a pursuit is not random, accidental, or coincidental. Wisdom is not what we aspire to in the good life, for wisdom is merely one of the means by which good may be understood and pursued, yet without wisdom and the exercise of rational insight we are not free to pursue the good. What is essential to wisdom is discipline or, as the Bible puts it, the "desire to learn." "The true beginning of wisdom," the Bible says in The Wisdom of Solomon 6:17(KJV), "is the desire to learn."

What Makes Us Happy?

Some years ago, in reading an obituary of a woman academic at Oxford, I noted that she attributed such success as she had enjoyed in life to Aristotle's definition of happiness. As that definition was both appealing and new to me, I jotted it down, and every year since I have entered it onto the flyleaf of my new appointment book. There it sits, together with a few other aphorisms protecting me, as I imagine, from the tyranny of the calendar. As I copied it from the *London Times*, it reads:

> *Happiness: the exercise of vital powers along lines of excellence, in a life affording them scope.*
>
> ARISTOTLE

Lacking a sufficiently classical education, I had no idea where Aristotle said this, and for years it remained a floating aphorism and a handy classical illusion with which to impress friends and strangers even less classically literate than I. Then, in a forced march through Aristotle's great work *The Nicomachean Ethics* in search of something else, I found it, or something very close to it. Thus, in a more thorough way, I became reacquainted with Aristotle and with his notion of the good life.

To the person untrained in philosophy and with only a vague recollection of some long dead men from survey courses of long ago, the very name "Aristotle" conjures up sensations of skimmed reading assignments and being unprepared in class. Most often, my reaction to Aristotle is that other people, usually smarter people, know more about him than do I. As he belongs to a period and a profession far removed from the ordinary concerns of ordinary people, it comes as something of a surprise to most people who don't know it, to discover that Aristotle's entire effort in his great book on ethics is to answer the question: "How can I make my life a success?" To some, that question is both too crude and too self-interested. Seen through the lenses of contemporary careerism and the tyranny of what William James once called "that bitch-goddess Success," Aristotle's question seems almost too gritty, even parochial, for what we imagine high-minded, serious philosophy to be.

That image and perception notwithstanding, Aristotle is determined to ask the basic questions that everyone really wants to ask, which are: "What will make my life worth living? What counts as success?" As a young man, Aristotle wrote an essay entitled "The Exhortation to Philosophy," in which he noted that those things generally counted as valuable in this life, namely wealth, health, strength, beauty, influence, power, and ability, have no real and lasting value if the soul is not good. They are things that may make for a living, and indeed for a good and a successful living as the world counts success, but for Aristotle the difference is between making a living and making a life. The quality of the soul determines the quality of the life, and thus it is to the nature of the soul that we first must look if we would look toward living the good life.

The soul has a rational and an irrational part, and just as the soul is superior to the body, so is the rational part of the soul superior to the irrational part. Our purpose — *teleos* is the Greek word Aristotle uses — is to use the rational part of the soul, the better part, to learn of the good things we need to know. The rational part of the soul allows us to discern and to distinguish, and thus separates us from inanimate objects incapable of such behavior. It also allows us to exercise control over the irrational parts of the soul that can give us temporary pleasures and satisfactions, which, if unchecked, provide us with distorted and partial knowledge and thus deprive us of whole and balanced knowledge. Just like the passions, they have their moments, and, like passions, they both distort and are impermanent.

In Aristotle's view, the only way we can appreciate our human nature is to appreciate our divine nature. To exercise the mind, the rational part of the soul, is to encounter the permanent, which is the divine. Reason is the means by which we achieve the happy state of the gods, for as Aristotle says, "Man deprived of perception and mind is reduced to the condition of a plant; deprived of mind alone he is turned into a brute; deprived of irrationality but retaining mind, he becomes like God."[4] Thus, to live well, according to Aristotle, is to live one's life under the guidance of the virtues of the rational soul.

Living under such guidance is called "contemplation," which is in some sense an unfortunate choice of word, for in English it suggests passivity, even inaction. It is like the word "meditation," which to the uninitiated in the art and skill of meditation also suggests to the overworked Western mind the absence of action, or doing nothing. Just as meditation properly practiced and understood is doing something quite profound but very different from ordinary activity, contemplation, as Aristotle uses the term, is an activity, a process of the highest order. Contemplation allows the use of the highest human resource, the rational part of the soul, to consider the highest object of human enterprise, the divine, and the highest element in us is life devoted to the contemplation of the divine.

Such contemplation is neither an abstract nor a merely "spiritual" exercise, in the sense of being without form or substance. We are aided in the activity of contemplation by the intellectual and the moral virtues. The intellectual virtues give us knowledge of the truth and are acquired by learning at the hands of teachers; the moral virtues dispose our emotions to respond correctly to practical situations and are acquired by practice. Such knowledge and habits afford the one who has them happiness, or *eudaimonia*, the Greek word Aristotle uses. This definition of "happiness," however, is not what our English word suggests, that is, "pleasure" or "contentment." Aristotle's "happiness" is more nuanced and can be translated as "flourishing" or "well-being." One commentary suggests that it is closest to meaning "whatever makes a human life good for the person living it."[5] Another rendering of "happiness," in this sense, is "the good life: the complete good, that is, what is most good, most noble, most pleasant." St. Thomas Aquinas, in his *Commentary on Aristotle*, parses "happiness" as "an activity flowing from virtue." Another rendering of *eudaimonia* that avoids the English problem with "happiness" altogether calls it "success," which in this sense means entirely excellent activity. Perhaps the simplest concept of the term is "living well and doing well," which is possible only from activities that flow from the intellectual and moral virtues. Thus, the person who lives such a life is happy, and the life so lived is good.

Now back to the epitaph for the English academic and Aristotle's definition of happiness that, without benefit of the preceding exegesis, I so slavishly copied into my appointment book: "Happiness: the exercise of vital powers along lines of excellence, in a life affording them scope." At the end of Chapter 10 of Book 10 of *The Nicomachean Ethics*, Aristotle writes:

> What is to prevent us, then, from concluding that the happy person is the one who, adequately furnished with external goods, engages in activities in accordance with complete virtue, not for just any period of time but over a complete life?

"Happiness," here in our several nuanced renderings, is a consequence, a result, of the opportunity that a certain sense of worldly security affords, to engage in activities informed by the exercise of the intellectual and moral virtues acquired by learning and by the practice of good habits over the course of an entire lifetime. The person who is able to do this is good, and the life thus led is the good life. The person is good in the sense of virtuous, happy in the sense of doing what a good person does, and successful, that is, consistent, in the perception and performance of excellent activity. Another way of putting it is this: the good person is one who is good at being a person.

This sounds annoyingly like one of those tautologies that one is supposed to tease out on the verbal part of the SAT exam, and is likely to drive people away from rather than drawing them nearer to a cogent definition. Just at this point, as if recognizing the sounds of the cracking thin ice of the definition that will send us to the philosophical bottom, Aristotle offers us an illustration. He says that a good flute player is one who is good at playing the flute, just as the good person is one who lives the good life well, that is, one who combines reason and activity with excellence.

Purpose and Function

Aristotle wants us to understand that for him fulfillment or satisfaction means being good at what one is meant to do. Here we have to understand the difference between the use of "good" as a moral quality, e.g., Mother Teresa went about doing good; and "good" as the excellent fulfillment of a function, e.g., Stradivarius made good violins. Both people were good at what they did, but one was so in a moral sense and the other in an aesthetic or performative sense. Aristotle is closer to the latter than to the former. Taking note of Aristotle's musical example, I offer two of my own in the hope of clarifying what he means to say. Many years ago, I first heard Jessye Norman sing in Elgar's oratorio *The Dream of Gerontius*. I sat in the second balcony of Boston's Symphony Hall on a Good Friday afternoon, and with Norman's final note at the end of a timeless three hours I felt as though in her voice I had heard the most sublime sound of my life. I had never heard of Jessye Norman, but at that moment I was convinced that she could do nothing better than what she was doing, that nobody could do it better than she, and that she was the very incarnation of excellence itself. That was not a moral decision, for I knew nothing of her character or personality or whether she was a good or a bad person. I simply knew that she was good, indeed excellent, at what she did. That is the sense in which Aristotle uses the notion of excellence and good: the good singer is one who is good at singing, and reason and activity with excellence make it so.

Among the pleasures of my life is a long friendship with the cellist Yo Yo Ma. I have known him since he was a freshman at Harvard over a quarter of a century ago, and I remember as if it were yesterday the first time I saw or, I should say, heard him in action. It was at an undergraduate master class with the great Russian cellist Rostropovich. Ordinarily I would not have attended a Saturday morning session to listen to Harvard's seven best undergraduate cellists as they sawed their way through their repertoires in the presence of a Russian maestro, but one of the cellists, not Ma, was a student friend of mine and I, along with others from his undergraduate house, had come to offer moral support. Each student played a piece, and at its close the maestro, speaking through an interpreter, would say a few things, suggest a twist here, a turn there, and then move on. Our young man seemed to do quite well, and we were pleased for him. The maestro seemed mildly bored by the whole thing, but he gave a good show of artistic temperament, his Russian language not failing to communicate his pleasure or dissatisfaction.

The next to last contestant was Ma, and I was one of few in the audience who did not already know of his reputation as a prodigy. He began to play, and when Ma plays, his whole being becomes an extension of the music and of the instrument; rather than being solely an instrumentalist, he is instrumentalist, instrument, and, indeed, even conductor. The late great trumpet player Armando Ghitalla, of the Boston Symphony Orchestra, used to say that some musicians play the notes, others the rhythm, and some, finally, the music. Ma plays everything, is everything, and well before he had finished—in that particular Saturday morning session—the maestro jumped up, gesticulating wildly, and, in a torrent of Russian too fast for translation, forced the young player to stop. We were stunned. Was he pleased, impressed, angry, dismayed? He took the bow from Yo Yo and, playing over his shoulder, did something that appeared to be a correction of bowing or of interpretation. Yo Yo did as instructed. A few more measures, and the scene was repeated. We could tell that Rostropovich was excited beyond words, and we thought he was about to throw a tantrum. The encounters between the two of them became intense and physical, and we onlookers were witnessing some form of transformation. The poor translator could not get a word in edgewise. At the end, Yo Yo finished with a flourish, and the maestro, throwing all of his European reserve to the winds, flung his arms about the neck of the slight young man and showered him with kisses. The other cellists burst into applause, the audience jumped to its feet, and although no one knew quite what had happened, all were conscious of the fact that they had witnessed something extraordinary. Only in the wake of the pandemonium did the translator have a chance to say that the maestro had said he had never before heard such playing in his life and that he, the maestro, was in the presence of genius.

How does one describe such a moment? It was, as Aristotle said, "Happiness: the exercise of vital powers along lines of excellence, in a life affording them scope." The good cellist is one who is good at playing the cello, just as the good person is one who is good at being a person, doing what is most good, most noble, and most pleasant. What the good person and the good musician do is perform virtuously, and the virtue of something is related to the notion of its ability to perform excellently its characteristic activity. The characteristic activity of a musician is to do music excellently, and the characteristic activity of a human being is to be human excellently: the effective discharge of this function is the only real happiness. We do not do virtuous things in order to be happy; rather, we are happy because we do virtuous things; and we are only truly happy when we are doing what we are meant to do and being what we are meant to be.

Limitations on the Life of Virtue

For Aristotle, the virtuous life was not necessarily an easy life, and he accepted the wisdom that one should never call a person successful until his life is over. Discipline and education are essential to the virtuous life, and also essential is sufficient opportunity of both time and means to be able to engage in the discipline and education that encourages virtuous activity. Not everyone has the natural talent or the opportunity to pursue it at the highest level of excellence, of a Jessye Norman or a Yo Yo Ma, and yet success in life, the living of the good life, is not measured in comparison with the lives of others, but rather by what one does with what one has in one's own life. The good life depends upon the qualities of one's activities, and a virtuous person cannot fail to lead a good life, because by training and habit that person will choose to do only virtuous things.

Aristotle was an elitist, for the virtuous life as he described it was available only to those who could afford to think about it. He was, after all, a teacher of aristocratic young men who had, by virtue of their social position, only three career options:

1. They could engage in pleasant amusements and refined pleasures.

2. They could enter into public service and the realm of politics, seeking to gain honor and reputation.

3. They could engage in philosophy and attempt to understand the universe.

The person who worked or was poor or had bad luck was excluded from this process. The political, economic, or wisdom skills required of someone responsible for a political community, a household, or his own soul are qualities or goods that in Aristotle's time fell to gentlemen who, in addition to those skills, also required some degree of good fortune. Someone obsessed with economic survival or at the beck and call of somebody else simply could not afford to be a gentleman, which in Greek is translated literally as someone who is "noble and good."

Is virtue, the good life as elucidated by Aristotle, possible for those who would be automatically excluded from it by Aristotle's own worldview? For example, although when Aristotle uses the Greek word for "mankind," the term means "humankind" and not simply the male gender, Aristotle himself was speaking and writing only for members of the male gender. Is the good life available to those not included in his cultural frame of reference? To answer this question we will have to turn to subsequent developments in antiquity to which Aristotle's world was first compared, and then under which it was subsumed.

The Judeo-Christian tradition is no less concerned with the question of what makes a life good and how one pursues it; and while the questions of happiness, success, purpose, and good remain at the center of human inquiry after more than mere survival, the answers are transformed by the experiences of those who enterprise new relations with themselves, with one another, and with the one whom they will come to call "God." There is a shift in emphasis from self to the other, from the "good" to "God," from the good life to eternal life, and from duty to altruism. Virtues are redefined in light of these shifts, and the result is an acknowledgment of the limits of human perfection and the redefinition of what is good from a philosophical concept to a relational one that extends both God-ward and human-ward. It is this tradition, the result of these several transformations, that becomes normative in the West and is virtually equated with what was once easily called "Western civilization." For the student of the good life, what is now of great interest consists in what is retained from the classical system, what is changed and transformed by the encounter with Judeo-Christian tradition, and what emerges as a new and distinct way of asking the same old question: "What must I do to be good?"

What We Know and What We Need to Know

The question of the "good life" in the tradition of Plato, Socrates, and Aristotle was always the question of what creates a life worth living. What is the nature of success and happiness? What is good, and how do I pursue it? Often the questions seem to have lives of their own—a philosopher's paradise—and, as we have found with Aristotle, the answers often lead to even more complexity. Moral education in the Greek or Athenian tradition was not easy, and it certainly was not a pastime for the average person.

In the Christian tradition, with its appropriation of much of the moral education of its Hebrew antecedents, both questions and answers seem clearer, if not easier, although the application of what is known to the practice of living is an equally demanding, and at times frustrating, enterprise.

The question of what is good is implied in that most famous of all ethical passages from the Hebrew Bible. In Micah 6, the prophet asks if God will be pleased with the traditional variety of offerings and sacrifices, with the abasement of the worshiper, and with expressions of Eastern homage. The conversation of Micah 6 is in the form of an indictment against the people of Israel for their lack of gratitude toward God, and their sin is a sin against love. God has shown his love to them over and over again, by sending them able leaders, delivering them from slavery, guiding them through the wilderness, and performing numerous and unambiguous acts of kindness and benevolence toward them; and for his pains in doing all of this, the people respond with indifference. By the offended tones of God toward the people, who continually fail to remember all that they owe to God, we learn that God has feelings, senses a personal and ethical injury, and experiences the bitterness of ingratitude.

Being God may mean having the right to expect people—the object of divine benevolence—to be grateful, but now even God knows that people do not like to feel grateful. Gratitude is a cold virtue. Why? Because the person who shows gratitude acknowledges obligation, necessity, or even inadequacy. Although people are always relieved to be given assistance and are even thankful for it, they do not like to be reminded of it, especially after the period of immediate need has passed. By the very act of receiving it, the recipient of an act of mercy or of kindness is placed in a relationship of obligation to the giver of it. This might even be described as a "power" relationship. To acknowledge the power that helped you is also an acknowledgment that you stood in need of help, that you are not as powerful or independent as you had thought, and that despite your present circumstances of relief you could fall into powerlessness again and again require rescue at the hands of another, to whom you would then owe an obligation.

This large ethical issue with which Micah contends can be seen on a more intimate and domestic scale in ordinary life, where routinely we do our best to deflect such seemingly harmless things as social compliments. For example, when you are complimented on your appearance or performance, cultural etiquette requires that you both accept and deflect the compliment at the same time. "You sang wonderfully today," is said to the diva, and she replies, "Oh, not at all, but thank you so very much." "What a magnificent party," you say to your hostess on your way out, and her response is, "You are so kind. I'm delighted you enjoyed yourself, but you are the great party-giver." At first these little exchanges sound like so much "sociobabble," but in fact they constitute a deadly game of "Don't get caught with the compliment."

A story is told "down Maine" illustrating the so-called problem of obligation. Two Yankee fishermen were far out on the water when they became enveloped in a thick pea-souper of a fog, and soon they heard the ominous sounds of a big ship headed in their direction. As they could neither see nor be seen, it was very likely that their little craft would be sliced in two by the Bangor packet boat bearing down upon them. One man said to the other, "I'll work the oars, and you know what to do"; the other immediately assumed the posture of prayer. Just as he was about to begin to pray, however, the fog lifted, the big boat swerved, and they were saved and not swamped. The Yankee at the oars said to the Yankee about to pray, "Now don't you say a word: no need to be beholden."

The problem is not that we forget our obligations. It is human nature to want to avoid obligation, not because we don't want to be "beholden," as the Yankee fisherman said, but because of it we are reminded of our powerlessness.

Thus, when God constantly reminds people of all of his mercies and blessings, of how he has saved them from this, that, and the other—drumming up gratitude, as it were—the people are not always grateful. The people in the book of Micah, however, are forced to acknowledge their guilt, which consists in their failure to remember. Reminded of this by the prophet, they plead that they do not know how to approach, much less to placate, the God whom they have offended and who has a right to be offended. What will be an acceptable sacrifice? What will be a show of good faith? In the language of modern negotiation, "What will it take to put this right?" Conventional wisdom suggests some kind of ritual response well known in the history of the people. Will personal homage, the offer of animals, or even the sacrifice of one's firstborn achieve it, after the historic model of Abraham and Isaac?

The conventional reading of the text at this point suggests that God prefers righteousness to ritual, and thus that tribal sacrifice is not acceptable. What is more interesting here, however, than a conventional move toward ethical behavior is the fact that the prophet says to the people that they already know from God what God wants: "He has showed you, O man, what is good." You do not have to have secret discernment or sophisticated wisdom to know what it is that God requires of you, for God has said it all before. These verses from Micah 6, which introduce the summary of ethical obligations toward neighbor and God, are part of the Torah, and well known to every Jew. Micah uses the language of Deuteronomy 10:12, which says:

And now, Israel, what does the Lord your God, require of you, but to fear the Lord your God, to walk in all his ways, to love him, to serve the Lord your God with all your heart and with all your soul . . .

All these things in Deuteronomy 10:12 are themselves a summary of the values previously affirmed by Moses: fear, love, deeds, service, and complete commitment.

Thus Micah, many generations later, is invoking a code and reiterating the good, as it were, that should have been by that time innate. This is no novelty: the obligation is not simply to remember what God once did, but to remember what God then and now requires as an expression of response to God's goodness:

He has showed you, O man, what is good;
and what does the Lord require of you
but to do justice, and to love kindness,
and to walk humbly with your God?

MICAH 6:8

The ethical demand is a summary of accumulated ethical wisdom not simply from Deuteronomy, which we find in the Torah, but from the prophetic predecessors of Micah. It is Amos who demands justice (5:24), Hosea who requires mercy or kindness (6:6), and Isaiah who insists upon humility in the face of the exalted God (2:11). Justice, kindness, and humility might well be called the "three historic Hebrew virtues," and although "virtue" is admittedly a classical and not a Hebrew term, those three, together with the summary of the law as love of God and love of neighbor as oneself, provide the ethical norm of Hebrew scripture and, by extension, of Christian scripture as well. The substance of these virtues is enormously significant: here is a code of conduct, not of belief, and one that is both inclusive and absolute. Yet, of even greater interest is the conviction that this is not new knowledge, but is well and universally known, and to know that one knows it is not only to define how one is to behave, but who one is. We already know what the good is: the task now is to perform it, or, as my colleague Bishop Krister Stendahl once put it in an epigram that I paraphrase imperfectly: "The demand of [Christian] ethics is to act upon what we have always known."

We Know What Is Good

The contemporary search for virtue and the hope for the good life do not take place in an ethical vacuum. It is not the case that we have forgotten the old standards or that we never really knew them. We know full well that it is better to tell the truth than to lie, better to be loyal than disloyal, better to love than to hate. We know that the Golden Rule ought still to be the standard by which we live and expect others to live; and we believe that we believe in humility, modesty, honesty, integrity, fidelity, fortitude, and courage. We are not ignorant of the virtues of classical antiquity, nor even, in this decidedly secular age, are we uninformed of the Christian virtues.

The question is not whether these virtues are true. The question is, for many a modern: "Can I afford them if they are?" Most people are perfectly aware of the traditions of the good life. They may not have read the classical literature, but they know something of the heroic qualities idealized in antiquity, and they admire such people as Jesus and Mother Teresa. Epic movies like *Braveheart* and *Gladiator* still make money from people's admiration of the heroic, and in television and film no one needs a primer to determine the identity of the villain or the hero. One of the reasons the cowboy epic and stories of the Mafia have enormous appeal in America is that they play out in black and white the moral areas that for most average people are merely gray. The enormous appeal of the television series *The Sopranos* has not so much to do with brilliant writing or interesting plots as it does with the fact that in our day we have what Shakespeare had in his: upon the stage — in our case the television stage — a morality of good, bad, and ambiguity with which we can clearly identify is writ large; and what we seek but cannot necessarily achieve in our own moral pilgrimage toward the life of virtue, the good life, we see played out before us in a parable we can understand, if not always emulate.

My argument is that we want to be noble, heroic, honorable, decent people. We want to be better than we are, and we know right and wrong when we see it. Our question, I suggest, is whether we can afford the values to which we aspire. In a dishonorable world, will the honorable be disadvantaged? If "everybody's doing it" and I don't do it, what happens to me? Socrates was forced to drink hemlock for his pains. Jesus was crucified. Abraham Lincoln and Martin Luther King Jr. were assassinated, and Joe Bloggs loses his job for blowing the whistle. How can I adapt the values and virtues of the good life for my life and world, which are less than perfect?

In order to answer those questions as we seek to frame a life and not just a living, a life that is worth living because it is good and therefore good for us, I suggest that we are going to have to learn something about failure and success as two constructive elements of the good life and to come to terms with both discipline and freedom as means to the end of living a good life. It is to these matters that we now turn.

PART II

THE GOOD LIFE

TOOLS FOR THE JOURNEY

CHAPTER 4

FAILURE

WHAT'S GOOD ABOUT IT?

When you're successful you don't appreciate all the magic that
went into that success as much as when you've gone through
failure. When you try something and it doesn't work, you
have a tendency to spend time reflecting.
JASON RASKY, COFOUNDER,
FAILURE MAGAZINE, 2001

All of my life I have lived with the shame of my first conspicuous failure, for I was required to repeat the second grade in an age long before social promotion and was known then on the playground as "Peter the Repeater." The day on which I got the dreadful news is as clear to me as yesterday, and I hadn't seen it coming. In my young life I had always enjoyed some success in charming my elders, and as I was a reasonably bright hard worker and generally a "good kid," success as one knows it at age seven had generally attended my way. On the last day of school before the summer, however, Miss Cassady, our formidable second-grade teacher in the Mount Pleasant School, conferred on me and on my good friend Alfred one of the greatest honors a second grader could get: she asked us to clap the erasers outside and to help her with cleaning up the classroom. Then, in the nicest possible way, she told us that we would each have the pleasure of her company for another year. We were to be kept back; and thus we would be branded forever as not up to par with our peers. In a grammar school with six grades and twenty-five pupils per grade, the environment was of some considerable intimacy, almost a closed community, and from it no secrets could be hid. Alfred and I were companions in shame and terrified of what our parents would say to us when they found out what had happened—although, unknown to us, they had already been informed by the efficient Miss Cassady. It was a very long walk home that day, as I carried with me my first significant experience of failure.

My parents were wonderful about it, and it was only years later that I realized they had been in cahoots with Miss Cassady. I, too, got over it and on with it and, determined to prove myself more than "Peter the Repeater," I became something of the ambitious overachiever known so well ever since to my contemporaries. The fact that I deserved to fail, that I was better off for repeating, and that I made something of myself with this second chance may well serve to illustrate the therapeutic virtues of failure, an important moral lesson in life. For me it was not a pleasant lesson to learn, I have resisted its implications all of my life, and I resent the sense of shame I still regard as the first of many blemishes upon my life's experiences. I do not like failure, but I have come to see its value in the ongoing search for the good life.

As the earliest days of my school career were lived under this cloud, so too were the closing days of my high-school career. Among the people in my family and my school there had never been a question of "whether" I was going to college, but rather of where I would go and how; and I had my heart set on Bowdoin College, in Brunswick, Maine, the "Harvard of the North," as it had aspired to be since its founding toward the close of the eighteenth century. A Plymouth friend of whom I thought the world had gone there, and thus I had been encouraged to think of Bowdoin.

I lent every effort to that goal, even ruining three years of perfect attendance in high school in order to attend the required on-campus interview. My parents forsook their work, drove me to Brunswick, Maine, and sat in the waiting room as I went in to see the admissions officer. He was a trim, tidy man with a bow tie, the perfect picture of the Yankee schoolmaster; we sat opposite one another across a table, and I was prepared to like him and all he stood for. After some desultory conversation, however, he leafed again through my folder, closed it, clasped his hands, and, looking at me dead in the eye across the table, said, "Mr. Gomes, I don't think you are Bowdoin material." The rest was a blur, the only focus of which was to make as graceful and efficient a withdrawal from that room as possible. I managed it. My eager parents wanted to know all, and fast, expecting only the best, and finally, after some exasperating procrastination, I told them that I wouldn't be going to Bowdoin as I had failed to be admitted. This time, not having had the benefit of Miss Cassady's forewarning, they were truly understanding.

We went on to my second choice, Bates College, in Lewiston, Maine, which generously took a chance on me, and I have been grateful to the admissions office ever since. Bates, by any standard, was the best place for me, and the Dean of Admissions, Milton Lindholm, remains to this day my hero and my friend. This all happened forty years ago and yet it remains vibrant and fresh, not so much for the success that came from the Bates experience, but because of the experience of failure that promoted it. When several years ago I was awarded an honorary degree from Bowdoin, I thanked the college for not having admitted me so many years earlier, as the result of that decision had facilitated some of the happiest choices of my life.

As examples of the Christian virtue of the second chance, the experience of what William James called the "twice-born man," I have used these illustrations of personal failure, for in each case what had looked like a disaster and a dead end had turned out to be a means for an improved situation. Religion is nearly always the experience of the twice-born, the second birth, the new creation, the reprieve, and the renewal. When, today, my students, for example, do not get their first choices in life, when the doors of opportunity are slammed shut in the faces of adults, or when failure looms inevitable and unavoidable for friends or acquaintances, I haul out these autobiographical bromides, and by and large they work. There is something very American, very "can-do" about them, and the easy moral is that the villain failure is properly overcome and defeated.

The older I get, however, the more I am persuaded that the true story has less to do with overcoming failure and what follows it, than with failure itself, with what it does to us and for us, and with what we can do with it besides quickly distancing ourselves from it. The shame of failure, for that is how I have always felt about it, is that it makes us appear not necessarily incompetent, but unnatural. Success, as we understand it in the culture of American and Western self-actualization, is normal and hence normative, and given the proper opportunity, there is no excuse for anything but success. Failure is thus either a moral defect or a bit of bad luck. To fail is to be less than we are meant to be, and thus failure is to the soul what disease is to the body: just as we would not encourage a culture of disease, so do we not encourage a culture of failure. In our culture of self-esteem, which derives from our insistence upon equity in the pursuit of happiness, a pursuit that is often confused with the assurance of happiness, we are complicit in the desire to construct a failure-proof culture. Failure in school now is rare, and when it happens, more often than not it is an indictment of the teacher and not of the taught. Some academic colleagues of mine dislike giving what we used to call "pop quizzes," reasoning that some students would be better prepared than others, which would lead to inevitable failures, which would then be unfair to those who, being less well prepared, failed.

Such a situation invokes the memory of a legendary Bates professor at the turn of the twentieth century, George Millett "Goosey" Chase, famous for his Christian charity in the difficult business of teaching Greek to undergraduates. Also famous for his pop quizzes, he always looked on the bright side of even the worst performances, seeking to encourage whenever he could. Of one dismal student he is reported to have said, "You have done quite well, sir. A remarkable improvement, sir. Yours is quite the best grade . . . of those who failed."

Such mitigation in failure is as rare as it is laughable. In a culture ruled by success and by the appearance of success, the reality of failure is unacceptable, and the current controversy in academia concerning what is blithely called "grade inflation" suggests two things in this regard. First, presumably more people are now getting higher grades, not because they are smarter than their predecessors, but because the culture will not permit their teachers to give out failing grades; nor will it permit students to accept them. Success, as defined in terms of high grades, is now normal and natural, and thus to give someone less than the normal or the natural grade is to brand that person as less than normal or natural, and to do it will cost him or her more than a few moments of self-reflection as well as a loss of self-esteem. When grade inflation first began in the mid-1960s, it theoretically was to keep white middle-class boys out of the draft pool, and hence from almost certain death in Vietnam. The famous "gentleman's C" was now almost a death warrant, and who would want to be responsible for that?

The phenomenon of grade inflation is not, alas, peculiar to American universities. Writing on the education pages of the *London Daily Telegraph* on July 21, 1999, Dr. Andy Martin, a lecturer in French at the University of Cambridge, observed:

If Cambridge were a hospital, no one would die anymore; the corpse would simply be "declared to have deserved life.". . . There is a broad inflationary pressure on educational institutions to be seen to be doing well. And so they do. The problem is that we are devaluing the currency. . . . This is not the end of civilisation as we know it, but we are opening ourselves up to incredulity from the outside world.[1]

In commenting on Cambridge honors-degree holders and their inability to spell or construct a decent English sentence, he noted that, unlike in Japanese universities, where people still fail their degrees, "in the West it appears that we are afraid to fail anymore. Yet without failure, we can neither measure success, nor, perhaps attain it." He concludes: "I want to propose that universities bring back failure. . . . If the Government is serious about raising standards, I can think of no better barometer of quality than the quantity of failures."[2]

The English, it seems, are just catching on to what has long been an American problem. Today the argument that says we have in effect banished failure means that greater scrutiny must be applied to what passes for success. Thus academic purists, not willing to believe the press notices of their own admissions departments, decline to admit that the students now are brighter and smarter and prefer to believe that standards somehow are now less demanding. In essence, they argue that credible failure is essential to credible success and that the quality of the "A" is dependent upon the quality of the "F." They partake of the logic of Gilbert and Sullivan's notoriously snobbish Grand Inquisitor in *The Gondoliers*, who famously sings, "If everybody's somebody, than no one's anybody." Failure is not good in its own right, but it is useful insofar as it benefits the good of success.

Failure as an aberration or failure as simply the device by which to maintain the purity of success does not take into account the moral benefits of failure and what can be learned from it. In an age of ever expanding prosperity and cultural optimism, when, as General Electric used to tell us, "Progress is our most important product" and we could all believe it to be so, failure could be branded an Old World, un-American activity. For example, criticism of the failure of the American dream to deliver the goods to many of its own people could be, and frequently was, construed to be unpatriotic and, indeed, un-American. When in the period between the two world wars, two great African Americans, the intellectual W. E. B. Du Bois and the singer Paul

Robeson, charged white America with a failure to live up to its promise for its African American citizens, each was denounced as a traitor and a communist sympathizer and generally hounded out of public life. When they both praised socialist possibilities over American realities, in the eyes of their patriotic critics, who could not bear the suggestion of democracy's failures, their foreign and seditious sympathies were exposed for all to see.

When, at the start of the twentieth century, Dr. Du Bois said that the problem of that century for America would be the problem of color, he stated by implication that failure to address the failure of race relations in America would prove to be our culture's fatal flaw. He understood that in society, as in personal experience, it is in our nature to avoid hurt, pain, sorrow, suffering, or even the hint of failure. We are averse to pain, and even when the failure we suffer hurts ourselves as well as others, it is our human tendency to avoid it, pretend it isn't there, or to do anything to avoid the reality of failure and dysfunction. This is why we are so reluctant to visit the dentist, for there is pain to be found there that is perhaps associated with our failure to keep up our dental hygiene, and we would rather suffer the pain that our failure has caused than endure the pain of the dentist, which will serve as a cure.

It was in 1901 that Du Bois made his famously trenchant remark about the social pain ahead for America for its failure to address its own failures. In quite another connection, in that very same year the man under whom Du Bois had studied at Harvard in the last years of the previous century also had something to say about pain and failure. William James, in *The Varieties of Religious Experience*, derived from his Gifford Lectures given at Edinburgh in 1901–2 and destined for iconic status in the young field of the psychology of religion, in Lectures VI and VII on "The Sick Soul," spoke of the utility of failure: "Let us see whether pity, pain, and fear, and the sentiment of human helplessness may not open a profounder view and put into our hands a more complicated key to the meaning of the situation."[3]

William James is perhaps most famous for his delineation of two major religious temperaments: the one he calls the healthy-minded and the other, the sick-minded. To our contemporary minds the terms seem simple, and if a choice is to be made between them we will naturally choose to be healthy-minded over sick-minded. These terms in themselves, however, do an injustice to the subtle distinctions James wishes to make between them. The so-called healthy-minded outlook, a temperament with much in common with optimism and high-mindedness, is good as far as it goes, for it gives people a cheery purchase on the world and a sense of possibility, the "can-do" spirit. James characterizes this position as "The once-born and their sky-blue optimistic gospel." These are the ones who, despite all appearances and indeed even evidence to the contrary, continually cry, "Hurrah for the Universe! God's in his Heaven, all's right with the world!" This temperament, argues James, "has a constitutional incapacity for prolonged suffering," and this incapacity becomes the basis for a peculiar type of religion, "a religion in which good, even the good of this world's life, is regarded as the essential thing for a rational being to attend to." The religion of healthy-mindedness, James argues, is connected to happiness, and happiness is for many the chief object of life: "How to gain, how to keep, how to recover happiness." With the relationship between religion and happiness established, James suggests it is not surprising that people come to regard the happiness that a religion can afford as a proof of its truth. If a creed makes a person happy, that person will believe it to be true and thus adopt it. This is understandable, for in many persons happiness is innate—"congenital" is the word James uses. They enjoy "cosmic emotion," which expresses itself in them as enthusiasm and freedom. They look on the bright side. The glass is always half full rather than half empty. Where many see problems they see possibilities, and they believe that in the long run all will turn out well and that things are better now than they once were.

James took as examples of this kind of thinking such apostles of nineteenth-century New England optimism as Ralph Waldo Emerson and Theodore Parker and the liberal religious tradition, the so-called Boston religion, that was inspired by their writings. These stood out as the high point of the theological, cultural, and intellectual revolution that had been raging for nearly three hundred years against the dark-sided Calvinism of New England's Puritan background. The stern, judgmental God of retribution and absolute power has yielded to "the animating Spirit of a beautiful harmonious world, beneficent and kind, merciful as well as pure." He cites as typical of this once-born soul the woman who described the pleasure it gave her "to think that she could always cuddle up to God."

In some sense, James did not need to persuade his Scottish Presbyterian auditors in Edinburgh University of the thinness of the once-born soul, and they themselves would have been among the first to sense the inadequacy of an inadequate doctrine of sin. It is James's own New England location, and the American culture it spawned, that exemplified the once-born tradition. Quoting no less a paragon of New England virtue than Dr. Edward Everett Hale, the famous chaplain of the United States Senate and author of the patriotic fable "The Man Without a Country," James cites his view on child rearing and theology:

> A child who is early taught that he is God's child, that he may live and move and have his being in God, and that he has, therefore, infinite strength at hand for the conquering of any difficulty, will take life more easily, and probably will make more of it, than one who is told that he is born the child of wrath and wholly incapable of God.[4]

Of Emerson, Parker, Hale, and the rest of the apostles of the once-born, James notes: "One can but recognize in such writers as these the presence of a temperament organically weighted on the side of cheer and fatally forbidden to linger, as those of opposite temperament linger, over the darker aspects of the universe."[5] For some, he says, such optimism may become quasi-pathological, and even temporary sadness "or a momentary humility" is denied them by what he calls "a kind of congenital anaesthesia."

What makes James interesting here is that he is not trying to make a theological or a doctrinal point. His is not a debate between Calvinism and liberalism. He is making a psychological point, which, insofar as it goes, is that the religion of healthy-mindedness, the religion of the once-born, is fine, but that its fundamental flaw has to do with its inability to account for failure, evil, and what the religiously orthodox would call sin.

Religions of optimism prove inadequate when unavoidable melancholy enters in and, indeed, evil, sickness, and failure, the sources of melancholy, are realities and not illusions in the world. To fail to take them into account is to fail to take the world seriously on its terms, and in failing to do that, one misses the opportunity to learn the essential lessons that such things teach. Truth, for example, is not the absence of falsehood or error: it is the means by which falsehood and error are seen to be what they are. There can be no light without the darkness out of which it shines. Good requires evil by which it can define itself and against which it can defend itself. Theologians of a certain stripe have always been pleased to suggest that the Devil's greatest contribution to the human predicament is the human argument that the Devil, and hence his works, could not possibly exist.

While James argues that the world is far too complex, even mysterious, to be seen simply as an opposition between healthy-minded optimism and sick-minded pessimism, a distinction he might have called "simple-minded," he nevertheless commends the temperament of the twice-born, the sick-minded. Such persons are those who, having discovered the limitations and deceits of the first birth, the first life, the world of optimism, are delivered from that into a twice-born state and are thus able to see the situation in which they find themselves as whole and complete. Real life by this definition is one that encompasses both good and evil. The method of averting one's attention from evil, and of living simply in the light of good, is splendid as long as it works, but it breaks down impotently as soon as melancholy comes:

> And even though one be quite free from melancholy one's self, there is no doubt that healthy-mindedness is inadequate as a philosophical doctrine, because the evil facts which it refuses positively to account for are a genuine portion of reality; and they may after all be the best key to life's significance, and possibly the only openers of our eyes to the deepest levels of truth.[6]

Systems that fail to account for evil facts, including failure, are therefore less than complete, because evil and failure are as real and as rationally significant as good and happiness. Thus, if one is going to take the whole of life seriously, as indeed one must if one is to attempt the good life, then failure, among the other distempers of life, must not be acknowledged by one as an essential part of the whole, but also one must discern what can be learned from it. This is the human situation.

What Can Failure Do for Us?

Over the years, I have given many commencement addresses and preached many baccalaureate sermons, and I have learned that the one thing the candidates for degrees least expect to hear from the speaker of the day is a candid assessment of their chances for life. Most frequently, the platform has been captured either by some celebrity figure who uses the moment to float some policy balloon or by someone who wishes to offer his or her potted philosophy for success, fun, or the quick fix. The best address I ever heard was also the shortest, when, many years ago, George Plympton advised a Harvard graduating class,

"Don't go. It's terrible out there." I have tried to learn from my mistakes and the mistakes of others on those occasions, and so in recent years I have aimed my talks pretty close to the emotional nerve of the graduating class. Rather than preach to their strengths and pander to their vanities, as so many of their colleges, alas, have done, I speak to what I have come to discover is their chief anxiety—failure.

Most of the students have been led to believe that, for the amount of money their parents are paying, failure is impossible. As the "brightest and the best," they believe that they have a right to expect choices between the good and the better for all of their days and that they are destined to be "masters of the universe," in Tom Wolfe's sardonic phrase. The world awaits their talents, they think, and will reward them handsomely for them. Most of them have been led to believe some version of all of this but, increasingly, more and more do not. They themselves know something of the uncertain, if not fraudulent, nature of the transaction whereby with the toss of a tassel or a mortarboard they become educated men and women. Most of them know that getting into college was a lot harder than getting out of it, and that getting through college was an exercise set to prove that it was still possible to fool a lot of the people a lot of the time. Now, as they are about to enter an unsubsidized world, the more thoughtful among them wonder when and how they will be exposed, and how they then will cope.

My opening gambit has become this: learn how to profit from your failures, for in life most of you will know more of failure than of success, and if you can learn from your failures, you will have learned much. That usually gets their attention. In recent years, I have had some powerful assistance from people in a world where failure is not easily tolerated, such as Harvard Medical School's Dr. Judah Folkman, one of the world's leading cancer researchers who, in an article in the *Boston Globe* on his work, opened with this disarming declaration: "I learn more from my failures than from my successes." When somebody in medical science says that, we tend to listen.

In another example, in the spring of 2001, there appeared on the Health/Science pages of the *Boston Globe*, under the banner headline "The Forgotten Man," an account of the difficult career of Dr. William DeVries:

> He used to be the world's best-known heart surgeon, and maybe its best-known doctor. That was two decades ago when, with Ravel's "Bolero" booming in the operating room, Dr. William DeVries raised the hopes of millions of cardiac patients by stitching a man-made heart into the chest of Barney Clark, a retired dentist from Seattle.[7]

Clark died a little over one hundred days later, and following the deaths of three more patients after DeVries had installed in them his Jarvik-7 mechanical heart, the government made him destroy fourteen unused mechanical hearts, his license to experiment was lifted, and his former partner branded him in public as a second-rate surgeon. DeVries sank from sight. After two decades, however, he was back, but as an onlooker at someone else's success with the implant of an artificial heart. Successful surgery occurred in the summer of 2001, and the initial success of that effort brought DeVries's original failure to mind. According to the newspaper account, DeVries still bears the scars of his very public failures in the artificial-heart business; yet despite them, he offered the following advice to those who were now searching for a suitable candidate for the newest implant: "I learned more from my mistakes and failures than my successes, so I would tell them they're going to be disappointed."[8]

Then, with reference to the race among five cities to be the site of the first implant, and sounding very much unlike the stereotype of the egomaniacal surgeon, Dr. DeVries said, "If you're dealing with science, it's better to be second, third, or fourth." Perhaps he was mindful of the old adage that it is the second mouse that gets the cheese, not the first.

Those of us with little knowledge of science imagine it to have a low tolerance for failure, as we remember how intimately acquainted with failure we became in our failed laboratory experiments in high-school chemistry and biology. For those of us who are uninformed humanists or simply scientifically illiterate, what we know of science are its popular successes: the triumphant discoveries, the cures, the vaccines, the heroic procedures; and we actually believe the surgeon jokes. In the cafeteria line in heaven, a man in a white coat cuts in and grabs all the food, to everyone's annoyance. "Who is that?" asks an irritated newcomer. "Oh, that's just God," comes the reply. "He thinks he's a surgeon."

The essence of good science is competence and a patience that pursues success in the contemplation of failure. A surgeon colleague of mine at Harvard Medical School, world famous for his skills both as a surgeon and as an innovative researcher in the medical stabilization of surgery patients, was also equally famous for the care and candor of his morbidity reports. He would not tolerate the minimizing of mistakes or the natural desire to regard death as failure. His own reputation grew in proportion to his conviction that failure was an essential ingredient in teaching, research, and learning and ultimately in advancing health and life; and medical science is famous for the fact that most visible scientific successes are built upon a firm foundation of invisible but essential failures. The experimental life that comprises science and medicine illustrates Jason Rasky's point, given at the opening of the chapter:

When you're successful you don't appreciate all the magic that went into that success as much as when you've gone through failure. When you try something and it doesn't work, you have a tendency to spend time reflecting.[9]

When Things Fall Apart in Private

In over thirty years of ministry in the same place, I have prepared hundreds of people for marriage, for it is one of the things ministers do. Early on, though I knew next to nothing, I was anxious to be as helpful as I possibly could be to couples not much younger than myself; and because I was a minister they assumed I had the answers to a successful Christian marriage in which God would be pleased and they would be satisfied. Marriage counseling was, and remains, an awesome responsibility, and I adopted as my own the medical dictum that says, "First, do no harm." I tried not to do any harm, and I first began in the marriage business at a time when that very institution was coming on hard times. When I was young I had hardly known anyone who had been divorced, and there had been something sensational and scandalous about the very word "divorce" in the small-town circles in which I was brought up. The church, and particularly the Baptist church of my youth, frowned upon it because the Bible stated in no uncertain terms that divorce was wrong and that Jesus himself disapproved of it. Divorce was the stuff of movies and novels I was not allowed to see or to read, and the few divorced people who moved in my family's social circle were mildly tolerated, although their "circumstances" were never discussed. Apart from those we heard about in Hollywood, the most famous divorced person in the world in my youth was Wallis Warfield Simpson, the Duchess of Windsor, whose several divorces cost Edward VIII his throne and empire.

Marriage was for life. We all knew people stuck in bad marriages, and in abusive, unfulfilling relationships that made a mockery out of all of the marriage vows except the one that said "Till death us do part." We all understood the not so apocryphal tale of the Irish Catholic woman who was brought up on charges of murdering her abusive, layabout husband. When asked in the Dublin court why she didn't simply divorce him, she replied that while murder was a crime, divorce was a sin, and she was, when all was said and done, a good Catholic.

When I was ordained and acquired a "license to solemnize matrimony," in the archaic language of the Commonwealth of Massachusetts, I resolved to take seriously my duties in this regard, and to try to be as helpful as possible to the mostly young people who came to see me in their preparation for marriage. Already the phenomenon of "living together" was becoming almost normal, and initially, when before their marriage my rather old-fashioned secretary took down the vital information for the first appointment, the couple would blush just a bit when they gave the same address for the man as for the woman. My secretary, a woman of Presbyterian scruples but well seasoned in the world, would invariably comment, "A boardinghouse, I presume?"

Trying to be as trendy as possible, I would ask such couples why they would want to ruin, by entering into marriage, what appeared to be a good friendship. Shocked by the question, they would reply that "living together was a way to test out the relationship"—"like science," as one of them said. "Then, when we find what works and what doesn't work, we'll get rid of the bad and concentrate on the good." It was on the basis of that "good" that they now wanted to make permanent and public their relationship.

As our conversations continued over several weeks I would ask them to describe their "worst-case scenarios" in the marriage they were contemplating. This question was usually unnerving, because they were accustomed to testifying to all and sundry about their hopes and successes and were glad to offer evidence of their mutual endearments. Having been asked earlier about good and bad role models of marriage among their acquaintances, including their parents, however, they should have been prepared for this inquiry into their own future anxieties, but until they were pressed, they demurred in glittering generalities. It was at that point that I was able to confront them with the hard realities of the vows from the classical liturgy by which they would be wed in The Memorial Church at Harvard, "for better for worse, for richer for poorer, in sickness and in health . . . till death us do part."

While these vows, derived from the Latin liturgy of the Roman Catholic Church and frozen in the priceless language of the sixteenth-century Anglican *Book of Common Prayer*, did not contemplate divorce, despite the awkward truth that the English church was founded on the fact of Henry VIII's determination to have a divorce, they did contemplate failure. That is to say, the classical marriage vows assumed both the good and the bad in marriage, and assumed that although one would enjoy the good, one could endure the bad, and it would take nothing less than a lifetime to live out the implication of all the promises. Failure was not overcome by the promises: the promises embraced failure, and the psychologically insightful assumption was, and remains, that one would learn from both good and bad and thus would provide by precept and example the firm foundation for the generations yet to come.

"What will happen when the looks fade, the waistline expands, the hair and the teeth go, the money doesn't turn up as expected, the children take their toll, sex becomes routine, and the routine becomes burdensome?" I ask my soon-to-be-married couples. Those are not questions that the young, the beautiful, and the excited like to consider, especially when posed by an interfering clergyman, but it seems to me to be my duty to ask questions that only they can answer and that only they can discuss between themselves. As many couples have said to me over the years, their best discussions occurred after they left my study. I do not put these questions to discourage them from marrying each other; I simply want them to realize that their marriage needs to be able to accommodate the reality of failure within it, and that failure, frustration, and disappointment are interior to marriage and not exterior to it.

That concept was, and remains, a losing one. Marriage has so long been the captive of the notion of the fairy-tale ending, "and they lived happily ever after," that anything less than happiness is defined as grounds for separation and divorce. William James did not have marriage in mind when he made his distinctions between the once-born and the twice-born, the healthy-minded and the sick-minded, but those distinctions can easily be applied. Once-minded marriages are those that cannot encompass the possibility and reality of failure; and when failure enters in, however defined after a season of denial, there then comes the temptation to dismiss it by turning away from it. The marriage itself cannot comprehend failure for it is by definition "good," and thus if the marriage is "bad," there is no marriage. That is the logic by which people define their bad marriages as "no" marriages or "unreal" marriages, and by implication that is also the logic of the principle of annulment in the Roman Catholic theology of marriage, whereby an impediment must be proven that declares the marriage null and void. This was what, in 1527, Henry VIII sought of Pope Clement VII.

"Tough love" is a concept that has come to the fore within the context of a culture of addiction, suggesting that, for the benefits of the long term, in the short term we should have zero tolerance for the bad behaviors and addictions of those whom we love the most. In the intergenerational culture of drugs, alcohol, and other abuses, "tough love" was hailed as one of the few strategies of promise and hope; when I use the term "tough love" within the context of a conversation about marriage, I do so with quite a different content and intent in mind. Marriage is tough love, not in the sense of how one deals with an abusive or abused loved one, but in the simple fact that it is tough, that is difficult to love under all circumstances all of the time. Therefore, in marriage, learning to live through, and not simply with, one's failures and those of others is one of the essential ingredients in putting failures and disappointments to good use. Marriage will not necessarily always turn out well. There is the cautionary tale of the Scottish crofter in the remotest part of the Outer Hebrides who lost his wife of sixty-three years. The minister came to see him six months after the funeral, prepared to console him in the loss of his helpmate. "You must miss her," said the parson. "Aye," responded the widower, "but I never really liked her."

Marriages fail more often than not because too frequently the parties do not know how to take account of failure within the marriage. I am not arguing for or against divorce as a solution to the problems of marriage; I am saying that the ease with which divorce is contemplated as a solution to the problems of marriage suggests a cultural inability to contemplate the reality of failure and what can be learned from it. The culture of divorce is not a culture of failure, but rather a culture that fails to take failure seriously. Surely some marriages will properly be dissolved and end in divorce, and, wisely, within most religious traditions provision is made for that sad reality; but just as failure is an essential ingredient to ultimate success in science, so too is failure in one's personal life, if properly used, essential to the construction of the good life and, by extension, in the construction and maintenance of a good marriage. Marriage itself contemplates that constructive use of failure: "for better for worse, for richer for poorer, in sickness and in health . . . till death us do part."

When Things Fall Apart in Public

Race is America's unfinished business. William E. B. Du Bois said as much when, in 1900, as William James was busily preparing his Gifford Lectures in his Cambridge study, he wrote, "The problem of the twentieth century is the problem of the color line." Sadly, events of the past hundred years would prove him right. For one shining moment, however, at mid-century, as a result of improved conditions and increased social agitation to secure civil rights for black Americans, it looked as though the problem of the color line was finally to be resolved, with liberty and justice for all. Between the wars, and often under less than ideal conditions, the race project was prosecuted by

Dr. Du Bois, the NAACP, and hundreds of other reform-minded blacks and whites. When Marian Anderson gave her song recital at the Lincoln Memorial on Easter Sunday afternoon, 1939, after having been denied the use of Constitution Hall by the Daughters of the American Revolution—which denial caused First Lady Eleanor Roosevelt to resign her membership in the DAR—at the very heart of the nation's capital a symbolic blow for civil rights was struck. The admirable service of black soldiers, sailors, and airmen, in a still segregated American military, in a war against totalitarianism and racism around the world forced President Harry S. Truman to issue the executive order by which the military was desegregated. Then followed the series of court cases, acts of civil disobedience, and the moral confrontations that came to their symbolic head in the great march on Washington on August 27, 1963, the very day on which Du Bois died at age ninety-five in Ghana, where he had gone to live after renouncing his American citizenship. The next five years, from 1963 to 1968 and the death of Martin Luther King Jr., would witness the second American civil war, this time led not by generals and ground troops but by preachers, students, social agitators, and the combined consciences of young and old, white and black. For many, these years were the defining years of their lives, and for the nation and the century it was the defining moment of the American experience.

From the distance of thirty years later, it is difficult to remember the intensity and optimism of that period and the sense that not only the race but the nation itself was getting a second chance, having a conversion experience, coming to terms with the reality of both evil and hope in the temperament of James's twice-born man. What helps us to remember, and what informs those now too young to have anything to remember from that period, is that remarkable achievement of television journalism Henry Hampton's epochal series *Eyes on the Prize*. A camera was running throughout the long years of "the movement," and what it recorded would be edited and adapted for the American medium of television, thus assuring that this narrative, America's own passion play, would not be forgotten. Eleven volumes of archival film, sometimes terrible to behold, included lynchings, riots, the killing of the little black girls in the Sixteenth Street Baptist Church in Birmingham, and the murders of Emmett Till, Medgar Evers, and Dr. King, and were all the more horrible to see again for the second time. Yet, throughout it all, there were overwhelming moments of dignity, pride, and hope. Hampton captured the innate bravery and dignity of those young college students conducting their sit-ins at Southern lunch counters and the moral vision of those Montgomery domestics who, after the example of Rosa Parks, refused to ride on the buses until they could sit where they pleased. The films captured the simple purposefulness of hundreds of church folk determined to act as Christians in a war they could hope to win only by love and law.

The films also captured the bestiality and veniality of white oppressors such as Ross Barnett, Bull Connor, George Wallace, and the nameless sheriffs, their deputies, and the howling mobs. No one who was there can say "I wasn't there," for it is all on incriminating film, and it ought to be required viewing annually, in every school. If it is useful for Americans to regularly see the horrors of the Holocaust in Europe, it is even more useful for Americans to regularly see the horrors prosecuted in their own name, by their own people, on their own people.

Henry Hampton died in December 1998, much mourned and lamented. When he was asked what he hoped he had accomplished in his series *Eyes on the Prize*, he answered that he had wanted to capture the perseverance of his people as an essay not simply in law or in political strategy or as a social movement, but as a sustained series of actions over many years and generations that could be described as "The sure conviction nourished in discouragement."

For many, sure convictions are often made less sure by discouragement and failure, and in looking at *Eyes on the Prize* in the closing years of the twentieth century, an entire generation removed from the last events of that formative period, discouragement is an easy sentiment to summon. Much of the public oratory on Martin Luther King Jr.'s birthday is an annual lament on how far we have fallen from "The Dream," and on how much harder it seems to achieve the dream today than it was forty years ago; and now there is no Martin Luther King Jr. to help us along the way.

No one knows more of failure in America than the African American. By this I do not mean to suggest that the African American is a failure or that success is unknown to the African American. What I do mean to say is that for no one more than the African American has the American hope or experience failed in its ability to deliver on its promises. We did not ask to come here, nor, with the possible exception of the "Back to Africa Movement" of Marcus Garvey, did we seek to leave. Excepting Nat Turner's "rebellion," we did not take to our pitchforks as did the peasantry of France in the eighteenth century or the black Africans in Zimbabwe in the twenty-first century. We have believed the promises of America and have tried to live up to them, even offering our service in segregated armies and accepting humiliating social conditions as the reward for our sacrifice. The calls for revenge and redistributive justice from the Black Panthers, the Nation of Islam, and other militant black groups in the late twentieth century stand out only because they are in stark contrast to the vast majority's desire to accept and enjoy the rights of life, liberty, and the pursuit of happiness. That white America still resists this, albeit less blatantly than in the days of the Ku Klux Klan, is a continuing paradox. The artful campaign against the notion of "affirmative action" as an effective remedy to centuries of white benefit at black expense is really not a debate on a flawed policy: it is a fear, and it is a failure to recognize the fundamental flaw that cries out for redress.

A further paradox is contained in the sad story of race in America. Du Bois argued that the failure to address the failure of the American experience's ability to deliver on its promises for its most visibly disadvantaged people would mean that the nation would never know any real peace or social cohesion. In 1917, in the context of overtly racist treatment of black troops in World War I and the outbreak of race riots in the industrialized North, when whites decided to prevent African Americans from taking more industrial jobs, the racial situation could not have been worse. One of Du Bois's confederates wrote a widely circulated paper in which the fate of the Negro and Western civilization were conjoined:

> We are perfectly well aware that the outlook for us is not encouraging. . . . We, the American Negroes, are the acid test for occidental civilization. If we perish, we perish. But when we fall, we shall fall like Samson, dragging inevitably with us the pillars of a nation's democracy.[10]

Failure may well be un-American, but it is an ineradicable part of the fabric of the American experience. Thus, we take seriously that most American of all twentieth-century American writers, F. Scott Fitzgerald, when he says, "Vitality shows in not only the ability to persevere, but in the ability to start over."

It is the ability both to persevere and to start over that is most desired in order to heal the cultural and psychic wounds opened up in America by the calamitous events of September 11, 2001. It is almost blasphemous, and perhaps even treasonous, to suggest that failure of some sort was involved in those attacks upon the twin towers of the World Trade Center on that lovely September morning, but, at the very least, some have suggested fault with our intelligence-gathering sources, fault with our immigration policies, and fault with our airport security. All of those systems failed us when we needed them most. Epochal moments such as the sinking of the *Titanic* and the attack on Pearl Harbor, the assassinations of John F. Kennedy, Martin Luther King Jr., and Robert F. Kennedy, and the crash of the *Challenger* and the bombing in Oklahoma City are moments when our "congenital optimism," as

James would call it, fails us, and we are forced to incorporate sobering and often terrifying experiences of evil and disaster into our frame of reality. It may seem easier if we are simply fatalistic and pessimistic, accepting the fact that bad things happen not only to bad people; but what is more realistic and characteristic is our determination, at least for a time, to examine ourselves, our circumstances, our hopes, and our fears, and to ask what we can learn from present troubles and what, if anything, we ought to do. These are what Pope John Paul II calls "teachable moments," because they force us to reflection and, possibly as a result, to amendment of life. It is still too early to know in any definitive way what we have learned about ourselves and the world from the events of September 11, 2001; most attempts to do so at this stage are either premature or transparently opportunistic. Yet we dare not wait too long, for moments of cultural and personal introspection, especially where bad news is concerned, are short-lived and fragile.

What, then, are we to do when things fall apart and the center does not hold? In her little book *When Things Fall Apart: Heart Advice for Difficult Times*, Pema Chödrön, an American Buddhist nun and resident teacher at the Gampa Abbey in Nova Scotia—the first Tibetan monastery in North America established for Westerners—provides an answer that, though written in 1997, seems remarkably apt for a world now never the same after September 11, 2001:

> When things fall apart and we're on the verge of we know not what, the test for each of us is to stay on that brink and not concretize. . . . Right now—in the very instant of groundlessness—[we] see to taking care of those who need our care and of discovering our goodness."[11]

Speaking against the culture of violence, panic, and fear, she reminds us pleasure-principled Westerners of the very first of the Buddha's noble truths, which points out that:

Suffering is inevitable for human beings as long as we believe that things last, that they don't disintegrate, that they can be counted on to satisfy our hunger for security. . . . From this point of view, the only time we ever know what's really going on is when the rug's been pulled out and we can't find anywhere to land. We use these situations either to wake ourselves up or to put ourselves to sleep.[12]

Failure almost always brings with it a sense of loss, such as in a lost opportunity, a lost moment, a lost friend, a lost confidence, or a lost life, and to deny that failure, that loss, is to lose even the benefit of the loss. Such a time Pema Chödrön calls a kind of testing: "the kind of testing that spiritual warriors need in order to awaken their hearts."[13]

For most people, the time of failure is the most important time of testing in their lives. Margaret Thatcher once said that "Failure is not an option," by which she meant to imply the inevitability of success, but the truth of the statement transcends even her own meaning: we do not willingly choose failure, but our moments of testing and maturity will be determined by how we choose to deal with the failures that are inevitable. We might say that where there is failure, there is life; and it is failure in life, as in science, that will help us to redefine what success is, and what success can be.

CHAPTER 5

SUCCESS

HOW DO I KNOW
WHEN I'VE MADE IT?

You can't be good unless you love it.
CAPTAIN BILLY TYNE OF THE *ANDREA GAIL*,
IN *THE PERFECT STORM*, SPEAKING OF THE
DANGERS OF COMMERCIAL DEEP-SEA FISHING

Success as a moral concept is difficult to classify. One will not find it on any classical list of virtues, moralists tend to avoid it as a subject, and theologians seem more comfortable discussing failure than success. In the more than eight hundred pages of anthologized moral wisdom in William Bennett's enormously popular work *The Book of Virtues*, "success" appears only once in the index, and that in reference to a four-stanza extract from an obscure poem by Henry Wadsworth Longfellow entitled "The Ladder of St. Augustine," which includes these cautionary lines:

The heights by great men reached and kept
Were not attained by sudden flight;
But they, while their companions slept,
Were toiling upward in the night.[1]

William James, in a famous letter to H. G. Wells in 1906, credited what he called American "moral flabbiness" to "the exclusive worship of the bitch-goddess Success. That—with the squalid cash interpretation put on the word 'success'—is our national disease."[2] Those were, and remain, very strong words, suggesting as they do that success is corrosive of virtue because we more often than not yield to the temptation to make a virtue of success, and when we do not know the content of success, we are in serious trouble.

For example, we wish people success. Does that mean that we wish them the ability to achieve whatever it is they wish to achieve? Do we wish them to do well what they do? Do we wish them to find and to do well the right thing? Success is one of the staples we offer from the larder of clichés at graduation time, when we encourage the young to be successful and the young congratulate themselves on already having achieved a singular degree of success. Over the years I have watched with a fascinating horror the developing phenomenon of self-congratulation at commencement time, when students, who were once meant to be the objects of the congratulations of their teachers, parents, and friends, have now become their own loudest cheerleaders and, regarding themselves as the home team, cheer for themselves accordingly. It almost seems as if they do not expect others to appreciate their achievement, and that their "success" will go unnoticed unless they cheer themselves hoarse for themselves. Many are like the egocentric actor John Barrymore, who is said to have remarked that his only regret after a long career in the theater was that he had not had the pleasure of seeing himself on the stage.

Advice from the Well-Heeled

Not many years ago, a book called *Graduation Day* appeared in time for the annual spring season of congratulation- and success-mongering. Its subtitle was *The Best of America's Commencement Speeches,* and its list of speakers included the hit parade of current American celebrities: Jodie Foster, Sting, Ted Turner, Ben and Jerry, Barbara Bush, Alice Walker, Toni Morrison, Bill Clinton, and many others. American college students rate the "success" of their graduation by the star power of the speakers on their graduation day, and this list indicates the ability of modern academia to lure big names to campus. The exchange is crudely simple and usually entails awarding an honorary degree for a splash of name recognition and a bit of self-aggrandizing self-deprecation. It works only too well.

Naturally, success is one of the recurrent themes of the day, and it is exemplified by the proven success of the speaker and the hoped-for success of those listening to the speaker. In a section entitled "You Will Succeed," Garrison Keillor, Andy Rooney, Patrick Stewart, Hank Aaron, and Ross Perot address the young. A little more than halfway through his long and rambling speech at Boston University's 1994 commencement, Ross Perot addressed the subject of success:

> Now anytime I'm with a group like you, they always say, "Now, Ross, we want to be successful." Well, okay, we'll talk about that, but what is success? You say, "Well, success is making a lot of money." I say no, you're on the wrong track. Success is being the best at whatever you do.[3]

In the minds of many of his young listeners, and presumably among the less subtle reasons for his invitation to address them, was the fact that Perot was outstanding by his own definition: he was the best at whatever he did, and what he did best was to make money, which made him one of the wealthiest and most successful men in the world. Had he been poor, it is unlikely that many would have taken his homilies seriously, much less his presidential ambitions, but because he was fabulously wealthy and therefore "successful," that is, the best at what he did, he could afford to tell people that "financial success and happiness are unrelated."

I've had the interesting opportunity to know most of the people that you would think of as the wealthiest people in the world. A huge number of them are very unhappy. I am no happier today than I was as a boy in the Depression in Texarkana.[4]

The wealth of his youth was because of his parents, and his wealth today, as opposed to his money, is in his wife and children. Knowing that his ambitious young listeners were not yet prepared to consider the moral distinction between wealth and money, he went on to say about money:

No, after you make it, about all you can do is give it away to good causes, and interestingly enough you've got to be careful it doesn't ruin your children. . . . And there's a final story here: it's harder to give it away intelligently than it is to make it. So it's kinda interesting.[5]

As with most commencement talk ideas, Perot's were not new, although they may have sounded refreshingly novel in the America of the mid-1990s, when no one dared, in Haynes Johnson's trenchant words, "to pierce the illusions of America Rex," and whose ever increasing prosperity and material achievement stimulated not only the economy, but also an increasingly dangerous and diverting sense of security and invincibility. Perot doubtless knew something of *The Gospel of Wealth*, a set of essays on money and good works by his capitalist ancestor, Andrew Carnegie. By 1901, as the result of the sale of his company to J. P. Morgan for $480 million, Andrew Carnegie had become the wealthiest man in the world but, as Perot would observe nearly a century later, Carnegie knew that the hard part of his life was just beginning, and that his success would be determined not by what he made or kept, but by what he gave away. As early as 1868, when he was only thirty-three years old and had an annual income of $50,000, a sum beyond the dreams of avarice for most of the Western world, Carnegie was determined not to be ruled by his money. He drew up a set of rules for his life not unlike those of Benjamin Franklin and George Washington, although he had infinitely more money at his disposal than they ever could have imagined. The first of his rules read: "Make no effort to increase fortune, but spend the surplus each year for benevolent purposes. Cast aside business forever except for others."[6] Further instructing himself, Carnegie wrote:

> Man must have an idol. The massing of wealth is one of the worst species of idolatry . . . no idol more debasing than the worship of money. Whatever I engage in I must push inordinately, therefore I should be careful to choose that life which will be the most elevating in its character.[7]

Anticipating the problem of giving it all away to suitable causes, Carnegie made for himself and for any others who might care to follow his example a list of seven objects of philanthropy, which included the founding of universities, libraries, medical institutions, parks, public halls, swimming pools, and, lastly, churches. Over the course of the first half of the twentieth century, scarcely an American town or city of any municipal ambition lacked an object of Carnegie's philanthropy; and his philanthropy touched even myself, for when I was a young man I became organist at The Memorial Methodist Church in Plymouth, Massachusetts, presiding over an impressive little two-manual Estey tubular pneumatic pipe organ that had been obtained for the church in 1900 through the Carnegie Trust. Always called the "Carnegie organ" by the old-timers, it was an object of great pride to everyone, and especially so to me.

Perhaps the most famous American who determined to do good after having done well was John D. Rockefeller, whose success at accumulating wealth was exceeded only by his son's success in giving it away.

Both men, motivated by religious principle, were determined to demonstrate that riches were merely a means to good, and that success was to be defined contrary to the American gospel of acquisition and greed and in terms of moral as opposed to material success. It was as if they were all trying to demonstrate that they were the exceptions to William James's indictment of "moral flabbiness" and the squalid worship of material possessions.

For most of the twentieth century, the temple to the success of American capitalism was not the World Trade Center and its twin towers, which proved so susceptible to the destructive envy of Islamic terrorists, but rather midtown New York's Rockefeller Center on Fifth Avenue, with its famous ice rink and Christmas display. While Ross Perot was a precocious little boy in Texarkana and just before the American entry into World War II after Pearl Harbor, John D. Rockefeller Jr. participated in a radio debate about America's interests in the war. Out of this came what was called his "creed," and on the balustrade in front of Rockefeller Center he later had the creed engraved for all to read.[8] The World Trade Center and twin towers are now gone, but Rockefeller Center and the creed continue to attract the millions along the Avenue. It begins: "I believe in the supreme worth of the individual and in his right to life, liberty, and the pursuit of happiness."

Among the set of ten credal social convictions are these following, which are meant to help define civic and individual success in moral rather than material terms. For a nation creeping out of its worst economic depression by dint of World War II, its worst war yet, these views of one of the richest men in the world must have had quite an impact. Seeing them for the first time, as I saw them less than a month after the destruction of the twin towers, I found that still to be true:

I believe that every right implies a responsibility, every opportunity, an obligation, every possession, a duty.

I believe in the dignity of labor, whether with head or hand; that the world owes no man a living but that it owes every man an opportunity to make a living.

I believe that thrift is essential to well-ordered living, and that economy is a prime requisite of a sound financial structure, whether in government, business, or personal affairs.

I believe that the rendering of useful service is the common duty of mankind, and that only in the purifying fire of sacrifice is the dross of selfishness consumed and the greatness of the human soul set free.

These creeds of the rich do their best to liberate the notion of success from the merely material. As Andrew Carnegie would have it, anybody could make money, and success in doing so was not a moral quality. Morality enters when one determines a worthy purpose for the use of the money one has been successful at making, and a successful person is therefore one who recognizes money as a means to a greater end. Some critics would say that the moral question comes in earlier than at the point of philanthropy: How, for instance, did one make the money that one now endeavors to give away? The moral ends may be clear, but what about the morality of the means?

John D. Rockefeller Sr., founder of the family fortune, was seen in his dotage as a kindly old gentleman, bald as an egg, who encouraged thrift and gave away dimes. Many, however, could not take him seriously as a philanthropist because they were aware of the way in which he had made his money. Ida Tarbell and her fellow muckrakers had told the world of the perfidies of the Standard Oil Company and about how competition was squashed and good men driven out of business, how monopolies in the absence of restraints refused to inhibit their rapacious powers, and how workers as well as competitors found themselves squeezed by the relentless profit-making machine of Rockefeller money. When Rockefeller's pastor, the Baptist preacher Owen Gates, warned him that his wealth would kill him, Rockefeller attempted a serious reconciliation of his business principles with his religious scruples. It would be the son, however, John D. Rockefeller Jr., who as his full-time vocation would put into practice the philanthropic ideas begun by his father and earlier enunciated by Andrew Carnegie. No better expression of John D. Jr.'s view of the world and his duty toward it can be found than in the creed in front of Rockefeller Center. The next to final statement in this secular creed might well be understood as a definition for the living of a successful life:

I believe in an all-wise and all-loving God, named by whatever name, and that the individual's highest fulfillment, greatest happiness, and widest usefulness are to be found in living in harmony with his will.

Rich for a Purpose

Success is here defined as living with a purpose, and that purpose in harmony with God's will, and money and material prosperity are the means to fulfill that purpose. From this definition easily came the notion that the more money one had, the more good one could do. Thus, poverty was not so much a sign of God's displeasure as a lack of human ambition to do good. In an age and a place of opportunity, poverty was no longer a virtue but, by the lights of capitalist America, a positive hindrance to virtue. Charles Wesley, the founder of Methodism in eighteenth-century England, was fond of saying to his people, "Get all you can . . . so that you can do all you can." Success by this view was to turn prosperity from a soul-destroying obsession with things, a condition against which Jesus warned, into an opportunity to do as much good toward others as possible. This was an expression of the basic principle, familiar to generations of the privileged young, "From those to whom much is given, much is expected."

Even Aristotle argued that in order to pursue the good life a little money would do no harm; it should not be so much it becomes an obsession, but not so little that one's mental and spiritual energies were misplaced in worrying about basic necessities. Aristotle was then speaking to aristocratic youth; he did not see his invitation to the contemplation of the good life in populist terms. The Christian tradition of the good, addressed as it was to all, but with a clear preference for the dispossessed and the expectations of a life to come beyond earthly needs and ambitions, was not meant to survive on the terms of this world. In some very real sense, success in the earliest Christian tradition was defined as a triumph over the visible and material world. True, God's greatest act, as recorded in the Bible, was to come into the world in the form of Jesus, but the entire direction of Jesus' ministry was to save or redeem that world from itself and for something better. Success, therefore, does not consist of an accumulation of things or of an interest in things. In one of his most famous moral maxims, Jesus makes this point abundantly clear:

> *Lay not up for yourselves treasures upon earth, where moth and rust doth corrupt, and where thieves break through and steal; but lay up for yourselves treasures in heaven, where neither moth nor rust doth corrupt, and where thieves do not break through nor steal. For where your treasure is, there will your heart be also.*
>
> MATTHEW 6:19–21, KJV

By the early decades of the twentieth century in America, the good news preached was neither this dispossession gospel of Jesus and the early church nor the philanthropic gospel of Carnegie and Rockefeller, but a definition of success that defined wealth as opportunity and poverty as a rebuke. The most well known exponent of this was a Baptist preacher, Russell H. Conwell, who became famous and rich on the basis of one sermon that he preached over and over again, all across the land. It was entitled "Acres of Diamonds," and its essential thesis was: "Get rich, young man, for money is power and power ought to be in the hands of the good people." This was addressed to Christian people who were defined as good, and in order for them to do good as well as to be good they needed social power, and money was the means to that power. Lest there be any doubt about what his meaning was, Conwell said in that famous sermon:

> I say you have no right to be poor. . . . You and I know that there are some things more valuable than money; nevertheless, there is not one of these things that is not greatly enhanced by the use of money. . . . Love is the grandest thing on God's earth, but fortunate is the lover who has plenty of money.[9]

As Ross Perot and others point out, it is difficult to disassociate notions of success from notions of material prosperity. One of the reasons Russell Conwell's sermon can be described as perhaps the most "successful" sermon of the twentieth century is that it proclaimed a truth people believed implicitly, wanted to believe, and wanted to prove and practice for themselves. The combination of realism, idealism, and materialism was designed to flourish in the American culture of success and opportunity; and yet, as a young Christian MBA student once said to me after a Bible study class in the Harvard Business School, "There must be more to success than 'stuff.'"

Jabez and the Selfish Prayer

At the start of the twenty-first century, people who have never heard of Russell Conwell and "Acres of Diamonds" have been running to the bookstores in droves to buy the single most popular book on religion available today. It is a slender little volume of fewer than one hundred pages, not much larger than a Palm Pilot, entitled *The Prayer of Jabez: Breaking Through to the Blessed Life*. Written in 2000 by Bruce Wilkinson, founder and president of what he calls "Walk Thru' the Bible Ministries," *The Prayer of Jabez* is a brief commentary on one verse from the Old Testament book of 1 Chronicles. Wilkinson says, "What sentence has revolutionized my life the most? The cry of a gimper named Jabez."[10]

Jabez is not one of those biblical people with whom to reckon, as he is mentioned only once, and then in passing. The Hebrew from which his name comes means "one having been born in pain," and all we know about him we find in two verses (4:9–10). The first describes him simply: "Now Jabez was more honorable than his brothers, and his mother called his name Jabez, saying, 'Because I bore him in pain.'" The second verse is the actual prayer of Jabez, which reads:

> And Jabez called on the God of Israel saying: "O that you would bless me indeed, and enlarge my territory, that your hand would be with me, and that you should keep me from evil, that I may not cause pain." So God granted him what he requested.

Wilkinson writes that he discovered this prayer in the course of his Bible study and that he has prayed it ever since. He regards it as a model prayer, as effective in life for himself and for hundreds of others as it was for Jabez. The one-sentence prayer has four parts, and it is on these that Wilkinson writes his succinct commentary:

1. That you would bless me indeed

2. And enlarge my territory

3. That your hand would be with me

4. And that you should keep me from evil

Reminding us that Jesus encouraged his followers to "Ask, and it shall be given you; seek, and ye shall find; knock, and it shall be opened unto you" (Matthew 7:7, KJV), Wilkinson argues that we should be more "selfish" in our praying; that is, we should not be afraid to ask God for what we want. It is our nature to ask and God's nature to give, and so false modesty and a spirituality so pure that it is of no earthly good should give way to a bold request for God to give us as much of what we desire as God is willing to manage. Jabez provides us with a perfect, efficient, and effective example of how to do this. Wilkinson reminds us that prayer of this sort is not asking for more of what we could get ourselves. It is asking for what we need, and indeed want, which only God can supply. That is what a blessing is. The enlarged territory sounds very much like the "gospel of more," but it is understood here as a greater scope for doing good. He further asks to be encouraged by God's presence and restrained from doing evil or harm as his circumstances change; and perhaps the most important thing to note here is that God says yes to his prayer.

On the surface, *The Prayer of Jabez* and its phenomenal popularity in the bookstores might suggest just another scheme to combine prosperity and piety. The phrase "enlarge my territory" is susceptible to the level of a "God-help-me-to-win-the-lottery" piety, but Wilkinson, in a creative and demanding way, makes much more of it than that. The creative part is to reaffirm the legitimacy of need-based prayer. In much of contemporary Christian piety, asking for things for oneself is regarded both as being selfish and as telling God what to do, the first of which is morally suspect and the second, theologically suspect. Wilkinson argues that not only is it all right to pray for what we want; it is absolutely essential that we do so, especially when we cannot supply that want on our own. Prayer that presupposes neither need nor supply is not really prayer, but just so much formulaic talk at God. What Jabez's prayer models is the notion that we should know what we need and not be afraid to ask God for it.

The demanding part is making sure that what we ask of God is what God wants of us: "The Jabez blessing focuses like a laser on our wanting for ourselves nothing more and nothing less than what God wants for us."[11] Our desire is to receive what God wants us to receive, so that God's will can be accomplished through us. We must know what God wants us to be in order to ask God to help us to become it.

This may seem a concession to weakness. It is how, for example, many people see the prayer of Jesus in the garden on the night before his crucifixion. First he asks that "this cup," the suffering that is to come, should pass from him, but then he says, "Not my will, but thine, be done" (Matthew 26:39). That seems like "giving up," as I have heard more than one Christian say on Holy Thursday before Good Friday, or "wimping out," in another way of putting it, making the religion of the crucified a religion for losers. Later we will discuss how such a loss as the cross redefines both failure and success.

In the context of the Jabez blessing, to pray properly is to ask God's power to enable us to be and to do what God wants: "If seeking God's blessing is our intimate act of worship, and asking to do more for Him is our utmost ambition, then asking for God's hand upon us is our strategic choice to sustain and continue the great things that God has begun in our lives."[12] Wilkinson calls this "the touch of greatness" and reminds us that in the Jabez blessing we do not become "great," that this is not a prayer about mere self-aggrandizement. Rather, we become dependent on the strong hand of God: "Your surrendered need turns into this unlimited opportunity. And He becomes great through you."[13]

Unlike much of the literature of spiritual self-help and success, *The Prayer of Jabez* deals honestly with the fact that success—that is, in the terms of the prayer, "blessing"—nearly always comes at a very high price. As we know, there is always the problem of unanswered prayer, but even greater problems develop when prayer is, in fact, answered.

The old adage holds a powerful spiritual truth: "Be careful what you pray for, for you just may get it." Spiritual success always stimulates a higher degree of spiritual opposition. Success raises expectations, both on the part of the one who is succeeding and on the part of those forces that seem always to rise to frustrate. For everything you gain, you now have more to lose. Every victory anticipates a greater defeat. As my mother used to say about a lovely sunny day in the changeable climate of New England, "We'll pay for this."

Spiritual success, then, does not make us immune to future conflict and trouble, and at its best such success helps us only to better accompany to the conflicts and failures that inevitably attend our way. Success thus defined is not the surmounting of tribulation for all time; rather, it is the capacity to better cope with tribulation as its strategies increase in proportion to our strength. The secret is that it is not our strength, but our dependence upon the strength of God that enables us. Success is not what we do or get for ourselves. Success is our willingness to struggle to discern and then to achieve what God desires for us. In this sense we understand Jesus' Holy Thursday night prayer not as a cry of desperate resignation, but as a willing submission of a weaker will, his own, to the greater will that is God's. This is the ultimate empowerment, the ultimate enablement, the ultimate liberation, and the ultimate success.

One can see the appeal of *The Prayer of Jabez* to a people confused about what success is, who intuit that true success may not be as it is popularly supposed, and who wish to be successful at something that is "more than stuff" and that endures. Any little book that helps us to move beyond James's "moral flabbiness" and "squalid cash" in our search for success in living the good life is bound to attract attention. It was so before the collapse of the twin towers, but after that physical and psychic calamity, the yearning for something more, other, and better is now of epidemic proportions.

This Life or the Next?

Half the battle for a success that counts and endures is to know what we don't want, what doesn't work, and what cannot satisfy. A *New Yorker* cartoon of the last decade about an epitaph on a tombstone says it all. The epitaph reads:

Tuned in,
Turned on,
Dropped in,
Dropped out,
Worked out,
Saved up,
Dropped dead.

With the possible exception of the first two, these sentiments embrace the qualities, diversions, and prejudices of the various lifestyles by which late-modern men and women—presumably the kind who read the cartoons in the *New Yorker*—so capriciously defined themselves. Each one of the sentiments was an aspect of the good life to those who embraced that particular aspect, but in rapid succession and with the inevitable end despite what preceded, the epitaph was in essence an epitaph on serial perceptions of the good life. At first glance, we laugh. At second glance, we recognize one or two of our friends along the way, perhaps some who are still trapped in or deluded by one of those ephemeral moments. Then we recognize ourselves, or at least a part of ourselves. Depending upon how well read we are, we recognize this as similar to what that cynical preacher in the Hebrew Bible wrote when he said, "Vanity, vanity, all is vanity," or to the succinct advice of an old aunt or grandmother who said, "Here today, gone tomorrow."

One of the points of the good life is to help prevent us from thinking too much of the rather morbid notion that life itself, whether good, bad, or indifferent, is inevitably short and its end arbitrary. In the end we are all dead or, more elegantly put in the words of John Henry Cardinal Newman in the nineteenth century: "Life is short. Death is certain. And the world to come is everlasting." For Newman and the tradition in which he stood, his words were meant to be an encouragement and, amazingly, to cheer people up. The point of the world to come was to provide a permanent assurance of goodness that could not be compared with the less than ideal circumstances under which most people lived in the world. The good life couldn't possibly be this life, for at least two reasons.

The first reason is that there is just too much trouble and trial in the world. No less a good person than Jesus himself argued that, "In the world ye shall have tribulation," and the only way he could deal with it was to leave this world for a better one, thereby trumping reality with goodness: "But do not be dismayed, I have overcome the world" (John 16:33). This didn't mean that good ultimately triumphs over evil in this life; this is not a Hollywood motion picture convention of the happy ending. The once-born man, in James's phrase, who does not recognize that things as they are will never be any better could hardly accept Newman's words as anything but resignation, denial, or threat.

For those, however, for whom this life could never be good enough, the fact of the brevity of life, the certainty of death, and the never-ending nature of eternity was good news. It made this imperfect life bearable, if not good.

The second reason believers could not possibly confuse this life with the good life is the fact that we ourselves are simply not good enough on our own to make it so. Try as hard as we may, we are not capable of self-perfection; for example, think about what goes on when we try to lose weight. For a while, with the right diet and exercise plan, we lose it and are pleased with our exercise of self-discipline, the results of which are so clear and attractive for all to see. A sad and unavoidable fact in the history of American dieting, however, is that nearly all of the weight we lose we regain, and often with other debilitating side effects. Weight is the equivalent of sin in the American good life, and there are far too many people who suffer from obesity, and many more who for various reasons imagine themselves to be too fat. There are others for whom the thin ideal is their ultimate demon, which gives rise to such health problems as anorexia and bulimia; and there are those who lose the weight they wish to lose and then live in terror of regaining it, and thus subject themselves to draconian countermeasures. None of the runway models and ideal body types, male or female, can afford to remind themselves that, no matter what they do, they will all die and become food for worms.

The Greeks actually believed that there was a knowledge that, once mastered, would lead to the living of the good life. We saw something of that in our earlier discussion of Aristotle and his utter conviction that knowledge of virtue leads to virtue, and hence to the living of the good life. The enemy here was ignorance, the method, diligent instruction and sound learning, and the solution, all one needed to know in order to do the right thing.

One does not have to be religious, much less Christian, Jewish, or Muslim, at the start of the twenty-first century to realize how quaint, even naive, and certainly impossible such a program now sounds. If ignorance were the only problem, then the most educated and the most learned would be the most pious people and, as the Hebrew wisdom literature once put it, the multitude of the wise would indeed be the welfare of the world. Much of our secular culture still believes in salvation by education, and hence the opportunity for education is the only right worth insisting upon in the name of a culture of equity. Salvation for the most ardent home schooler and the most passionate advocate for affirmative education is freedom for education, albeit a particular form of education, which is understood to be the ticket out of ignorance and into the land of opportunity for the good life. One must believe it is possible if one is to have a chance of achieving it.

An Important Image

It would be first the Jews and then the Christians who would discover that knowledge is not wisdom, wisdom is not virtue, and virtue, as defined by the human effort to achieve, is not the good life. They did not need the philosopher's stone to teach them this: they needed only to look at one another, or at themselves. When St. Paul, for example, in 1 Corinthians, makes his famous reference about seeing in a glass darkly, a reference almost always overwhelmed by the sentiments about love that surround it, the commentaries faithfully point out that for all but the most exceptionally wealthy of people, men and women in Paul's day had to make do with imperfectly formed reflecting surfaces as mirrors, or looking-glasses. Thus, no matter how good the glass itself was, it would always reflect an imperfect, imprecise image, and no matter how good or noble the person looking in the glass was, that person could see only an imperfect refraction of the image from the glass. Thus, to "know thyself," in application of the classical Greek aphorism, was in the Jewish and Christian idiom not possible on the basis of self-instruction.

One of the essential qualities of self-knowledge was that pure self-knowledge was not possible, or at least not in this life. We could never see ourselves as we really were, and even if we could, we could not usually bear what we saw, for image and reality would be out of sync. That is always the case in this life. Psychoanalysis, the presumed great successor to religion in the twentieth century, promised the first real possibility of self-knowledge. Freud was to liberate humankind from the long dark night of self-ignorance by probing neither the heavens nor the philosophies, but the psyche; and what religion was said to have promised to our ancestors, psychoanalysis was now to provide for us: security in knowledge of self and the ability thereby to act wisely and well for self and others. Despite millions of patients and analysts, however, and billions of consulting dollars and hours, we still see through a glass darkly, and we respond imperfectly to imperfect images. Life is a fun house, and at the carnival the characteristic feature of a fun house is always the distorting mirrors.

So, if we define the good life as the ultimate good for ourselves and concede that such a life is unlikely to be attained easily, if at all, in this life, and if we are not prepared to speculate on the life to come or to live this life on the basis of such speculation, how do we define and measure success in our search for that good life here and now? Just because my students may mistake the good life for money, jobs, prestige, security, beauty, and even good works does not mean that they are any less keen to define the good life in qualities that endure beyond those. Therefore, part of their moral education is to learn how to distinguish between enduring truths and the illusion of truth.

In a book of sermons by the late Theodore Parker Ferris, famous rector of Trinity Church, Boston, in the middle of the twentieth century, I discovered a poem that describes the choice between alleged fact and elusive wonder:

FACT AND WONDER
Only the young possess the simplicity
To accept a truth transcending rote and rule,
So that, like star-led shepherds, children see
The fact of miracle.
But logic, the sophist, clouds the maturing life,
Caution replaces the fearless face of youth,
Till the skeptic mind prefers a plausible lie
To a fantastic truth.[14]

Plausible lies are part of the illusions of our culture, things that appear to be real, valuable, and permanent, designed to give us pleasure and satisfaction and to help us in the mastery of ourselves and our world. Goebbels, Hitler's minister of propaganda, perfected the notion of the "big lie," which, if told often enough, would be accepted by people as truth. Plausible lies about the good society and the good life have flourished in an age of material comfort that has developed the science of advertising, which invents both solutions to needs and needs that then require invented solutions. The power of mass advertising, notably on television, and the creation of a desirable, attainable, and a steadily improving standard of living, together with the planned obsolescence designed to stimulate rather than to feed appetites, meant that the good life was no longer a philosophical abstraction upon which the leisured and the lettered could contemplate, as Aristotle had assumed. Now it was a social opportunity and an economic necessity. Envy was no longer simply one of the seven deadly sins: it was now an ingredient essential to the success of the consumer society. Success, then, was attaining one's fair share of what this consumer society determined it to be, and that determination was usually in tangible, material things that were universally recognized and valued, such as a late-model car, a house in the suburbs, a college education, a sound pension plan, or a perfect lawn. For the children, first came Little League, then onward and upward they went to soccer, dance lessons, and appropriately themed summer camping experiences. The television shows of the 1950s, which have an eternal existence in the nostalgia TV industry, played these aspirations out before a willing public: happiness was the pursuit of the American dream, and increasingly it was within reach of the millions who traded what few convictions they had about the next life for the pleasures of this one.

Another new means developed to secure these goods was the notion of credit. Once upon a time, in the American Protestant and immigrant culture, credit was something available only to businessmen and through prudent bankers, and other people who did business on credit or on the cuff were usually described as "on the road to ruin." To borrow was a concession to defeat, and to pay on "time" usually meant that people were encouraged to buy what they couldn't afford. The new

economy for the new consumer could not wait for the thrifty house-
holder to save up sufficient funds to buy what was wanted in cash and
all at once. Thus, when banks began to create installment loan departments for ordinary consumers, and the green-stamp industry under
Sperry and Hutchinson created a secondary currency actually called
green stamps for the purchase of consumer goods, thrift, as our grandparents knew it, was held hostage to consumption.

As a child of the 1940s and early 1950s, I watched this transformation work out its conflicts in our home. My mother, born in 1901 and
formed both by the parsonage in which she had been raised and the
Great Depression from which she had emerged as a single woman with
a good job, while inherently frugal was very much a creature of the new
economy. She knew how to "make a nickel do a dollar's work," as she
would say, but she was also enchanted by the new ways to get new
things. She knew, therefore, how to make stamps, installment loans,
and other consumer inducements work for her; she never lost money
and was never late on a payment for anything, which was a point of
pride with her. My father, on the other hand, had grown up in the agri-
cultural barter economy of the Cape Verde Islands before immigrating
in 1924 to this country, and as a young man here he worked odd jobs in
immigrant communities before settling down to married life, raising a
family, and giving his life over to growing cranberries. He was suspicious of credit in any form, as he had seen what it could to people's spirits when their goods and services were indentured to a capital
lender—which he regarded as peonage. He didn't trust the apparent
altruism of banks, for he had seen many people lose their money in the
crash of 1929, and he did not like the idea of owing anybody anything,
because it compromised his dignity and his independence. Thus he
was a cash-on-the-barrelhead kind of man, and until his older years he
was suspicious even of checks and of money orders. Most of the older
Island men who were contemporaries of my father's father kept their
money in coffee cans buried beneath the woodpile in the back garden;

my father was not quite as conservative as they were, but he appreciated the ability of those old fellows who, when they went into town to buy something, whether a can of stewed tomatoes or a second-hand model A Ford, could peel off the correct amount of cash from a thick dirty bundle.

Needless to say, my mother and my father had different views on the purpose and use of money, but they were agreed, as was nearly everyone else, that money was indispensable to the good life, which, in their case, they wanted not so much for themselves as for their son, and they succeeded in maintaining for me the illusion of affluence. That there were people who had much more than we had and had had it for generations, I knew, and rather than feeling envious of the gentry, I quite admired them; but years later, when I commented to my mother that I had not realized that we were poor, she replied in some heat and with no sense of irony, "We were *not* poor: we simply didn't have enough money." That was her way of affirming the larger principle that money is not the same as wealth, and that the lack of money is therefore not the same as poverty. Success, even with the prevailing standard of material goods, was to be measured in other ways.

Plausible Lies and Fantastic Truths

One way of measuring success was being able to distinguish between the illusions that gave apparent, superficial pleasure and the realities, the fantastic truths, that sustained when all else failed. There was always available in small-town America the moral example of the old family that had once had all of this world's goods, but that now was living in genteel poverty. The family's members were still "quality" people, for they still had about them their dignity, their sense of responsibility, and a *noblesse oblige* even when they couldn't afford it; and even in their reduced circumstances they were always deferred to because of what most ordinary people referred to as their "quality factor."

Then there was the vivid example of the *nouveau riche*, the country-club set, easily lampooned as "Babbitts," whose money was so new and abundant that no one, including themselves, could get beyond it. They were rich, but not wealthy, and certainly not, as we used to say, "well-to-do"; and they were too nervous about their origins and the stability of their fortunes to be able to do much good for anyone other than themselves. Not only were they therefore selfish, but ordinary people liked to believe they were fundamentally unhappy and unfulfilled and lacked the depth of meaning that their means afforded.

Eventually, in the 1950s, social critics began to point out the cultural differences between affluence and happiness, which were not hard to see. In the period between 1945 and 1960, America enjoyed a robust postwar economy so strong as to stimulate the wholesale invention of the suburbs and a federal highway system designed to facilitate the breakdown of regional insularity. Television and advertising came of age, and as a result of both in the late 1950s came the development of an economically independent teenage consumer culture just in time to sustain such teenage "industries" as the drive-in movie, the fast-food restaurant, and, most important of all, rock-and-roll music.

Among the beneficiaries of this rich and expansive time were the religious communities of America, and particularly America's "established" religious community, the mainstream Protestant church. The Protestant churches were determined to extend their influence to the ever expanding suburbs, and all across America new churches followed the movement of the people in a syndrome that *Time* magazine, in a famous cover story on the religious revival in the America of the 1950s, called "America's Edifice Complex."

Writers such as sociologist Vance Packard, economist John Kenneth Galbraith, and theologian Reinhold Niebuhr pointed out in their books the fatal flaws of a consumerist culture, especially one that favored individual indulgence over social responsibility. Most people, however, preferred the more soothing nostrums of Dr. Norman Vincent Peale and his *Power of Positive Thinking* and the rousing crusades of the charismatic young preacher Billy Graham, who could fill Madison Square Garden with his appeals for "decisions for Christ." Only in the nihilism of the increasingly strident songs of youth, and their indulgent, sardonic take on what passed for polite society, was it suggested that the good life as lived and experienced was not all that it had been cracked up to be. When Britain's Harold Macmillan won reelection for the Tory Party on the materialist slogan "You Never Had It So Good," at the height of Carnaby Street and British rock's social revolution, it didn't occur to anyone that his government would be brought down by a torrid sex scandal that served only to emphasize the growing credibility gap between perceptions of the good life and the sense of having a life that counted.

The Grand Illusions

Few preachers were prepared to take on the perceptions and deceptions of a culture that defined success in terms of excess. Most were content to take whatever benefits they could and, besides, it had become the conventional wisdom that it was society that was to be saved, and not individuals. To reform the world was prophetic; to engage in individual reformation was simply interference. It was the very society that the poet T. S. Eliot had envisioned a generation before, when he observed that people would "dream of systems so perfect / that no one need ever be good."

Out of all of this came a modest collection of sermons written by a British preacher now serving a large and influential church in Toronto, Ontario. A. Leonard Griffith had previously served as minister of the City Temple, in London, England, a nonconformist congregation not to be confused with the more famous Temple Church, located within the Middle Temple, in the Strand. Griffith's London church was an old-fashioned preaching station with a reformed and evangelistic feel to it, which attracted large Sunday congregations of regulars as well as American tourists who came to hear sound preaching, and very good music under the direction of the well-known Eric Thiman. Griffith knew and preached in London at the height of its "Carnaby Street" phase in the trendy "Age of Aquarius," that time in which one of the Beatles said, to the consternation of only a few, that his band of rockers was more famous than Jesus Christ.

From this setting Griffith accepted a call to Canada, and in 1969 he published a book of his sermons called *Illusions of Our Culture*. It was a *cri de coeur* of a committed and articulate Christian who saw the world seduced by illusions that were infinitely more appealing than the hard truths the church had to offer, for not only was the church eclipsed in terms of what it had to say, but it was completely outclassed by those who offered a competing vision. "I am concerned," he wrote in his preface,

> that our culture is shot through with illusions which, if they are believed, will endanger society and deprive the individual of self-fulfillment. The reason for their presence is that so many of the spokesmen of our culture—broadcasters, lecturers, writers, editors, poets, philosophers and artists—are not men of deep religious faith.[15]

What these people have to say about religion may or may not be true. The fact that they may know next to nothing about religion will not prevent their speaking on the subject, and whatever they say by way of enforcing the comfortable illusions of a secular age will, as Griffith said, "exercise a greater influence on popular thought than do all the spokesmen of God put together. Obviously, the Church is no longer a match for them." Out of that concern came his arrow against the wind.

His chapters concern themselves with the self-deluding illusions of affluence, security, neutrality, independence, maturity, and progress, among others; and he notes that such illusions are the marks of a civilization that has come to believe its own press clippings. It was the early Christian theologian Tertullian who first used the phrase "men already civilized and under the illusions of their very culture," when writing of the pervasive self-confidence of Roman civilization. Griffith's people would find Tertullian's alternative to their illusion not simply distasteful, but impossible to hear, for they felt they had need of no ideas other than their own.

If we were to think of Griffith's book as an establishment critique of the so-called counterculture, we would be mistaken. It is an establishment critique of the establishment, with its smug self-satisfactions, its capacity to substitute convenience, and its all too eager willingness to compromise in favor of the passing definition of cultural success. "No wonder the hippies protest against the values of our bourgeois culture!"[16] Griffith remarks. They see what a later generation would call the "disconnect" between what we aspire to and what we are used to. In their eyes, as in Tertullian's, the worst that one can do is to settle for an illusion instead of a reality and be content to live with a plausible lie rather than to accept the demands of a fantastic truth. The good life deserves no less than the pursuit of that fantastic truth, no matter how trendy the times or appealing the lies.

What Is Worth Doing

On June 14, 1914, fewer than two months before the guns of August would announce the start of World War I, Abbott Lawrence Lowell, twenty-second president of Harvard, took the pulpit of Appleton Chapel to deliver his baccalaureate sermon to the Class of 1914. The president took "success" as his topic, noting:

The men who make a rapid success in their first venture in life are not numerous, and some of them actually are injured if they do. A young man must perforce choose his career before he has tried it. He must estimate his own qualities, with which he is still only partly familiar; and he must guess how well they fit him for an occupation of which he has had no personal experience.[17]

To many, the success of Harvard graduates in 1914 would appear to be practically automatic. Harvard, the oldest and richest college in the land, and both its friends and its critics would appear to have the Midas touch, for not only had all that Harvard touched turned to gold, but all who were in any way touched by it seemed destined for what the world would regard as "success," and intellectual, social, scientific, and political eminence seemed an assured part of the best education that money could buy. Lowell, himself a Harvard aristocrat and heir to a Brahmin entitlement of nearly five generations, was the iconic embodiment of an American elite. Although he was wealthy, he did not speak as a wealthy man, but as the president of what many considered to be "a rich man's school," and his discourse on success would be heeded if not in Cambridge, where it might seem superfluous, then certainly in the broader and more ambitious world of rising American expectations.

Thus it is interesting to note that for him, "Success is an illusive thing, very hard to measure, and sometimes a man does not himself know whether he has made a success or not." Success was also an elusive thing:

Does it [success] mean the mere satisfaction of desires or ambitions, whatever they may be? If a man's desire is to gratify immediate cravings for pleasure with as little exertion as possible, and he does so, has he made a success of his life? Certainly not. The mere satisfaction of desire, then, is not success unless the object desired is worthy.[18]

Lowell's Puritan inheritance and his sense of Yankee rectitude did not permit him to accept the pleasure principle as a sufficient definition of success. "True success does not depend upon achieving the objects a man has set before himself at the outset of his career, on the satisfaction of ambitions, or aims, or on being contented with what he has attained."[19]

The world is full of people who have attained what they wanted and are neither happy nor satisfied. Mere competence, or even excellence, in a chosen field of endeavor is an insufficient basis for success, for they do not take into account questions of worth, value, or merit. In short, they fail the test of goodness, and certainly success cannot be said to be gained without some sense of the good of the thing at which one is successful. Thus, the mere making of money, the gaining of power or influence, the achievement of a reputation, and the accumulation of honors and distinctions may be regarded as accomplishments, but whether the one who has gained these accomplishments can be regarded as successful in the moral and not simply in the achievement sense is another matter, and hence the burden of Lowell's address.

Only in the final paragraph of his tightly argued sermon does Lowell provide his working definition of success:

> True success does not consist in doing what we set forth to do, what we had hoped to do, nor even in doing what we have struggled to do; but in doing something that is worth doing.[20]

For such a long time and for so many people, success has been defined as the achievement of that which gives the most pleasure and happiness to the individual—success in relationship to the attainments of the interior ambition—that it sounds strange to have success defined as other and outwardly directed and not necessarily readily detected. Lowell observes that those people whom we call saints often died thinking themselves unsuccessful, or even failures. Many died without realizing their own life goals or without realizing that for which posterity would remember them. Lowell does not mention Mozart in this regard, but although Mozart had no small opinion of himself in life — a point made with exaggerated brilliance almost to the point of buffoonery in the play and movie *Amadeus* — at his premature death he was buried without much ceremony in a common grave, and no one yet realized for what great things he would be remembered.

Lowell is not advising his young charges to wait for posthumous glory and recognition, for he is, after all, interested in the practical side of life on this side of the grave. His intention is to guide his materialistic, ambitious, and perhaps anxious young achievers into the notion that if the good life, that is, the life that can be called a success, is to be lived now, then such a life must be lived beyond the simple compass of self-gratification: "The man who sees clearly how and why the object of his life lies outside of and beyond himself, and to whom the solution of the problem has become a deep conviction in the innermost recesses of his world, has the greatest sustaining power this world affords."[21]

With that sentence, which was not the clarion call to action that one might expect on such an occasion, but an invitation to the contemplation of interior priorities by which to make a life, and a good one, and not merely a living, Lowell concludes his sermon. We have no idea how it sat with his listeners, for, as with most commencement oratory, it was probably forgotten by lunchtime the next day. Yet, in its demand for an austere introspection, with self sublimated to value and worth, Lowell's sermon defines success not in what we do, but in the value, the worthwhileness, of our doing. By this measure, some of what the world regards as manifest failure might well be seen as success. Although Lowell makes no mention of Jesus in his sermon, and certainly would not have wanted to be seen as imparting any of the theological particulars of any religious denomination, this latter point might well be illustrated by a very conspicuous Christian of the next generation, the German Lutheran pastor and martyr Dietrich Bonhoeffer. Hanged by the Nazis within weeks of the end of World War II, it was Bonhoeffer who said, "The figure of the Crucified invalidates all thought which takes success for its standard."

Such an antidote to the "moral flabbiness" of success falsely conceived and worshiped, again in James's analysis of the American "national disease," requires that we come to know more of discipline and freedom and their relationship; and to this we will turn on to what we should know about the good life.

CHAPTER 6

DISCIPLINE

THE PRACTICE OF PERFECTION

If you are willing, my [child], you will be instructed;
if you give your mind to it, you will become clever.
ECCLESIASTICUS 6:32 (KJV), Apocrypha

The true beginning of wisdom is the desire to learn . . .
THE WISDOM OF SOLOMON 6:17 (KJV),
Apocrypha

Train up a child in the way he should go;
and when he is old, he will not depart from it.
PROVERBS 22:6 (KJV)

I remember very well the visit: he had come to see me about arrange-
ments for his memorial service although he was not ill or given to a
morbid compulsion. He was simply sensible, prudent, and practical,
like all of his ancestors, for the man who had come to see me was
Charles Francis Adams. In Boston, when people see the name Adams,
they ask, "Is he a *real* Adams?" by which they mean a descendant of the
two presidents Adams, and of Henry, of Brooks, and of the whole talented tribe. My visitor was not only a "real" Adams in every sense, but
he was the spitting image of his father's grandfather, John Quincy

Adams. After we had settled the efficient details for the memorial service, we came as close to small talk as an Adams can. I ventured to ask what it was like to bear so famous a name, and Charlie replied, quite simply, "It's a lifetime job." Then, as if recalling a recent conversation with his father, President Coolidge's Secretary of the Navy and now dead for nearly a half century, Charlie said that on his first day of work following his graduation from Harvard in 1932, his father looked him in the eye and said, "You have inherited a great reputation for truth: God help you if you lose it."

Of our public families, the Adams family has until quite recently been generally neglected. Certainly we know a great deal about the Roosevelts, the Kennedys, and the second father and son presidency, the Bushes; and William Henry and Benjamin Harrison continue in death to occupy the minor roles they played in life. We always knew that we ought to pay more attention to the Adams family, but in a celebrity culture they lacked dash, wit, and image. The second and sixth presidents stood for those sulfurous New England virtues, the Yankee rectitude against which this country has been in continuous rebellion for most of its existence. How ironic it is that the Adams civic legacy should have been rehabilitated at the very point of the Clinton presidency's disarray, as David McCullough's heroic biography of John Adams became nearly a cult best-seller, and from this renewed and compelling attention came federal commitment to a suitable memorial to John, Abigail, and John Quincy Adams on the Mall in Washington, in an obligation long overdue.

What is it that makes us admire John Adams and John Quincy Adams? They were not wealthy, but neither were they fashionably poor. John Adams lost out to a much more wealthy and clever man in Thomas Jefferson, and John Quincy Adams to a heroic populist and friend of the poor, Andrew "Old Hickory" Jackson. The Adams men lacked charm, were physically ungainly, and tended to sulk when they did not get their way. As flinty as the soil from which they sprang, they brandished as weapons their well-justified reputations for plain living and high thinking, and although they were not lovable, they became the kind of ancestors that everybody would like to claim.

Why? Because of character—not because of personality or celebrity, the essential criteria of this tabloid culture—but because of character. As the famous aphorism states: "Reputation is what the world knows of you, but character is what God knows of you." In an ideal world the two are consistent, with reputation serving as the shell that houses the living ingredient, the character; and as character is not neutral and everybody has character, the possession of a good character is essential to the maintenance of a good reputation. For this to be the characteristic of an individual is a situation worthy of praise, and of such individuals Plutarch wrote in his famous series of lives. For a family dynasty to have such a reputation is even more unusual, for it is both a privilege and a burden, and it was of this that the young Charlie Adams had been reminded by his father. Character, as the father had said of the vocation of being an Adams, is a lifetime job.

The Medicine of the Soul

When earlier we looked at the little book on courtesy and manners that Sister Mercedes wrote for her schoolgirls in California and at the rules of LaSalle Academy for boys in New York City, we understood that these were efforts not simply in intellectual content, but in moral formation as well, as in the making of character. Thus, if education is a key component in the good life, and a key component of education is the formation of good character, we must ask what the essential ingredient is in that character formation that will help to perpetuate the qualities we admire in the Adams family, and in others perhaps less famous, whose characters we would choose to emulate and to have reproduced in our children. In other words, we must ask what virtue it is that, if cultivated, will most help in the development of a good character capable of coping with failure, success, and freedom.

The answer, I suggest, is discipline, which helps to form the character by the application of external exemplary examples and the suppression of those internal instincts that may compromise the moral ambition of the individual. It was St. Augustine who called discipline "the medicine of the soul" and gave to it two functions: restraint, implying fear, and instruction, implying love. For Augustine, those two qualities are emblematic of the two testaments of scripture. The Old Testament, with its emphasis on law, is an exercise in restraint, where fear functions doubly, in the fear of breaking the law and in the consequences of breaking the law. Thus, one is restrained from evil or bad character not because one is good or strong, but because one fears alienation and estrangement from God and from the good, which evil provokes, and the consequences of it, which is the loss of the divine society and the impairment of the human will. When in the wisdom literature of the Old Testament we read that "The fear of the Lord is the beginning of wisdom" (Psalm 111:10), we understand the pedagogical function of discipline, of which restraint is one expression. From this notion of discipline as a function of law that leads to liberty, we get the description of law as "those wise restraints that set us free." Restraint, then, is a preventative of evil, a preemptive strike against the consequences of the lack of control. In the medical analogy that we may extend from Augustine's notion of discipline as the "medicine of the soul," we may say that restraint is to the soul what physical exercise is to the body. We may think of exercise as a positive thing, and it is, but its function is a preventative one, which is to say that it is intended to prevent the body from falling apart. When we jog, or pump iron, or do circuit training on the Nautilus machine, we are in preventative mode, fighting against the things to which the flesh is naturally heir. Health in this case is going against the inevitable direction of nature, and the inevitable direction of nature is decay, atrophy, and death. Discipline helps us to retard that inevitability.

The second property of discipline as the "medicine of the soul" is instruction, and what fear is to restraint, love is to instruction. The operating rule of the New Testament is the new commandment that Jesus mandates for all of his followers: that we should love one another. All of the New Testament and all of Christian ethics are to be read through the new mandate, or commandment, that Jesus gave to his disciples on the night in which he was betrayed: "This is my commandment, that ye love one another, as I have loved you" (John 15:12, KJV). If fear is reactive, love is proactive. For Augustine, then, the one who would lead a good life and exercise discipline as the virtue essential to the formation of character will first fear God and then love him:

> And as regards the mind, his endeavors are in this order, that he should first fear, and then love God. This is true excellence of conduct, and thus the knowledge of the truth, of which we are ever in pursuit, is acquired.[1]

Self-discipline begins with self-knowledge, imperfect as that knowledge may be, for in attempting to know who and what we are, we become aware of who and what we are not. Self-awareness is the place where the internal moral education begins, and it is not always pretty. This, for example, is the burden of perhaps the most famous account of self-awareness in human experience, the experience of Adam and Eve in the Garden of Eden.

Original Self-Awareness

Let's not waste time on whether the story, as recorded in the book of Genesis in the Bible, is true, for that is a false issue that serves only to distract from the substance of the meaning the story is meant to convey.

The story itself does not begin with the story, as there is something before it that provokes it, a situation that requires explanation, a question that demands an answer. We should be concerned first with what that prior situation was, and then with the adequacy or acceptability of the answer that the story in the Genesis text provides. Even more than asking truth questions of the text, we should ask how, for thousands of years and for millions of people, the questions and answers the Genesis texts provide have defined subsequent questions and answers and the behaviors derived from them.

If we look at the story of Adam and Eve in the Garden of Eden as telling a moral story and not a scientific one, we can see that the elements of human behavior it seeks to address have to do with the developing awareness of the sense of the self. Presumably the question asked, to which this narrative is an answer, concerned how human beings became the complex moral beings they are now, what they were like before this, and what the consequences, opportunities, and remedies are of this condition.

In the Genesis account, Adam and Eve become aware of themselves, which is to say they acquire self-consciousness, at the moment they discover their nakedness. We might think that they became aware of self when they assented to the blandishments of the serpent, but at that point they were ignorant of the knowledge of good and evil. Literally speaking, they did not know any better. They knew simply that they were to be obedient and to do as God said, and God told them to do two things: to till the garden and to not eat the fruit. The serpent, described as "subtle," which here implies not only an acute knowledge of his own powers but an even more acute insight into the weakness of others, offers Eve the opportunity to be like God. Who would not want to be like God? Because God had formed man out of the dust, man was therefore literally a creature of sand, spit, and spirit; and woman was formed from man. Thus they each reflected God's handiwork and in theory, at least, the serpent offered them both self-knowledge, for in becoming like God and in having the knowledge of good and of evil, they would become even more like the one who created them. What could be wrong with that?

Unaware of self, or incompletely aware of self, Adam and Eve lived in innocence, which here is clearly morally the same as ignorance. They were naked, Genesis tells us, and of their nakedness they were neither aware nor ashamed until the moment of self-awareness. They ate the fruit, and "The eyes of them both were opened, and they knew that they were naked" (Genesis 3:7, KJV). They had been naked all along, and it had been, as the twentieth-century buzzword has it, "no problem"; but when they became aware of the fact that they were naked, both their nakedness and their awareness of it became a problem.

We may well ask why. Augustine and other Christian moralists have argued that panic set in when they became aware of their sexual identities and saw their sexual organs, which Augustine goes so far as to call "instruments of shame" because they behave not at the behest of the will, but with a mind, as it were, of their own. Sexual arousal is a visible, unambiguous response to passions and forces beyond the rational control of the will. Adam and Eve, however, are not simply aware of their sexuality, but now of themselves as beings capable of the good and the evil of which they have just acquired knowledge. They know they have disobeyed God; they know they have done the one thing God did not want them to do, and thus they now know disobedience, shame, guilt, ingratitude, and fear. The results of this unsettling knowledge lead to more bad behavior and, having lived intimately with God in the garden, Adam and Even in their new knowledge now become ashamed and furtive. First they hide from themselves, and then they hide from each other by sewing together fig leaves and making themselves aprons to cover their "private parts," as they will always be known. Presumably, before this what we call "modesty" had been unnecessary, as nakedness was neither a threat nor a temptation and therefore nothing of which to be ashamed. It is the self-awareness that the forbidden fruit induced that caused those primal humans to hide from themselves, then from each other, and finally from God: "And they heard the sound of the Lord God walking in the garden in the cool of the day; and Adam and his wife hid themselves from the presence of the Lord God amongst the trees of the garden" (Genesis 3:8, KJV).

As the narrative progresses we discover that they hide from God because their new knowledge tells them that if God sees them not naked, but covered up, God will know that they have disobeyed. Interestingly, God is not put off by the nudity of his creatures, which is a sign to him of their obedience. It is their clothing, minimal as it is, in the form of the fig leaves, usually represented as covering the loins of the man and the woman, but not the breasts of the woman, that informs God of their disobedience. They hide not only because they are aware of their nakedness, but because that awareness, and their feeble attempt to literally cover it up, communicates the larger sin. That whole awareness generates a terrible sense of fear and apprehension, for what else would make the creature fear the creator? Surely a part of that fear was the sense that the creatures had disappointed the creator, that there would be consequences to follow that disappointment, and that their own ability to make sound judgments in their own best interests had now been impaired. Would the impairment be permanent, or was it merely an aberration? Were there things, actions, behaviors they could undertake to put any of this right? Knowing now what they knew about God, themselves, the serpent, and their situation, could they ever again be innocent, happy, or good? If not, whatever would become of them?

One of the things they anticipated was punishment, for they knew they had disobeyed an order of God. "You may freely eat of every tree of the garden," says God in his initial instructions to Adam, "but of the tree of the knowledge of good and evil you shall not eat, for in the day that you eat of it you shall die" (Genesis 2:16–17). Death was the punishment, and it seemed a swift and immediate sentence, like sticking one's finger into a live electrical socket. As my colleague James Kugel points out, however, in his lively discussion of the problems with the Genesis text, they did not die, or at least not immediately. According to Genesis 5:5, Adam went on to live to the age of nine hundred thirty years, which is not a bad tenure, and as the death of Eve is not recorded, we may assume that she shared much of her husband's time.

Some critics suggest that the notion of "day" should be expanded in the same fashion that it is in the "seven-day" creation narrative, while others suggest that it is the fact of mortality and not the precise moment of death that is the fulfillment of the promised punishment.[2] I suggest a slightly different reading: within the context of this self-induced self-awareness, the first thing Adam and Eve come to know about themselves is the fact that they will die sooner or later, but ultimately. The knowledge of death, a reality greater than the knowledge of disobedience, shame, and fear, now becomes the context within which life must of necessity be lived and by which it must forever be defined. To know that one is to die is the fundamental truth of human identity and the basis of all human knowledge and behavior. The knowledge of personal, existential extinction is the first fruit of the garden; and whether death is a punishment, a natural conclusion, a disaster, or a fate, it is an unalterable fact of life. Thus, the story of Adam and Eve is not about sin, disobedience, sex, or shame, but is an attempt to explain the reality of death. The first lesson in this tradition having to do with living the good life is that life, however good, is finite, a limited resource, and that one does not have all the time in the world to discover what it is or how to live it. The first duty of self-awareness, therefore, is the knowledge of the fewness of one's days.

Living Within the Limits

This point is made variously throughout Hebrew scripture and perhaps most famously in Psalm 39:4, which has long been a feature of the Christian burial office. Here, the psalmist asks for explicit knowledge of his death date so that he may know how to order his life while he is still living: "Lord, let me know my end, and what is the measure of my days; let me know how fleeting my life is!" This information is sought not out of morbid fear, but out of a practical sense of adapting to the limits. The uncertainty of life is not a cause for fear, but a cause for modesty, which allows one time for doing the right or good thing. That uncertainty is made real by the illusions of earthly riches and power, in a vain effort to compensate for human insecurity by investment in the things that would appear to be permanent, and hence to assure permanence. The one who attempts this is warned later on in the same psalm (v. 6): "For man walketh in a vain shadow, and disquieteth himself in vain; he heapeth up riches, and cannot tell who shall gather them" (KJV).

Not only is the gathering of earthly treasure useless in forestalling the inevitable day of death, but even these seemingly permanent things are beyond the control of their owner after death. Wills, trusts, and lawyers are all designed to reach beyond the grave to give comfort to those who think they can dispose of their possessions, but the history of human experience demonstrates that there is nothing that can guarantee this, and the history of the law of probate is a living record of these frustrated ambitions. The awareness of mortality, the first fruit of the Garden of Eden, is one of the continuing themes of self-awareness, self-discipline, and moral intelligence throughout the Bible; and the awareness of death is the first key to the discipline that contributes to the good life.

Perhaps the most famous moral choice given in the struggle for self-awareness, and thus for the good life, is the one presented by Moses to the Israelites in Deuteronomy 30. Set within a context of blessings and curses, the choice between life and good, and death and evil, is given by Moses to his people just before they enter into the Promised Land, that place for which for forty years they have been laboring and toward which they have been journeying.

> *I call heaven and earth to witness against you this day, that I*
> *have set before you life and death, blessing and curse; therefore*
> *choose life, that you and your descendants may live, loving the*
> *Lord your God, obeying his voice, and cleaving to him; for*
> *that means life to you and length of days, that you may dwell*
> *in the land which the Lord swore to your fathers, to*
> *Abraham, to Isaac, and to Jacob, to give them.*
>
> DEUTERONOMY 30:19–20

Most simply put, the context of the choice is that if you obey God, love God, keep God's commandments, and do the right and good thing, God will give you the land and a good life to enjoy within it. If you do not do the right and good thing, you will lose the land, and your life, instead of being blessed, will be cursed. The best advice here is to choose life, that you and those who come after you may live.

It is an axiom of moral philosophy that the essence of freedom is choice. We will have more to say of freedom in the next chapter, but here we must ask if this choice that Moses presents to his people is a real selection between the two equally valid alternatives of life and death, blessings and curses. As if to emphasize that this is merely a theoretical choice, and essentially a freedom to do the right thing, Moses directs his people to the choice he wishes them to make: "Therefore," he says, "choose life."

The choice of life is here equated with the choice of good, and good is here defined as fulfilling the laws of righteousness, of doing the right thing not by intuition or good intention, but by following the clear prescriptions of the law that are laid out for all. In his commentary on the history of the interpretation of this passage, James Kugel points out:

Choosing the good would (quite apart from Israel's continued life in its homeland) allow a person to enjoy the rewards that God normally grants to the righteous in their own individual lives, since God's all-seeing eye monitors the behavior of each human being.[3]

This, then, is not just a cultural choice for a people, important as that is in the history of Israel's self-understanding, but it is also an individual, existential choice, a choice between two paths or ways of life. The book of the prophet Jeremiah states, "And to this people shall you say: 'Thus says the Lord: behold, I put before you the path of life and the path of death'" (21:8, Kugel version). Kugel even suggests the existence of a now lost standard list of dos and don'ts based on summaries of the law, which may have been widely circulated under the title "The Two Ways."[4]

In the Christian New Testament these two ways are described in the familiar passage about the gates and the road, in the book of Matthew (7:13–14, KJV):

> *Enter ye in at the strait gate; for wide is the gate, and broad*
> *is the way, that leadeth to destruction, and many there be*
> *which go in thereat; because strait is the gate, and narrow is*
> *the way, which leadeth unto life, and few there be that find it.*

The modern English of J. B. Phillips translation of this passage reads:

> *Go in by the narrow gate. For the wide gate has a broad road*
> *which leads to disaster, and there are many people going that*
> *way. The narrow gate and the hard road lead out into life,*
> *and only a few are finding it.*

By the time of Matthew, himself a Jew and writing largely to a Jewish audience, the choices between life and death that had seemed so artificial in Moses' orchestration in Deuteronomy now seem somehow more attractive. In fact, and inexplicably so, many more seem to have made the easy, the wrong, or the bad choice for, as Matthew's text points out, "There are many people going that way"; as for the difficult, the right, and the good road or path, "only a few are finding it."

The reward of life for choosing life may be variously interpreted. Life, as the concept offered by Moses in his choice between blessings and curses, life and death, may mean not just length of days, but the quality of those days, however long or short. In this is implied the subtle but essential distinction between mere existence and living, what we might call the quality of life or, in particular, the moral quality of life. In this context it is the good thing that makes for the life that is good; and the reward for doing the good thing is the good life. It is not immortality, for nowhere is one promised that death can be either avoided or evaded. What we perceive here is the notion that life itself is the context in which the good life can be pursued, and presumably the more lifetime one has, the more one has an opportunity to please God, and thus to live the good life—in the moral sense—here and now, and to prepare for the life that comes after death. The one who chooses life in this world, therefore, chooses to live a life so pleasing to God and so righteous, that after death the reward will be life not subject to death.

Interesting as it may be to speculate whether by life Moses meant this life, life as opposed to death, or life as the reward after death, the ethical implications are significant for those who would see in this choice between two paths or two ways only one, which leads to the pursuit of and end of the good life. What the self-aware mortal most needs is the constant reminder of his or her mortality, so that within the constraints of limited time he or she may order priorities aright in the pursuit of the good life, for not only is the reward of the good life the quality of the life now lived, but the promise of the life to come. As one of the familiar blessings of the Christian marriage service derived from the

Anglican tradition puts to the couple: "May you so live together in this life that in the life to come you may have life everlasting."

The question of moral choices about the good life described in terms of two paths, ways, or roads will remind many of Robert Frost's poem "The Road Not Taken," which begins:

> *Two roads diverged in a yellow wood,*
> *And sorry I could not travel both*
> *And be one traveler, long I stood*
> *And looked down one as far as I could*
> *To where it bent in the undergrowth . . .* [5]

Generations of high-school students have had to ponder the moral implications of the choice of the "road less traveled" and of why and how that choice "made all the difference." How much Frost drew on Moses' offer of choices in Deuteronomy or on the rich layers of commentary in and beyond the Bible, we cannot tell. The usual gloss on the Frost poem has more to do with freedom than with moral responsibility, and for many people neither Frost nor Moses is particularly helpful in this matter of choice. It is Yogi Berra's much-cited malapropism that becomes the inadvertent text for the times: "When you come to the fork in the road, take it."

The desire for discipline proceeds from the awareness of the existence of chaos and disorder both in the world and in one's self. Self-awareness tells the one who wishes to pursue the good life that there is not an infinite amount of time in which to attend to this ambition, that this ambition for goodness is thwarted by qualities interior to the individual and circumstances external to the individual, over which, without an imposed order—a discipline—the individual, no matter how morally ambitious, has no control. The self-aware person puzzles over the question that even though one wishes to be and to do good, one knows enough of one's own limitations to know that on one's own one cannot accomplish it. How, one asks, can I be guided in making the right choices? How can I restrain those impulses, within and without, that I know, by the history of others and through my own experience, will do harm to me and to others?

The fact of death and the knowledge of the good life are evidently not good enough to prevent us from making wrong choices. Self-awareness makes us mindful of the fact that, in William James's words, "There is something wrong about us as we naturally stand."[6] This is the conflict, or chaos, of the self divided between the "yearning for something more" and the sense of being less than good, which creates the desire for order, or cosmos, which is the opposite of chaos, or disorder. Thus, discipline is the process by which we restore or create order, imposing considered restraints upon our unruly and natural affections; in chaos we experience the loss of order, we feel a sense of things, people, self, and time out of joint, and all seems meaningless, impossible, hypocritical. Discipline becomes the way back, or the way forward, depending upon whether we speak of order as something lost or something yet to be attained. We understand order to be essential to the pursuit of the good, for without it we cannot tell good from bad, and that is the ultimate disorder.

The very word "discipline," however, is now a problem. Ask people what comes to mind when they hear or read the word "discipline," and most will reply that they think of some notion of punishment or sanction, or both. A "disciplinary committee" in a school or college usually has as its task the responsibility of assessing blame and determining punishment for bad behavior. A "good disciplinarian" is one who keeps order by the threat or the fact of punishment; vividly famous examples of those who used corporal punishment come to mind in such Dickensian cane-wielding schoolmasters as Wackford Squeers in *Nicholas Nickleby* and Mr. Creakle in *David Copperfield*. Corporal punishment enjoyed the moral sanction of the Bible, as in Proverbs

10:13 (KJV), "A rod is for the back of him that is void of understanding," and in Proverbs 13:24 (KJV), "He that spareth his rod hateth his son," both of which could be summarized under the rubric, "Spare the rod and spoil the child." Even in the New Testament, where the rule of love is understood to prevail over mere punishment and intimidation, in Hebrews 12:6 (KJV), we read, "For whom the Lord loveth he chasteneth, and scourgeth every son whom he receiveth."

Discipline in this sense seems powerfully negative and reactive, and thus it comes as something of a surprise that, to Augustine and other moral thinkers, discipline, like the law for the Jews, is not a reactive negation of prohibited behavior, but a positive encouragement for good, and even a manifestation of goodness itself. We have something of an aesthetic sense of this when, in evaluating a good performance of some act or art, we recognize and appreciate the discipline that has enabled the performer to do well. We say that a performer has mastered the discipline of his or her art; we admire the discipline of the athlete and of the soldier; and we used to say that the practice of the piano and the mastery of such rule-oriented foreign languages as Greek and Latin provided mental discipline for the naturally chaotic minds of youth. To this day unruly youth are sent off to military schools and "tough love" camps in order to provide them with a discipline otherwise lacking in their chaotic lives; and one of the popular refrains of old dons and mafiosi in American movies about organized crime is that the younger generation lacks respect, honor, and discipline.

Discipline, therefore, and especially self-discipline, must be more than a form of punishment, and there must be more to it than the imposition of order through pain and punishment. It must be discipline in this other, positive sense to which the wisdom literature of the Jews refers when it says, in Ecclesiasticus, "If you are willing, my child, you can be disciplined; and if you apply yourself you will become clever" (6:32, NRSV); and, in The Wisdom of Solomon, "The very true beginning of [wisdom] is the desire of discipline" (6:17); and, in Proverbs,

"Train up a child in the way he should go, and when he is old he will not depart from it " (22:6, KJV). Discipline is good not only for individuals, but individual discipline is essential for what in the military is called "unit cohesion," where all must depend upon the discipline of each for the well-being of all. The military is not the only place, however, where discipline has an intimate relationship with the moral success of the individual and the moral success of the group.

I remember as a child being both enchanted and intimidated by the covenant that the members of my church recited once a month just before the Communion service, in an intentionally solemn moment. The Communion table was laid with white linen and silver; the deacons, all solemn middle-aged men in ill-fitting suits, my father among them, stood at either side of the table; and the pastor stood in the middle. The members about to receive the commemorative meal of white bread and grape juice all rose and recited the pledge, or covenant, that had served our little church since 1809 with neither amendment nor addition, and its elegant, archaic, and profoundly biblical language gave a dignity, even a solemnity, to our small proceedings worthy of the greatest cathedral or basilica liturgy in the world. The covenant read:

> As we trust we have been brought by divine grace to embrace the Lord Jesus Christ, and by the influence of His spirit to give ourselves up to Him, so we do now solemnly covenant with each other, as God shall enable us, to walk together in brotherly love; that we will *exercise a Christian care and watchfulness over each other, and faithfully warn, rebuke, and admonish our brethren as the case shall require*; that we will not forsake the assembling of ourselves together, nor omit the great duty of prayer, both for ourselves and for others; that we will participate in each other's joys, and endeavor, with tenderness and sympathy, to bear each other's burdens and sorrows; that we will seek divine aid to enable us to walk circumspectly and watchfully in the world, denying ungod-

liness and every worldly lust; that we will strive together for the support of a faithful evangelical ministry among us; and through life, amidst evil report and good report, seek to live to the glory of Him who hath called us out of darkness into his marvelous light. (emphasis added)[7]

Even as I write these words I can hear the ancient voices and see the faces of my elders reciting a form of words whose sophistication was out of character with their very ordinary lives, but whose moral ambition reflected their own. Fiercely anticredal, as all good Baptists felt themselves to be, while they would not impose a doctrinal conformity upon one another, they quite freely imposed and subscribed to a mutual spiritual discipline that attempted to describe and prescribe a way of life for each individual as well as for the community of individuals. "Unit cohesion" was essential to the well-being of the community and to every individual member of it.

That point is made clear by the intimidating portions I have italicized for emphasis in the text of the covenant. What could possibly be meant by "exercise a Christian care and watchfulness over each other, and faithfully warn, rebuke, and admonish our brethren as the case shall require"?

Contemporary members of our church today think they know what it means, and they don't like it. They think it's a busybody's charter, a license to pry, snoop, comment, and hold some members up to the standards of others. "It makes people uncomfortable," one of my friends noted. Increasingly younger and more progressive pastors have become loathe to use the covenant in the context of the Communion service, largely because it tends to ruin the "feel-good" mood of the service. For many people Communion, despite the very meaning of the term, is private time, a time for personal reflection with God, not for public accountability to one another, and the ritual of public affirmation of mutual trust and responsibility has therefore gradually lost its claim upon our worship and its people. The disciplinary function that the covenant was designed to serve, and had served so well for nearly two hundred years, is now pretty much gone.

Yet the framers of the covenant, biblically informed as they were and modeling themselves upon what they believed to be the practice of the early church, had had no trouble submitting themselves to a spiritual and social discipline that would make them each responsible to one another and to God. The covenant, with its invitation to care and to watchfulness, was to them as the law was to the ancient Hebrews, and with that functional comparison in mind they could say with the psalmist, and mean it:

> *O how I love thy law! It is my meditation all the day. Thou through thy commandments hast made me wiser than mine enemies; for they are ever with me. . . . Through thy precepts I get understanding; therefore I hate every false way. Thy word is a lamp unto my feet, and a light unto my path.*
>
> PSALM 119:97–105, KJV

The process of warning, rebuking, and admonishing was known in the language of our church as "spiritual discipline," and it was a matter to be taken very seriously. As recently as in the 1930s, on the Thursday before the first Sunday of the month and its Communion service, the church would devote its weekly prayer meeting to what was called a "covenant meeting," in which members would prepare themselves for the coming Sunday service by clearing up among themselves any "covenant offenses" that needed attention. In the ideal circumstance of spiritual candor, members would confess their sins, especially those against their neighbors, and ask public forgiveness. Members who knew of offenses of fellow members were obliged to report them if the member in question did not confess, with the idea that both individuals and the body were to be cleansed of unaddressed and unresolved conflicts so that they could take Communion with one another with pure hearts and clean consciences. Staunch Protestants that they were, they would have been horrified to learn that their practice, a purely New Testament practice in their view, reflected the Roman Catholic doctrinal position that one cannot communicate until one has confessed. That particular usage, "being confessed," means that simply to confess privately one's sins was not enough: confession had to be made and heard, a penance imposed, and the sin absolved.

I very much doubt that my Baptist ancestors were familiar with Augustine's book *On Christian Discipline*, which he wrote circa A.D. 400, although they would have been pleased to note that he regarded the church, the community of believers, as the place where the faithful would "take instruction in the house of learning." The subject of his book is right living, what we have here been calling the "good life." A key to the good life, or right living, in Augustine's view, is the right kind of self-love, and the right kind of self-love is the kind that directs the heart to God and displays charity for all people. This is the self-love implied in the summary of the law that Jesus gives in the New Testament: "Thou shalt love the Lord thy God with all thy heart, and with all thy soul, and with all thy strength, and with all thy mind; and thy neighbor as thyself" (Luke 10:27, KJV). Modern commentators tend to place the emphasis either on the vertical direction, toward love of God, or on the horizontal dimension, the ethical demands of neighborliness, neglecting the basis of comparison that is the appropriate self-love. Augustine says that self-love is distorted when it becomes merely love of self, a form of narcissism that, when combined with the love of material things, is destructive and idolatrous. That is not what he means to encourage. Self-love, rightly understood, according to Augustine is self-love rightly ordered, or disciplined love. This disciplined love has as its primary focus not punishment, but improvement, and its purpose is to reprove, correct, warn, admonish, and reprimand. The engine that drives this kind of self-disciplined self-love is the engine of memory.

The logic here is that if we remember, or are reminded, of where we have gone wrong, we will learn from our mistakes not to repeat them, and from false starts or errors we will make progress in the right direction. In other words, the remembrance of disorder is therapeutic. Contrary to our natural tendency to get rid of the memory of bad things as negative memory, or "baggage," as we are likely to call it nowadays, the proper use of self-discipline requires that we remember our errors, disorders, and sins, if you will, as a means of going beyond them. Thus, true confession requires not only the will to amend one's life, but the remembrance of what it is that requires amendment.

This process of confession, together with the acknowledgment that on our own and by the power of our own will we are helpless to do anything about the disorder to which we confess, formed until quite recently a part of the historic confessions of the Anglican tradition. In the Order for Morning Prayer in the Episcopal *Book of Common Prayer* of 1928, the faithful repeated a general confession that included the following words:

> We have followed too much the devices and desires of our own hearts; we have offended against thy holy laws; we have left undone those things which we ought to have done, and we have done those things which we ought not to have done; and there is no health in us: but thou, O Lord, have mercy upon us miserable offenders . . .

On Communion Sundays, the Episcopalians confessed their sins with these words, again from the *Book of Common Prayer* of 1928:

> We acknowledge and bewail our manifold sins and wickedness, which we from time to time most grievously have committed by thought, word, and deed, against thy Divine Majesty, provoking most justly thy wrath and indignation against us. We do earnestly

repent, and are heartily sorry for these our misdoings; the remembrance of them is grievous unto us; the burden of them is intolerable.

In the general confession, we find that the source of the sins is the following of the "devices and desires of our own hearts," which is the wrong form of self-love, because it then permits sins of omission, those things that we should have done but didn't do, and sins of commission, or those things that we did do but should not have. So far, most people are prepared to recognize this pattern of behavior as self-destructive, certainly disagreeable to God, and contrary to the good life. The offense to the modern sensibility enters at the phrase "there is no health in us," which the liturgical reformers, for what they called "pastoral reasons," removed because they felt it suggested that people were "sick" and constitutionally incapacitated. Such a view, many suggested, was out of sync with mid-twentieth-century views of a psychologically healthy soul, and the resultant loss of self-esteem did no one any good. In the revised *Book of Common Prayer* of 1979, therefore, the offending phrase, with its subsequent description of the would-be penitents as "miserable offenders," was removed. William James would have had a field day with the motives of the reformers, for, in their desire to provide a confession suitable to be said by a once-born, healthy-minded soul, they failed to take into consideration the fact that religions with confession and amendment of life operate on the assumption of what James would call the "twice-born," or "sick," soul, for whom the question is how one can be healed if one declines to acknowledge that one is sick and that, as result of one's malady, illness, or condition, one is miserably unhappy.

In the confession to be made at Communion, the 1928 version—with the "grievous burden" of the remembrance of the sins confessed—is carried over as an option into the 1979 First Rite of the Holy Eucharist. What is striking is the notion of remembrance as a "grievous burden." It was once said that to remember a sin is to repeat it, and that thus to repeat it is to double the burden of it, which means that a person would want to be rid of that burden as quickly as possible. Confession is the means of ridding oneself of an unbearable burden.

To remember chaos, however, as Augustine would have it, is to long for and appreciate order all the more. From chaos to cosmos is not only the way of the world from creation onward, but the way of the soul toward redemption. This is a part of the project that animates perhaps the most famous of Augustine's works, his *Confessions*, in which he wrote:

> I wish now to review in memory my past wickedness and the carnal corruptions of my soul—not because I still love them, but that I may love thee, O my God. For love of thy love I do this, recalling in the bitterness of self-examination my wicked ways, that thou mayest grow sweet to me, thou sweetness without deception, thou sweetness happy and assured.[8]

Here, the function of memory, the recalling of "past wickedness" and "carnal corruptions," is not pathological; nor is it indulged in in order to revel in those wickednesses as if savoring past pleasures or conquests. Rather, the recollection is to remind Augustine of how far, by the grace of God, he has come from those wickednesses. Recalling in the bitterness of self-examination his wicked ways, Augustine is reminded of the presence of the sweet and happy assurance of God, a presence made all the more palpable, real, and immediate by comparison with the time of wickedness and corruption, when God was not a presence in Augustine's life.

The absence of God is a form of adversity, and in other parts of the Christian tradition the memory of adversity is a vital part of the self-awareness of the person who pursues the good life; the memory of adversity recalled is the basis both for thanksgiving and for perseverance. When, for example, after one disaster after another during the course of the first half of the nineteenth century, those Pilgrim Baptists whose covenant we have discussed were finally able to build a handsome new meetinghouse, complete with a Victorian Gothic tower in which to house the town clock, the church clerk, in the moment of dedication and prosperity, wrote in his spidery hand across the pages of the minute book on the day of the first service in the new church, "Our years of affliction serve to enhance our present joy."

Another instance of memory as an agency of discipline relates to the celebration of Thanksgiving in 1622 by the Pilgrims at Plymouth. Their first winter in New England was a terrible one for the Mayflower Pilgrims, who were hardly prepared for the ferocity of the weather and the hard work of establishing a new colony. More than half of their company died that winter in what was called the "starving time," when a ration of five kernels of corn was apportioned to each adult for a meal, and there was scarcely enough food to sustain life. The following year, things had turned around, and there was instead the abundant harvest festival with which we associate our American celebration of Thanksgiving. One little-known local custom today is that on Thanksgiving Day, amidst the riotous bounty of table and hearth, five kernels of parched corn are frequently placed upon a red maple leaf and set at each place to remind people, who now enjoy great bounty, of the "starving time" of long ago. We do not know what the Pilgrims and their New England descendants may or may not have known of the customs of the Jewish seder, but the relationship between memory and celebration, deprivation and joy, all made real in a ritual meal with family and friends, is a common bond between Thanksgiving and Passover. What holds the two celebrations together is memory, not so much as Augustine uses memory to recall his past carnality and wickedness, but memory as a means to recall the providence of God. As the Baptist church clerk wrote, "Our years of affliction serve to enhance our present joy."

Augustine observes that everybody desires happiness, and that in our impatience for what it is that we want, we rarely associate happiness with discipline. Discipline, however, is the only way toward goodness, and only the good, according to Augustine, can be truly happy. "All wish to be happy," he notes; "none will be so but those who wish to be good."[9] This comes from his commentary on Psalm 32, which begins, "Blessed"—or "happy"—"is he whose transgression is forgiven, whose sin is covered" (KJV). The subject of the psalm is promised instruction and teaching, and if one uses understanding, accepts the discipline of the Lord, and does not behave like brute beasts such as the mule and the horse, which have no understanding and have to be coerced by bit and bridle, one will learn what one needs to know. This is a case of the desire for the discipline that leads to a better thing: "You want to be better off; I know it, we all know it, we all want the same thing. Look for what is better than yourself, so that by that means you may become better off than you are."[10]

Discipline, the medicine of the soul, in its capacity to instruct and restrain is the key to living the good life. Such discipline lies at the basis of President Charles William Eliot's nineteenth-century definition of the purpose of Harvard College and, by implication, any institution of liberal learning for the young: "To cultivate within each of you young men and women the durable values and satisfactions of life."[11] Eliot did not provide a list of what those "durable values and satisfactions" might be, but he could easily have done so. The Christian tradition of St. Paul, in Galatians 5, speaks of the "fruit of the Spirit," which he compares with the works of the flesh. The works of the flesh, he notes, are plain, and include fornication, impurity, licentiousness, idolatry, sorcery, enmity, strife, jealousy, anger, selfishness, dissension, party spirit, envy, drunkenness, carousing, and the like. Such things are bad for one, and those who engage in them not only compromise this life, but forfeit the life to come. "Those who do such things," Paul says, "shall not inherit the kingdom of God."

The fruit of the Spirit, on the other hand, is love, joy, peace, patience, kindness, goodness, faithfulness, gentleness, and self-control.

"Against such," Paul says, "there is no law." When the Baptists, and others who maintain the tradition of the "covenant meeting," required a baseline for determining whether a fellow believer required the discipline of the community, these comparative lists of Paul were often used. The works of the flesh all reflect selfish interest out of control—personal and social chaos—and if everybody behaved in these ways, chaos would soon follow. The fruit of the Spirit, however, is behavior that is better than we are, and of a higher order. When Augustine, in noting our human desire to be better off, encourages us to "Look for what is better than yourself, so that by that means you may become better off than you are," he is encouraging us to model a life and adopt the disciplines necessary to achieve a life that is ruled by the Spirit and that therefore can produce these fruits.

Eliot spoke of the "durable values and satisfactions of life," the things that survive and help us not only to survive but to flourish under pressure and adversity. In 1913, Harvard professor Dr. Richard Clark Cabot published a little book with a title taken from a famous essay by Leo Tolstoy entitled "What Men Live By." A medical man and natural scientific observer, Cabot noted from his medical practice, and those of his colleagues in the Harvard Medical School and many Boston area teaching hospitals, a combination of qualities used with increasing success to help to get sick people back to what he calls "real life." The key, of course, was the appropriate definition of what constituted "real life":

> "Real life," then, if it is to mean the nourishing, sustaining, and developing of existence, demands work, play, and love, and so much of the material and spiritual conditions of existence as make these possible.[12]

Work, play, and love "emerge as the permanent sources of helpfulness to which parents, educators, and social workers are now turning with confidence, while over their shoulders they glance wistfully toward worship," he added. Cabot came to these conclusions first from a medical point of view, when he was considering the qualities that keep healthy people healthy and how they would be useful in making sick people well. Cabot was not a pill pusher and was suspicious of quack remedies within and beyond his profession, regarding material relief of the sick as only the first necessity. Without what he called the "vital nourishment" that work, play, love, and worship provided, "all material relief becomes a farce or a poison, just as medicine is in most chronic disease a farce or a poison."[13] This was radical stuff for an avatar of the Harvard medical establishment, but partly because he was a *bona fide* member of the Brahmin medical aristocracy people took seriously what he had to say. The world was becoming busier and noisier, and pain and pleasure each were more intense. Inspired by Tolstoy, who had become synonymous with the search for meaning and value amid the meaninglessness of materialism, Cabot wanted, on the basis of his medical observations and social convictions, to prescribe for the whole health of modern people.

Many years later, Carl Jung would write a famous book entitled *Modern Man in Search of a Soul*, which was a post–World War I commentary on the sad state of modern Western secular civilization disillusioned with itself. When the doctor examines his depressed patient, Jung asks:

> What will he do when he sees only too clearly why his patient is ill, when he sees that it arises from his having no love, only sexuality; no faith, because he is afraid to grope in the dark; no hope, because he is disillusioned by the world and by life; and no understanding, because he has failed to read the meaning of his own existence?[14]

Jung was writing in despair at the lack of significant meaning in life. Dr. Cabot, writing on the eve of the Great War, in which he would later serve in France in the famous medical unit of The Massachusetts General Hospital, was prescribing for the good life and the disciplines necessary to sustain it:

> Every human being, man, woman, and child, hero and convict, neurasthenic and deep-sea fisherman, needs the blessing of God through these four gifts [work, play, love, worship]. . . . With these any life is happy despite sorrow and pain, successful despite bitter failure. Without them we lapse into animalism or below it.[15]

Even to Cabot these values may have seemed simplistic or too easy, and, as if anticipating the distant thunder of the guns of August 1914 that would change the world forever, he notes:

> At this very moment we may be lurching over the smooth bend of a cataract that is to overwhelm us; but if so, it is because we have not enough of that unchanging valor which has preserved us so far, and will reconstitute us after our downfall. For work, play, love, and prayer are open to rich and poor, to young and old; they are of all times and all races in whom character is an ideal.[16]

In his book Cabot hoped to show the sacredness of work and of love, as well as the accessibility and universality of play and worship. Contrary to our secular habits, he suggests that "we are so close to worship that we may at any time abruptly fall into it." Play, and art, can be so closely woven into the fabric of work, "till drudgery is reduced to a minimum." Two additional propositions constitute Cabot's essential prescription for the good life: "Work is our key to the sacredness of material nature, and . . . affection can be disciplined only by consecration. These are my theses."[17]

All four of Cabot's categories—work, play, love, worship—both provide and require self-discipline, the sacrifice of short-term gain and

apparent pleasure for long-term satisfaction, goodness, and happiness—
the enduring values and satisfactions of life. Work, in order to be done
well and to give satisfaction to worker and employer, must be accomplished by both the discipline of the craft and the interior discipline of
the worker. Play has long been regarded as morally instructive, because
in order to play well together, to play the game properly, people must
submit themselves to the discipline of the rules and to the self-discipline
of playing by those rules. Even love has its rules, as St. Paul points out in
his famous chapter on love, or charity, in 1 Corinthians 13; and worship,
for Cabot, is the means by which we renew our relationship with God,
who has established the basis of our human endeavor and aspiration in
the first place. Cabot uses the terms "worship," "prayer," and "spiritual
dimension" interchangeably in discussion of the fourth companion to
work, play, and love, and each connects us to our origin. "The harder we
work and play and the more intensely we devote ourselves to whomever
and whatever we love, the more pressing is our need for reorienting,
recommitting, refreshing ourselves in an appeal to God."[18]

For years I have been preaching on the question of life after the fall,
and by this I do not mean the theological concept of the "Fall," as in the
"fall from innocence" on the part of Adam and Eve in the garden. No,
I was interested in preparing my young charges at Harvard, and their
able contemporaries elsewhere in the colleges and universities of
America, for the ways in which they would make decisions and determine success when the good times, which in the 1980s and 1990s
seemed inevitable and endless, would come to an end. The irony is
that when things are going well and have been going well for a very
long time, for as long as those to whom you speak have been alive, it is
difficult, as it were, to rain on their parade. In such times, when prosperity is everybody's sacred cow and the rule is "He who dies with the
most toys wins," the good life seems very simple and very available, and
even, as one looter said to another after an urban riot in the late 1960s,
"as much as you can carry." The good life is more of the same, and now!

Yet even in the midst of an endless good time many people knew that something was wrong, yearned for something more, and felt the fundamental deception of a rhinestone culture. What disciplines would be needed for the hard times, the moments of crisis, the times when time itself would crash?

The twentieth century has been a hard tutor in these matters. The shock of World War I created the situation of despair in Europe of which Jung wrote in 1931; and in the United States, the crisis of the Great Depression would test our capacity for the good life, as the crisis of Pearl Harbor would demand a new kind of discipline from a people unaccustomed to any discipline at all. In the fifty years since the end of World War II, and despite phenomenal gains in the quality of life and the reinvigoration of a more pluralistic and inclusive society, we still find ourselves surprisingly unsatisfied with what we can call upon from our interior life to help us to cope with the relentless demands of our exterior life. Home schooling, the rise of interest in values and virtue education, and the renewal of conservative religious and political movements with their demands and expectations are all responses to the perceived lack of discipline where we most need it in life.

One of my most distinguished predecessors in The Memorial Church at Harvard, Willard Learoyd Sperry, began his career there within a few years of the Armistice of 1918 and retired in 1953 with World War II still a recent memory and the Cold War a new fact of life. He called his years of active ministry years of disappointment, for so many great hopes had risen only to be dashed upon the rocks of crisis and frustration. Although disappointed, however, he never gave in to despair, and drawing upon his long experience, toward the close of his career he wrote:

We are told that in times of crisis and opportunity our conduct is seldom determined by our surface conscious thought. The whole deeper stuff of the mind takes control then. The yield of our accumulated living over the years decides what we shall do at such times.[19]

Sperry was writing out of the context of two world wars, a great economic collapse, and a disillusioned peace, but he was writing of what he called "the whole deeper stuff of the mind," which is the yield of a lifetime of experience, moral ambition, and self-discipline. What is increasingly clear to men and to women who want to live a good and whole life, even when circumstances force a redefinition of what good is, is that self-discipline. Augustine's "medicine of the soul" is the only way through outer turmoil to inner peace. Surprising ourselves by the discovery of our own spiritual ambitions and interior disciplines as we find ourselves in the first war of the twenty-first century, perhaps we are prepared—as were so many who came before us—to cultivate and depend upon the durable values and satisfactions that make a good life rather than just a good living. It is for that purpose that our freedom may now at last be put to use.

CHAPTER 7

FREEDOM

FROM WHAT AND FOR WHAT?

*For freedom, Christ has set us free; stand fast therefore, and
do not submit again to a yoke of slavery.*
GALATIANS 5:1

*Freedom is a dangerous word, just because
it is an inspirational one.*
SIMON BLACKBURN, *BEING GOOD*, 2001

I f freedom is all that it is cracked up to be and I, presumably, am free,
then why is it that I am neither happy nor good? Why is there never
enough freedom, and, at the same time, always too much? This may
very well be the fundamental question of those of us who, believing
ourselves to be free because we have been told so often that we are, nevertheless find ourselves bound up and tied down, hand and foot.

Aunt Hagar's Children

My maternal grandmother was born in 1869 in Richmond, Virginia, in
the black section of the old Confederate capital known as City Point.
She had been brought up by her grandmother, from whom she had
heard the details of emancipation of the slaves and the end of the Civil

War. Many of her people had escaped north via the Underground Railroad in the years leading up to the Civil War, and others, for various reasons and by various devices, had been granted their freedom and yet remained in Virginia. Because these people were issued documents testifying to their free status, papers that were subject to inspection on the demand of any white person, those black persons were known as free-issue Negroes, or, in the black vernacular, "free-ishy." In our family, from my grandmother's ears to my mother's lips, and hence to me, the story of emancipation and freedom was not what I might have expected. Instead of jubilation and liberation there was confusion and fear, and anxiety was high because of the consequences of the severing of old and familiar bonds, in some cases those both of kinship and of affection. While no one in the telling of the tale, at a remove from the experience, wanted to confirm Margaret Mitchell's *Gone with the Wind* theory of happy blacks and benevolent masters unwilling to part and united in fury against the barbarous Union Army, nevertheless, as Grandma heard it and Mother told it, freedom, whatever it was, was not all that it was cracked up to be, and a great deal of work and relocation were required to accommodate its influences, both disruptive and benevolent, in the real lives of the people to whom it had been quite suddenly granted.

Although many of my ancestors had long enjoyed their freedom in the North, and some even in the South, I have always considered myself an heir of slavery, for I am only two generations removed from it. Thus, the older I become, the more fascinated I have become with the ambiguity and opportunity of freedom. Black people among themselves have always referred to one another as "Aunt Hagar's children," a reference to the slave wife of Abraham, whose position, and those of her children, was usurped by his free wife, Sarah, and her issue. So, from the first acquaintance of our people with the great and formative stories of the Bible, and particularly with the stories of the enslaved Hebrew people, we have seen ourselves as heirs of the slave and not of the free.

In freedom, and with the free exercise of it, we naturally spend more time, rather than less, in musing on the nature of freedom and the ways in which it allows or inhibits the pursuit of the good life. However it works or does not work, freedom, whatever it is, is an indispensable part of any conversation on what constitutes the good life, and hence it is the final subject we must consider in this conversation about what we have to know.

Freedom, strictly speaking, is neither a classical nor a theological virtue. As it is a condition and not a quality, it is not included in the development of character education among such core values as compassion, courage, courtesy, fairness, honesty, loyalty, perseverance, respect, and responsibility; and yet it is impossible to conceive of the good life, and its pursuit, in the absence of a concept of freedom that, at the very least, allows us the notion of how we shall choose to be good. The relationship of freedom to goodness, happiness, and the good life is our subject, for just as we cannot think of success without failure, neither can we think of discipline without freedom. Freedom as an idea, however, is elusive and chameleon-like, yet within the context of our American and Western culture it is ubiquitous, with the word itself having almost the quality of a buzzword. As we consider how we wish to live, we must therefore consider freedom in its various guises: as an end, as a means, or as a process, and the distinctions between true and false freedom, limited and absolute freedom, freedom from and freedom for.

A Millennial Paradox

Whatever freedom is, we are supposed to have a lot of it in the America of the twenty-first century, and we are supposed to enjoy it. We can certainly think of it as a commodity, something that can be quantified, and on the Fourth of July and other patriotic occasions we boast that we have more of it than any other place on earth or in any other time in the history of the planet. Freedom is what it is all about. We are free to do as we please; we are free not to do what we choose not to do; and we are free from consequences and immune from criticism.

"The right to be left alone," opined Supreme Court Justice William O. Douglas in 1952, "is the beginning of freedom." It is hard to tell whether he was simply summing up the American conventional wisdom on the subject or he was a prophet of the societal trends that would, for better or worse, define the second half of the twentieth century, that age that would from time to time fancy itself as the "American century."

This was the age in which I grew up, and I knew freedom to be a civic value, for, after all, like all public-school children in the era immediately following World War II, I was taught civics as part of the public-school curriculum. We knew about freedom, for it was that for which the Pilgrim fathers and mothers had landed at Plymouth Rock, which is not far at all by foot from my front door. At Thanksgiving, we local Plymouth folk, young and old, celebrated not only our families and private blessings, but we were grateful for the fact that all that was good about America, including freedom, had begun right here in "America's Hometown." So, growing up in Plymouth, Massachusetts, in the middle part of the last century, I knew all about freedom.

I must confess, however, that I seemed to know very little about that freedom from restraint, that "right to be left alone" defined by Mr. Justice Douglas, that would be taken for granted as the generational right of those who would come to maturity just a few years after me. I remember thinking that all adults were combined in an authoritarian conspiracy to deprive myself and my contemporaries of any liberty whatsoever: it was not a harsh deprivation, but it was total, effective, and, as we were constantly reminded, "for our own good."

Postmodernist critics of the 1950s like to argue that we remember it as a golden age that never was. *Father Knows Best, Leave It to Beaver,* and *Ozzie and Harriet* were all clever façades facilitated by the new artful medium of television, not really the real thing at all; and it was against the phoniness of all that James Dean, Elvis Presley, and Marlon Brando—each for a considerable share of our material wealth—gave us in angst, sex, and rock and roll. Freedom of expression was the revolutionary mantra of the age, and it included the right to see the pelvic motions of the Beatles and Elvis Presley on the *Ed Sullivan Show*, and the right to foment generational rebellion in the movies and in the increasingly confrontational moral tales on black-and-white television. The freedom for which our parents had scrimped and saved, and for which many of them had died in World War II, was now the freedom to express how unhappy we were with them and with the world that they had fought to save.

That, however, was not the world in which I was brought up and in which I came of age. The astonishing thing is that I recognize my world in much of the nostalgia television of that period, as I suspect quite a few people do, for without that recognition there would be no market for a product that specializes in former lifestyles; and we certainly do very little, especially where the media is concerned, that is not market-driven.

The conspiracy of which I spoke was based on the cultural triangle of school, home, and church, and it was enforced by a culture of deference, subordination, and authority. The amazing thing about such a culture was that we young people entered into it willingly, and, accepting its premises and its promises, we saw ourselves eventually reaping its rewards.

I remember setting off for my first day of school in the first grade. My father had wished me good luck the night before, as he would long be at work before my hour to go came the next morning; my mother gave me her last instructions, telling me to stay on the sidewalk, remember to say "please" and "thank you," and remember that the reputation of the family—just the three of us—and of the whole race—a very heavy burden indeed!—rested on how I conducted myself. Then, to top all this off, like a general addressing his troops before they go over the top, she said, in words to this effect, "If ever there is a disagreement between the principal and you, your father and I will always believe the principal." Thus challenged, off I went, and I had no reason to believe that twenty other first graders who set out that morning for the Mount Pleasant School and the tender mercies of our principal, Mrs. Manchester, had not received the same instructions. We were not perfectly behaved, and those were not the most sophisticated of times, but it was clear to us that "they," that is, all adults in any authority over us, were agreed as to what was to be done with and for us and that our freedom, such as it was, consisted in conforming to those expectations. This clarity, of course, made mischief fun and disobedience thrilling, if you were prepared to pay the consequences. It also made us clever and inventive, for we had to work hard to outwit and outmaneuver so comprehensive and benevolent a tyranny, although we would not be so destructive of authority and so dismissive of deference that there would be none left for us when our time came to exercise the one and receive the other. We were the young heirs of a culture, and to destroy it, or even significantly compromise it, would be to destroy what would have once been ours to pass on to others.

I have always loved Thornton Wilder's 1938 play *Our Town*, for in Grover's Corner, New Hampshire, I recognized much of the Plymouth, Massachusetts, of my youth. When I was a young instructor at Tuskegee Institute in Alabama in the late 1960s, I assigned *Our Town* to my students in freshman English, partly because I thought it would be good for them to read an American classic about a world that most of my young black students would think they knew little about, and also because it would tell them a little something about me, their young "Afro-Saxon"—as they described me—instructor from the North, whom they, with a combination of affection and derision, called "Pilgrim." So we read of "daily life," "love and marriage," and "death," and of the character of the characters known as the Webbs, the Gibbses, Emily and George, the stage manager, and even of the dead in the village cemetery. My students found all of this boring. "Nothin's happenin' here," was the general opinion, and I was regarded more with pity than with contempt for coming from a place that could produce so boring an account of life as this. Perhaps the most unknowingly astute comment came from a female student: "This has to be fiction; there really couldn't be a place like that!" Yet I lived in such a place, or in a reasonably close approximation of it; and in an environment that to some, perhaps then and certainly now, might seem stifling, uncreative, and even repressed, I felt free to grow.

Those who chafed a bit at the culture of conformity in such times and places were known locally as "characters" or "free spirits," and every town had some of these people who did not live within the lines. There was Miss Ellis, "Amelia" to all and sundry, who during the day worked in the bank but on her days off frequented the library reading room, where she consumed local genealogy books, and on occasion she went to Boston, where she communicated with the dead by means of the palmists at the Tremont Tea Room. We took what she said about things to come quite seriously because she was rarely known to be wrong. Then there was Miss Osmond, daughter of the local rector, who had been "on the stage" in New York before she returned to work in the library, where she actually read all of the newest and most sensational fiction and gave recommendations to her favorite patrons. She too went up to Boston on a weekly basis, to the theater. She subscribed to the *New Yorker*, believed that Sacco and Vanzetti were innocent, and thought President Eisenhower dull. For all of this, together with her exotic makeup, she was described as a "free spirit" and a "character."

In the six grades of our grammar school, we were organized into "citizenship clubs" as part of our daily exercise in civics. We elected class officers who presided over our weekly class meetings, and more often than not I was elected president, because, as one friend of many years put it, I "could talk about anything to anybody." Our business was to define good citizenship, and then to congratulate those who practiced it and criticize those who didn't. Even as I try to describe the process, I shudder at how it must come across to a generation steeped in the traditions of individual rights, privacy, and pluralistic values. We would decide with no small guidance from our teacher that riding our bikes on the sidewalks was a bad thing, and then we would report anybody who did it. The "accused" would be able to respond by denying the charge, pleading guilty, or pleading mitigating circumstances. After a while, most of us discovered that it was easier to confess and accept group censure than it was to argue against it, and group censure was followed by a promise of amendment of life and full restoration. Later, in our morbid little morality, we could not wait to bring a charge against the person who had brought one against us.

Moral cases were brought up for debate and resolution. One such case, which arose when I was in the third or fourth grade, involved the proper course of action to follow when, in a game of kick-the-ball, the ball went over the fence into a neighboring garden where, in its crash landing to the ground, it did great damage to some beautiful flowers. Given that we should have been more careful, that the owner of the house and garden was a known grouch, and that it was the ball that had done conspicuous damage and not we ourselves, what should we do? Options were explored. We could sneak over the fence and retrieve the ball. We could wait until the owner was not at home and then go get it. We could forget the ball and hope the owner wouldn't notice. Debate was lively and, as one might expect, the discussion was not permitted to end until we had decided what the right thing was and had agreed to do it. In due course it was decided that the boy in question would go to the door of the house, explain the situation to the grouch, ask for the ball, apologize for the damage, accept such punishment as was proposed, and, in the hope that our honesty would mitigate against it, offer some form of restitution, and, also in the hope that it would not be required, promise never to do it again. We followed that course of action, and it worked. I know. I was the boy.

Our little moral consensus worked in these and other matters, more or less, because we were a small community where we all—children and parents alike—knew each other, and few of us were outside the influence of a church. The Protestants had the sense of Protestant sin with which to deal, and the Catholics had confession and the priests and nuns. What is more, we were told that we could be happy only if we were good, and that our consciences would tell us both what was good and what was bad, and in either case would not give us any peace. As we were all normal and wanted to be happy, we therefore wanted to be good, and to be good meant doing what good people—who by definition were our parents, our teachers, the cop on the beat, the clergy, the librarians, and practically anybody else older or taller than we were—told us to do. We were not without role models; they cluttered the landscape of our little universe.

This was a world peopled by "shoulds" and "oughts," and "dos" and "don'ts," defined carefully by rights, in the sense of obligations, not entitlements, and wrongs, not in the sense of grievances, but of violations of the moral order of things. Freedom, apart from the abstractions of patriotic holidays and the history books, was the responsibility of doing "the right thing." Everybody, it seemed, was intent on insisting that we do that.

A small dose of freedom came, I remember, when I turned sixteen. In those days, turning sixteen meant that you could pay fifty cents to see the adult movies in the local theater instead of just the children's fare at the Saturday matinees. Adult movies in those days did not mean pornography, but rather meant what your parents and teachers saw. I decided to test my freedom with an adult ticket to see the scandalous movie of the day, *The Sandpiper*, with Elizabeth Taylor and Richard Burton, which not only was about a dissolute priest of irregular life, but also starred two of the most scandalously liberated celebrities in the world. I wanted to see it, and as someone with a vague but well-known future interest in the ministry, I reasoned that perhaps I ought to see it.

So, furtively, with that Protestant conscience working overtime, I slid my money beneath the glass window of the ticket taker's cage. The ticket taker, herself a fixture of the little movie palace, was the sister of the superintendent of our Sunday school, but not a churchgoer herself. She held my money on the counter and said, "Your mother know you're here?" Then, before I could think of a suitable answer, she pushed my money back through her glass window and went back to her reading while awaiting the next real patron.

Now this is not a tale of her interdiction or of my cowardice, but in a small and contained community where values were not only clarified but defined and imposed, where good, evil, and ambiguity—which to many was a form of evil—played out in domestic dramas of extraordinary ordinariness, freedom was very differently experienced then than it is now. Beyond the indulgence of local experience the same values were played out in the increasingly influential medium of television, which, by the time I entered high school in 1958, was the new domestic hearth around which everybody gathered. These values were not simply in the simple morality plays of the Cleavers, the Andersons, and the Nelsons or the more sophisticated zaniness of the Ricardos and the Kramdens, but in the very edgy values displayed in *The Twilight Zone*, with its creepy "Mr. Rogers for adults," Rod Serling. Alfred Hitchcock's weekly half-hour mystery plays, whose macabre twists always packed a moral punch, reminded us, in the most artful use of this new medium, that the moral ambiguities of the human condition with which Aeschylus and Shakespeare worked were still available for our instruction, intimidation, and delight.

The curriculum of the English department of the high school probably had not changed in fifty years as far as the reading of the "greats" was concerned, for they were understood to be part of our moral as well as our literary education. Unlike the schools, colleges, and even universities of the late twentieth century, which are "under pressure to train a workforce rather than to educate a community,"[1] literature had a moral and a civic purpose. Each year we spent major time in a close reading of a big Shakespeare text. In the eighth grade we had *Julius Caesar*, which was to appeal, I think, to youthful bravado and to impart some classical history to those just beginning Latin. In the ninth grade we studied *The Merchant of Venice*, which was classified as a comedy, but it was here that we actually discussed anti-Semitism in the portrayal of Shylock. I played the part of the Duke in the end-of-year production. Then we went on to *Macbeth*, with more than enough gore to go around. By the eleventh grade we were thought hormonally secure enough to take up *Romeo and Juliet* without embarrassment; and the greatest of all moral endeavors, *Hamlet*, was reserved for our senior year. Except for the feeble productions we ourselves put on in the school auditorium, few of us had ever seen or heard a Shakespearean play. It would not be until college, and beyond, that many of us would see and hear what we had spent so much time discussing and debating, but it was a part of our moral education, and no opportunity was lost, ever, to discuss the ambiguities of motivation, the limits of human freedom, the relationship of fate to free will, and the conflicts of the vices and virtues in the construction of the human experience.

This was not the exceptional education of a well-endowed private school or academy: this was the basic diet of the local public high school, a school not at all unlike the Madison High in which Our Miss Brooks and Mr. Boynton taught under the benevolent dictatorship of Principal Osgood Conklin. Eve Arden did not take us out of our little world and into her television world of fantasy. Her television world of fantasy, if one can describe the network television world of the 1950s as having any fantasy at all, succeeded because it replicated and confirmed the world in which so many of us lived.

Seemingly, much of that world stood *in loco parentis* to us. Even for me, as a Negro—we were "colored" then—growing up in the majority white culture, that relationship was maintained and reinforced. In his essay "The Search for Identity," theologian Howard Thurman, writing in 1971 as the great chapter of the civil rights movement was winding down, describes the decline of these "Our Town" values in the black community. Often that community was the basic unit of identity and defense against a hostile white environment. Its values were essential to the defense and formation of the young, and the so-called conspiracy of which I spoke earlier was, in Thurman's analysis, essential and benevolent:

> For a long time the Negro adult in the community stood *in loco parentis* to any Negro child. It was not necessary to know who the child was or where he lived. This gave the child an immediate sense of being cared for, with positive results in his own personality. The individual life could not be easily separated from the whole. Any stranger who came into the community had to be given hospitality, for all doors outside of the Negro community were closed to him. Thus there was the constant experience of overall identification. And this was good.[2]

Howard Thurman ranks as one of the great American theologians of the twentieth century, one whom Martin Marty calls both a saint and a mystic though hard to locate by the conventional definitions of those terms. When it was not as fashionable a thing as it is now, Howard Thurman, a black preacher, philosopher, and theologian, served in the highly visible post of dean of Marsh Chapel, Boston University, in the very period in which I was coping with the vagaries of freedom in Plymouth, a few miles to the south. I cannot say I had ever heard of him; nor did I ever meet him or hear him preach. As a black preacher to a predominately white university, however, he anticipated by a generation a role I would come to know very well from across the river at Harvard; and although he grew up in a segregated world significantly different from my own, in writing out of that experience he describes what he calls a "strange freedom," which sounds strikingly familiar:

It is a strange freedom to be adrift in the world of men without a sense of anchor anywhere. Always there is the need of mooring, the need for the firm grip on something that is rooted and will not give. The urge to be accountable to someone, to know that beyond the individual himself there is an answer that must be given, cannot be denied. The deed a man performs must be weighed in a balance held by another's hand.[3]

He describes in *The Inward Journey* a world in which the solitary being drifts with no attachments, no obligations, and a sense that if this is freedom, it is a "strange freedom," and not good enough to satisfy the natural need of society, accountability, and evaluation. Freedom in this sense cannot exist in isolation. "The very spirit of a man tends to panic," he writes, "from the desolation of going nameless up and down the streets of other minds where no salutation greets and no friendly recognition makes secure. It is a strange freedom to be adrift in the world of men."[4]

To be alone is what Thurman calls a "strange freedom," for on first glance one would assume that being alone, or in the solitary state, would be the ultimate expression and experience of freedom, because there is nobody to tell you anything or require you to do anything. Henry David Thoreau perhaps put it best when he said that he had three chairs in his little hut in the woods: one for solitude, two for company, and three for society. It was clear that he preferred the one and was at ease in his own company.

In the first paradise, Adam should have been quite happy and content with being alone, with no idle chatter, no conflicting values, and no one to intrude upon the space that was his to tend and enjoy in solitary splendor. The old and politically incorrect joke has Adam speaking with his children about life before Eve: "It was great," he says. "I had the place all to myself. Then your mother came along and ate us out of house and home." Eve's arrival, however, according to the Genesis account, was meant to be a blessing and not a curse, a gift from God who, in perhaps his first second thought after creation, determined that for the man whom he had just created, "it was not good that he should be alone." So Eve was created, either on her own or out of Adam's rib, depending upon which creation account in Genesis we read, to keep the man company and to impinge upon his "strange freedom."

This certainly is how Thurman would read Genesis and how he would address the problem of the strange freedom: "Always a way must be found for bringing into one's solitary place the settled look from another's face, for getting the quiet sanction of another's grace to undergird the meaning of the self."[5]

Why? Because "to be ignored, to be passed over as of no account and of no meaning, is to be made into a faceless thing, not a man."[6] A man of Thurman's spiritual sensitivity, of his deep and existential holiness, might have made him both off-putting and lonely. He knew of the need for the expression of freedom as a social act, an act of community, of freedom not as a splendid, autonomous isolation, but as a mutual, accountable participation in the lives of others. On a personal level, such an isolation is destructive; on the social level, something as profoundly separating and isolating as racial segregation would be the moral crisis of a civilization. It is out of both of these contexts that Thurman speaks of this "strange freedom," which runs counter to our ambitions for liberation and self-centeredness.

Small-town, "Our Town" America was for me not as claustrophobic or even as parochial as this narrative might at first suggest. I knew happiness in the sense that Willa Cather means it in *My Antonia*, where she has one of her characters say: "That is happiness; to be dissolved into something complete and great"; and the freedom I knew was not the "strange freedom" that Howard Thurman decries, but the exact opposite: participation, recognition, and affirmation in something greater than myself.

Also I knew something of that other freedom, that basic freedom for which the country was founded and that, beyond the reaches of my town, was routinely denied those people to whom I belonged. Oh, we had our little incidents of local racism, and probably more of them than I can remember, as it would have been the policy of my parents to protect me from such unpleasantness. I can recall eavesdropping on their whispered conversations with their friends about how badly some member of the community had been treated on account of race, and I knew that there was envy on the part of some whites that the local colored people had so much of this world's goods and were so solidly middle-class and comfortable. I remember my parents, especially my mother, bearing with dignity the little indignities and perceived slights that came her way, and making sure that none of them came my way. We were, however, kept aware of the larger battle for the larger freedoms for our people through the private circulation of the black press in our community and through the annual onslaught of summer visitors from the wider urban world of black America.

In Plymouth's local population of 12,500 people, approximately fifty were, as we would say today, persons of color. They included not only African Americans, but people of mixed race—what was left of the Native American population—and a large racially ambiguous community of immigrants from the Cape Verde Islands, which in those days still belonged to Portugal. To this last group my father belonged. The dominant minority population, however, was African American, and many of their ancestors had settled in town more than a century earlier and were thoroughly well established local citizens—"black Yankees," as they might well have said. It was with this group that my parents most identified.

Race was not a big deal in the sense that it was much talked about, but we were kept informed through the one or two members of the community who subscribed to such black periodicals as the *Pittsburgh Courier*, the *Boston Chronicle*, and the *Amsterdam News*. When John H. Johnson began his publishing empire in a successful attempt to become the Henry Luce of black America, some of us subscribed to *Ebony* and then to *Jet*, and, as the local newsagents did not carry these papers, they were either obtained by mail or brought back to town from occasional visits to Boston. The papers were avidly read and then circulated in plain brown wrappers throughout the black community. There was many a Sunday when, after church, we would find on the front seat of our car a paper bag full of magazines and newspapers, very much like a "zucchini attack" in suburban parking lots in summertime. In this way, through the often lurid accounts in the black press, we learned of what was going on in the outside world, which was sometimes cause for great joy, especially when we got pictures and details of the triumphs of black athletes and entertainers. Maya Angelou's account of the radio broadcast of the fight in which Joe Lewis beat Max Schmelling brought home to me how an account of events far off, reflecting to the benefit of the race, did us in our racial separation a power of good.

There would also be bad news, of black-on-black crime and atrocity in the big cities, the bizarre and macabre sensations of the black tabloids upon which *Jet* fed, and the terrible behavior of some murderer, robber, or kidnapper of whom we had perhaps heard little or nothing in the majority press. Whenever there was a sensational crime in the majority papers and the identity of the perpetrator was not yet known, a common sentiment frequently heard in the black community was, "Let him not be black, Lord, please let him not be black."

Then there were the summer visitors. In those days, the Plymouth and upper Cape area was a destination for well-to-do summer people from "away," who came for weeks and months at a time to set up housekeeping in the big summer houses near the sea. They came with their household staffs, many of whom in those days were black, and these entered into our little community of color and swelled our ranks. They came from New York, Washington, Philadelphia, Detroit, Atlanta, and other—to us—exotic places, and on Thursday and Sunday afternoons, the traditional "maid's days off," not only the maids, but the cooks, chauffeurs, nannies, and other assorted domestics filled our little downtown area with unaccustomed color and were warmly received in our homes. They brought to us tales of life in black America, and they were the city mice to us country mice. They enlarged our universe; and by their presence the notion of community, and who belonged to whom, was expanded. As Dr. Thurman would later observe in quite another context, "The individual life could not be easily separated from the whole. . . . Thus there was the constant experience of overall identification. And this was good."[7]

Freedom From

We have grown accustomed to looking upon the "sixties" as the beginning of an age of continuous liberation from old shibboleths and bad habits. The natural tendency to periodization and our ability to formulate catchy shorthand titles to encapsulate a period tempt us to actually believe that such neat and tidy periods existed as the "Roaring Twenties," the "Silent Fifties," the "Sizzling Sixties," the "Age of Aquarius," the "Seedy Seventies," the "Greedy Eighties," the "Needy Nineties," and so forth. Similar designations, such as "Baby boomers," "Gen X-ers," and now the newest, the "Millennials," give us a false sense of security in our ability to characterize generations and define eras.

The special character of the "sixties" is impressed upon our consciousness because the "Baby boomers," the chief definers of that moment, are our present cultural custodians. They write the books, feature articles, and monographs that give definition and cultural weight to their own experience, and they continue to insist upon seeing the culture in terms of their own countercultural playbook. Thus, they see "Camelot" as a defining moment, the death of a Beatle in the same light as their parents saw the death of Roosevelt or Churchill, and

Vietnam and Nixon as roughly equivalent to Munich and Hitler. As a Southern critic once observed about those who wield the levers of cultural power, it was not the Northern army or Abraham Lincoln who won the Civil War; it was Harriet Beecher Stowe and the publishing houses of Boston and New York who created a South that could never win and a North that would never lose.

It is true that we can trace the growth and multiplication of freedom from this period: social and political freedom in the dismemberment of old European colonial empires, and finally the death of Communism and the transformation of the Soviet Union. Democracy is the prevailing form of government in the world today, and in the places where it does not prevail, as for example in the Muslim world, it is a continuing irritant in their culture wars. The growth of Islamic fundamentalism around the world in the last quarter of a century is not only a testimonial to the appeal of a rigorous, all-defining reading of the Islamic tradition, but a clear sign of the continuing appeal, and hence threat, of Western-style democracy, that is, a threat to all who will not conform to it. Occidentalism, that is, the sense in the East that the West is not simply different, or even corrupt, but a clear and present danger to every Oriental or Eastern value and as such must be resisted and, as with the World Trade Center, confronted, is alive and well. The Shah of Iran was done in not because he was a bad monarch, but he was a bad monarch in the eyes of the mullahs and ayatollahs because he wished to be a Western monarch.

Much of the increase we see in both political and social freedoms we can rightly view as a legacy of the American culture of liberation that took its full expression in the 1960s. True, the Beatles were English, but it was their acceptance and re-creation in the image of American pop culture that made them what they became. Had they stayed in England, they would have been to the world culture of liberation and entertainment what British sex symbol Diana Dorrs was to the American Marilyn Monroe: forgotten.

The movement for civil rights for black Americans coincided with the decolonializing movements, the so-called freedom movements, all over the world. What began with the end of the British Empire in the partition in 1947 of British India into Hindu India and Muslim Pakistan spread to Africa and to the end of colonial rule there throughout the 1950s and 1960s. It seemed that everywhere in that empire "upon which the sun never set," the British flag was being hauled down and some new indigenous people's government installed. Even the great de Gaulle could not retain the French presence in Algeria, nor, toward the end, could he keep the students of Paris out of the streets. Everywhere, authority and deference were shattered in the name of freedom. It was, after all, the "Free Speech" movement at the University of California at Berkeley, with its charismatic leader, Mario Savio, that "fired the shot heard 'round the world" and started the age of the campus rebellion.

Freedom was not, however, defined simply in terms of revolting students and nation-states. The civil rights movement, which was remarkably nonconfrontational given the egregious wrongs it wished to correct and the disproportionate violence used against it, gave birth to sharper cultural confrontations in the name of liberation and freedom. The feminist movement, in its early stages called by its friends "women's liberation" and by its critics "women's lib," went to the barricades in the wake of the civil rights movement and in the middle of the antiwar movement. The antiwar movement was more about freedom from conscription and involvement than it was for advancing any form of freedom in Southeast Asia, save perhaps freedom from the oppressive engagement of the United States in the Vietnamese civil war. The domestic expression of all of these movements in the name of freedom and liberation from old constraints finally manifested itself in the gay rights movement, and Stonewall took its place beside Birmingham and Montgomery as a sacred place along the *via dolorosa* toward freedom.

In colleges, closed communities where the cultural trends of the larger society are both anticipated and reflected, and with a greater intensity, the movement toward freedom and the consequential distrust of authority, convention, and eventually even of discourse resulted in, in rapid order, the end of compulsory chapel, the death of parietals—those old rules governing the social relations between the sexes—the abrogation of the long-standing principle of *in loco parentis,* and the systematic suspicion attached to a curriculum that by its very nature was the inherited relic of another and less enlightened age. Where authority was once the means by which one generation taught the other, the slogan became "Trust nobody over thirty." Where civil discourse and process were once thought to be part of the lubricant that kept the communal machinery of a college community well oiled and functioning generation after generation, both civil discourse and process were held in contempt as tools of a bourgeois establishment that used them to perpetuate their own selfish interests in the oppressive corporatist state. Against these no action was too outrageous, no provocation too small.

When, in April 1969, radical students seized University Hall at Harvard, they did so with two purposes in mind: first, to discover through poring over restricted files who was compromised by participation in the American military-industrial complex; and second, to radicalize the large liberal center of opinion upon whose outrage they could depend when they themselves would be forcibly ejected from the premises by the hated police. Not much came of the first ambition, but the second worked beautifully, and the revolution came home to Harvard Yard, and hence to the heart of the establishment. Nathan Marsh Pusey, Harvard's president, who called in the cops, was vilified for doing so by the radicals and abandoned by the liberals in the faculty who were quite prepared, at the sight of somebody else's blood, to offer up Pusey on the altar of political expediency. Roger Rosenblatt, then a young instructor, in his little memoir of that period called *Coming Apart,* said that the majority of Pusey's faculty thought him "a patrician pighead," despite the fact that he had come on a scholarship to Harvard in 1924 from the public high school of Council Bluffs, Iowa. His face, they said, resembled "an institution."[8] If ever there was a time *not* to look like an institution, it was in April 1969.

Freedom, from that moment on, became not simply the granting of rights that had been wrongfully deprived citizens, which was the agenda of the civil rights movement; nor was it the wars for the liberation of oppressed peoples who had been for too long victims of imperial ideologies. Freedom now became the warrant for self-expression, self-determination, and the ticket to what would be the new good life. In place of deference, authority, and community there arose a new ideology of the self: individualism. Always a vital force in the creation of the American character, a pioneer value essential to the creation of a new civilization now became not only the means to the good life, but the end, and the good life became, simply, "What's good in it for me is indeed the good life."

I Am, Therefore!

One of the more interesting opportunities that falls to me as Harvard University's preacher is to take part in the reunion activities of returning classes, which often involves conducting the memorial service for the dead of a class since its last reunion. When I began in 1970, I was often dealing with the fathers of current students, men who had graduated twenty-five years or more before. Now I am dealing with the sons and daughters of those then current students. Over the years, as I am one of the few general officers of the university still holding the same office I held when many of these returning alumni were students, I am asked to do more than bury the dead, and for the moment it is mostly a pleasant thing to be the common link between two Harvard generations. It is not, however, always an easy role to play.

At the twenty-fifth reunion of the Class of 1972 and at the thirtieth reunion of the Class of 1969, I took part on each occasion in a "Harvard Then and Now" panel composed of alumni, current students, and professors and deans. In earlier versions of these panels, particularly in the early 1970s, the conversations reflected the all too familiar ingredients of the generation gap. The parents, reflecting the values of the Eisenhower years, tried to understand their young, long-haired offspring, but it was clear that they and their children had experienced very different Harvards. The young were impatient with their parents and wondered why they were obsessed with the dangers of co-ed bathrooms and "living together," with the people they were dating, and with what they were planning to do after college. The parents were frankly bewildered by their own children. They spoke a different language, and discussions of politics and values only led to acrimony. In some sense, however inadequately, it was part of my job to explain each generation to the other.

Today that role has not changed, but the parts played by each generation in the process have. I remember the panel for the Class of 1969's thirtieth reunion. This was the class in whose senior year the famous "bust" had occurred and the police had cleared out University Hall. That spring was a defining moment for them; and for many, if not all, the lives that they built after that time incorporated many of the values that had formed them—most of them very good. They were now forty-something, and, as one parent, who described herself as an "agonized and unreconstructed old liberal," said half in jest and half in sorrow, "We have raised a generation we don't recognize, and, worse, that doesn't recognize us." She had to face the fact of all revolutions: the counterrevolution.

The students were not all young Republicans. They were not all headed for Wall Street. They were not all "concentrators," Harvard's unique word for majors in economics. Many of them were less than enthusiastic for the cultural and countercultural values for which their parents had stood in college and, in certain cases, by which some of them had been raised. After hearing war stories about the "bust," the traumatic spring of 1969, and the battles for social reform and self-discovery that, among other things, had brought down Lyndon Johnson and Richard Nixon, one student said simply, "That was then and this is now"; and while she was too polite to say what naturally followed that observation, she clearly meant, "so get over it."

The parents were not without a generational riposte or two of their own, calling their own children's generation selfish, corporatist, socially indifferent, culturally unaware, sell-outs to the industrial state. One alum, clearly not a parent but very much defending his cohort against the soon to be graduated seniors, said in heated frustration, "If the revolution depended on you, there wouldn't be any." Which was just the point.

Except, there was a revolution, and it was the most effective kind because it was going on beneath the radar, as it were, and it too had to do with freedom, with a revolutionary, redefining of freedom. An incident occurred after one of my classes on the history of the interpretation of the Bible, which I teach as I had been taught the *Odyssey* many years before, on the assumption that it is written in a foreign language and that nobody has read it. Out of a lecture course of about ninety students, less than one-third, by my informal and inexact survey, had read the Bible. "That's why I took the course," one student said to me. "I might as well read it for credit."

On this particular day, a pair of parents was seated in the rear of my lecture hall, which was not unusual as it was the beginning of Freshmen Parents Weekend in late October, the first parental visiting time since the early days of September. At the end of the hour they came forward with their freshman daughter, whom I did not know as she was not in my section. They thanked me for the lecture and said that their daughter insisted that they come with her to church on Sunday to hear me preach. I said I'd look forward to seeing them, they

showed up on Sunday, and we exchanged greetings at the door following the service. Then early in the week, and quite unexpectedly, they
telephoned to ask if they could come to see me, and as they lived
nearby it was easily arranged. I could not imagine what they wanted,
but I sensed trouble ahead: Was the girl about to join a cult? Did they
think me too liberal for a religious girl or too conservative for a secular
girl? Had I made some horrible mistake in either lecture or sermon,
and one or both of them was a theologian or philosopher in disguise?
Worse, perhaps they were lawyers and some form of discrimination stuff
was about to be laid on me.

Well, they came, and they began, as parents often do, autobiograph-
ically. They had each graduated in the early 1970s from respectable
small liberal arts colleges in the Midwest. She had early become
involved in the women's movement, and he, sadly, had missed the
heart of the antiwar movement, but they had been moved by social justice and environmental issues for all of their lives. They had been
forced to go to church when they were young, but college put an end
to that. They were determined to give their little girl, an only child, the
benefit of their experience, and, as far as religion was concerned, they
would impose nothing and wanted her to decide for herself. They liked
Harvard because not only was it "the best there was," but, at least in
their minds, it was, and, these were their words, "religiously neutral."
They were pleased that their daughter had chosen to take my course
and that she, as I recall, was also taking another religion course in
Hinduism.

Where this conversation was going, I could not tell. Then they told
me that, after the church service on Sunday over a good lunch in
Harvard Square, they had got into a terrible argument with their daughter that had ended with tears and acrimonious exchanges. They had
thought they were discussing the sermon and the lecture, but the argument turned on the simple fact that they, the parents, had been able to
follow the service fairly well even though they hadn't been to church

for years. They knew where to look in the Bible to follow the lessons, the hymns were familiar to them, and they remembered the Lord's Prayer. The rub was that the daughter knew none of it, and her anger was at the fact that she had been deprived of this tradition that they had retained, and against which she could not rebel, even if she had wanted to. She didn't want to of course, and thus she accused her parents of being indifferent toward the development of a very important side of her life. Why had they done that?

The parents made the best case they could. Freedom was mentioned frequently, but they were plainly worried, as all parents are from time to time, that they had done something very wrong. Was there anything to worry about? What should be done? What could they do?

It was one of those moments for which divinity school had not prepared me, but nearly thirty years of teaching, preaching, and living at Harvard had. What they had to remember was that college is always a time of reformation, and that usually it takes the form of rejecting what has come from home and of trying on new things. In "our day," for I was not too much older than they, but old enough to represent a slightly different generation, you rejected religion at college because that was your way of separating yourself from Mom and Dad. You went off to college to lose two things: your religion and your virginity, and the two were often related. These parents were not Southern Baptists, and so I could share with them the old Southern Baptist joke explaining that the reason the Baptists are so much opposed to sex is that it is so much like dancing.

Nowadays, instead of coming to college to lose religion, young people who come with no religious background at all, largely due to the courtesy of their secular parents, actually discover religion in the new world of the university. They find people deeply moved by religion, and they want to know what makes them tick. In the world's most pluralistic university, ordinary American kids come and discover that their Muslim roommate is quite serious about saying his prayers five times a day, and without shame; that Jewish students flock to Hillel and are enchanted, if not entirely persuaded, by the strictures of their orthodox friends; that the religions of the world are seen to be observed by otherwise intelligent people; and that evangelical Protestants and conservative Catholics swarm about on weekends like bees. There is hardly a religious revival, in the conventional sawdust-trail sense of that term, going on here, but religion—not just the study of it, but the practice of it—is a normal part of everyday life here at Harvard.

The parents wanted to know, quite sincerely, if their daughter's behavior was some form of pathological behavior or an acting out of some dangerous urges and needs. Were all these "religious" types of whom I was speaking "needy" types, and could they be characterized by intellectual ability, ethnicity, social class, or family background? The very questions suggested that, to their minds, "normal college-age kids" were not into religion. When they married, maybe, and had children or faced a crisis or two, then possibly they might be, even though that pattern was not the one they followed. These parents were not hostile. They were genuinely curious, and even perplexed.

I told them to relax, that their daughter was surely capable of managing her religious discoveries, and that she would very likely get over her sense of being deprived. Then I told them to read the last lines of "Church Going," a marvelous poem by England's Philip Larkin about a cyclist who at first is indifferent and then becomes curious when he wanders into an empty medieval church for a quick look around. Musing at how long such an old place could continue to stand, still used for its original and now seemingly marginalized purpose, he asks, "And what remains when disbelief has gone?" His answer, after some oddly conflicted ruminations, constitutes the final verse:

A serious house on serious earth it is,
In whose blent air all our compulsions meet,
Are recognized, and robed as destinies.

And that much never can be obsolete,
Since someone will forever be surprising
A hunger in himself to be more serious,
And gravitating with it to this ground,
Which, he once heard, was proper to grow wise in,
If only that so many dead lie round.[9]

That surprising hunger to be more serious, that mood of discovery and encounter, is an exercise in freedom *for*, as compared with freedom *from*. It represents a desire, I think, to be reconnected, to see oneself as in pursuit of the good, and such a pursuit is not only freedom redefined, but it is the good redefined as well. Earlier we discussed the sense of cultural disenchantment on the part of the young. The young have always had seasons of cultural disenchantment; the French existentialists, the British "angry young men," and the American "beat generation" were all exercises in the cultural disenchantment of the postwar West. In the words of theologian Paul Tillich, much of this then modern cynicism is noncreative: "They try to undermine every norm put before them. . . . They courageously reject any solution which would deprive them of their freedom of rejecting whatever they want to reject." The modern cynic, he observes, does little to address the problem of meaninglessness: "Much compulsive self-affirmation, and much fanatical self-surrender are expressions of the noncreative courage to be as oneself."[10]

We have been long used to the freedom of rejection. What is new, the counterrevolutionary action, is the freedom of affirmation, the freedom to be included, the freedom to pursue that which makes for meaning in the things that endure and proves its greatest worth in times of greatest need.

Perhaps this freedom to affirm is best articulated in a slender volume by a very young recent graduate of Harvard. I never knew Jedediah Purdy in college: I wish I had, but I have come to know him a little through his first book, published just a year or so after he graduated. Purdy comes from West Virginia and was home-schooled by idealistic parents of the same generation as the parents of whom I earlier spoke. It would be wrong to depict him as some rural Rousseau, for he did have the benefit of some education at Exeter and Harvard did not appear to ruin him, yet he writes with an earnestness about the recovery of trust and commitment in America that would make an older, more cynical author blush. His heart is on his sleeve when he says, for his generation as well as for any other:

> Our liberty means unprecedented power to neglect the questions that tradition addresses, and that responsibility to any commons relies upon: What am I doing, and for what? What is the meaning of my work, and what are its purposes? What attachments—to people, to places, to principles—am I working to maintain, and why? Whose well-being is in my hands, and in whose hands is mine?[11]

Purdy may or may not be a religious man, I do not know, and he does not say, but these are religious questions, questions of purpose, teleological questions, as the Greeks would have it. Aristotle and Augustine would recognize them, as indeed would Howard Thurman. "We cannot answer those questions," he notes, "in solitude," without a sense of history and tradition, and yet, he goes on to say, we often begin the process of that consideration—contemplation, Aristotle would call it—alone.

> The circle of responsible work moves through the commons and the individual. It is in the individual that it can be decisively broken. Today it is the individual, moving from liberty into freely chosen circumscription, who can make it whole.[12]

Purdy's book may end up classified among the minor classics of civic virtue, a genre of ancient and enviable repute, and I hope we hear more from him, but I see it more as part of the continuing discussion of spiritual poverty that has become the major public discourse in American life as the new millennium and century move on, and certainly all the more since September 11, 2001. Purdy's 1999 book preceded by a year a much thicker sociologically rich pudding of a book by Yale's David G. Myers, in which nearly twenty years of conflict between material prosperity and spiritual poverty are documented for all to see. In *The American Paradox: Spiritual Hunger in an Age of Plenty*, Myers wants to know how it is that we can have so much and yet feel that we have so little. Why do we have more and do more, and enjoy it less? Therein lies the paradox:

> We now have, as average Americans, doubled real incomes and double what money buys. We have espresso coffee, the World Wide Web, sports utility vehicles, and caller ID. And we have less happiness, more depression, more fragile relationships, less communal commitment, less vocational security, more crime (even after the recent decline), and more demoralized children.[13]

Obviously these things no longer have the power to impress or to intimidate. As goals or badges of achievement or accomplishment, they are no longer the "toys" with which we wish to die. Once upon a time they did represent the good life, trophies of success in a world that defines success by what we have and boasts of a freedom that allows us to have as much of it as we can hoard. Long before the terrorist planes destroyed the twin towers, however, those monuments to our sense of material success, we knew that something was profoundly wrong.

I remember hearing the warning, now a quarter of a century ago, in Harvard Yard. The Commencement speaker for the Class of 1978 was Aleksandr Solzhenitsyn, and in the battle for celebrity speakers that year Harvard clearly had won. He spoke to a rain-soaked capacity audience on Commencement afternoon, and from where I sat the crowd was obscured by a sea of umbrellas, but nobody moved, nobody left, and everyone was transfixed by the icon of resistance to everything Soviet, although it was not about the failures of Russian Communism that he had come to speak. In a long and uncompromising address that would have made Cotton Mather proud, which was simultaneously translated from Russian into English by an incongruously charming young Japanese woman, Solzhenitsyn deplored the West's obsession with things, and goods, and material pleasures. Invoking a Puritanism that astonished the worldly Harvard audience, he said, "We have placed too much hope in politics and social reforms, only to find out that we were being deprived of our most precious possession: our spiritual life."[14]

Had I or any other cleric said such a thing to such an audience at that time, we would have been received with polite indifference and perhaps a little annoyance from the secular intellectuals who would have felt the occasion wasted by such pieties; and yet, arguably, here was one of the intellectual prizes of the West, literally biting the hand that was feeding him. Here was a man who had fled to "the land of the free and the home of the brave" and who was telling us that the freedom to get and to do and to have was insufficient in comparison with the freedom to be. In essence, we would be "rich in things but poor in soul," in the famous words of Harry Emerson Fosdick's hymn, until we were brought to our spiritual senses. In a world of rampant individualism and materialism, the freedom that seemingly makes all of that possible is a grand illusion, a plausible lie that is easier to believe than the fantastic truth it obscures. St. Paul writes in Galatians 5:1 that it was for freedom that Christ has set us free. The hard task is to use that freedom so that we do not become slaves to what freedom allows us to obtain. The new freedom is a freedom of affirmation, of affirming our pursuit of the good, and of affirming our participation in that good for others.

Jedediah Purdy suggests that in the end of our search for common things:

> We need today a kind of thought and action that is too little contemplated yet remains possible. It is the kind aimed at preservation of what we love most in the world, and a stay against forgetting what that loves requires.[15]

We are engaged, he says, in nothing less than in the maintenance of the world; and so we are. Yet in order to have even a modest chance of doing this, we will have to rediscover the freedom that disciplines and liberates at the same time. We will have to begin to make the distinctions between false freedom, which St. Augustine describes as freedom from responsibility and accountability, an illusory freedom that gives us, in the list of Gandhi's seven social sins: politics without principle, wealth without work, commerce without morality, pleasure without conscience, education without character, sciences without humanity, and worship without sacrifice.[16]

These things can destroy a nation, Gandhi said, and we know they can destroy people. True freedom is that which enables us to pursue the good life until the end, come what may. Christian liberty, Augustine reminds us, works to strengthen the will, for we are improved by the practice of improving habits; and even if we fail in this enterprise of true freedom, it is better to fail in what is worth pursuing than to succeed in what is not. Thus our freedom, rightly understood and rightly practiced, is a means and not an end, for its end is goodness, its result is happiness, and its process is nothing less than the good life. Freedom then becomes the means to help us to practice the three great theological virtues of faith, hope, and love. It is to these virtues that we shall now turn.

PART III

THE GOOD LIFE

THE GREAT VIRTUES

CHAPTER 8

VIRTUE

WAYS, MEANS, AND ENDS

INFERIORITY COMPLEX
If I had Solomon's wisdom,
Possessed all the power of Atlas,
And moved with Mercury's swiftness,
I'd find a way to mess things up,
Because I'd still be me.
ROBERT DONALD SPECTOR,
NEW YORK TIMES, JANUARY 7, 2002

Why is it important, even essential, to know that there are rules, ways, and means by which to achieve the good life? It is important because without them, alas, we would be doomed to things as they are, and ourselves to the way we are; and of ourselves, as William James pointed out long ago, we know "there is something wrong about us as we naturally stand."[1] Thus, we have always wanted to learn ways of self-improvement and self-betterment. It is an unthinking temptation to think of rules, laws, codes of conduct and behavior, and the like as externally imposed inhibitions upon our own freedom, and when we do, we see these things as unnatural and contrary to our state of nature. We do not need Hobbes or Locke or any other philosopher or theologian to tell us what we already know, which is that our state of nature— our natural circumstance, ourselves as we stand—is in disarray.

Although we may resent someone else's external imposition of order upon us as a restraint against our liberty, we are nevertheless naturally drawn to finding ways by which we can improve ourselves and provide for our own lives an order that makes sense and with which we can live. I think we are drawn to order as opposed to chaos in the same way that we prefer light to dark and breathing to not breathing, for as long as there is either order or the search for order, we believe ourselves to have a chance against the apparent disorder and chaos that surround us on every hand.

When little children, who have not yet developed a systematic code of ethics or given thought to chaos theory or to the teleological or purposeful objective of their lives, cry out in injured rage on the playing field at some perceived inequity, "That's not fair!" they are evaluating the moment of chaos by an as yet unarticulated but clearly felt sense of injured order. In other words, almost as if the child were in touch with the forces of a natural law that says order is better than chaos, the violation of that law in the eyes of the child means an appeal to that very law meant to restore balance and order both within and without. Thus, schoolyard codes of conduct appeal to the "fairness doctrine" as the most basic form of order, without which neither pleasure nor improvement can take place. Justice, the doing of the right thing, requires law and order to be done effectively and, once again, despite the elegant description of the law in the Bible as received downward from on high at the hands of Moses, that description itself does not come down from on high but up from below; it is an expression of that fundamental human need for an all-encompassing order—the law—that ascribes it to God. Let us make no mistake here, however: the law and its ascription to God come from our need of the law, and hence from our need of God. Thus it is a part of our profound need of a reliable guidance system that does not depend entirely upon ourselves, but recognizes and affirms that need as legitimate and provides a way for us to meet that need for guidance.

It has been my argument throughout this book that the search for order is as natural in our lives as is the reality of disorder. The history of our human experience has not been the escape from rules, laws, ordinances, and systems for the conduct of our lives; rather, the history of our human experience has been the experiment with various rules, laws, ordinances, and systems for the conduct of our lives that work and provide us with the ways and means to an ordered life that gives satisfaction to ourselves and to others. The struggle has not been between rules and freedoms; the struggle has always been between competing systems that can deliver us most effectively from the lack of order that inhibits our freedom and compromises our happiness. Interesting, charming, and intelligent as I may be, naturally or otherwise, I, nevertheless, would not dare to rely entirely upon those qualities of myself to deliver myself by myself beyond myself. It would be nice to have the benefit of the experience of others, both those who have failed in the same ambitions and those who have succeeded.

The Allure of Happiness

When I ask parents of undergraduate students what it is they hope for for their children, few have ever said that they want success, power, wisdom, or even wealth. They may have wanted those things along the way, and they may feel that those are the things their children deserve and that their tuition dollars ought to assure, but few parents, even in these bold and selfish times, ever state the acquisition of those things as the supreme good for their children. Nor do many offer goodness as a life's goal, which has an old-fashioned, wimpish sort of tone about it, a little like "Miss Congeniality" in the Miss America contest. No one wishes their children to be bad, but it is "uncool," so to speak, to express a preference for goodness. Nearly everyone, however, without regard to economic status, intellectual ability, or personality, wishes that their children will be happy. "I don't care what they do, as long as they are happy," is a familiar strain I have heard over and over again through the years. Also heard frequently is the correlative remark "If you're happy, you can do anything" or "If you're happy, it doesn't matter what you do."

To some, happiness as a life's goal seems somehow insubstantial, perhaps self-indulgent, frivolous, or the moral equivalent of a "happy face" decal and the ubiquitous admonishment to "Have a nice day." Since most people in the modern world know more of sorrow than of happiness, however, and hence are more practiced at dealing with depression than with elation, happiness seems both unreal and insubstantial; and how often we equate pain with reality: "If I hurt, then at least I know I am still alive." Happiness is so unnatural a state that the only way we know how to achieve it in the sophisticated secular West is by the means of such unnatural stimulants as drugs and alcohol. The epidemic use of drugs and drink in the twentieth century, often seen as a sign of our liberation and freedom from old taboos and our incessant quest for the ultimate "high," is really only a sign of our profoundly unsatisfying sense of the *status quo*, our distrust of things as they are and of ourselves as we are, and our notion that happiness is the illicit alternative to reality. The search for happiness, then, that constitutionally guaranteed American pursuit, is seen not as an objective, but as an escape, a diversion from objectivity.

Happiness as a goal, therefore, despite the culture of "happy talk" that reached epidemic proportions in the twentieth century, is both ubiquitous and suspect, and for people cut off from the history of their own moral traditions and ambitions this is a sad but understandable situation. Contemporary cultural icons of the secular world are always cast as frustrated or indefatigable in the search for personal happiness, and that is the theme of our soap-opera culture, with its beautiful, talented, but fatally flawed people who seek happiness in some form or other. Some of them deserve happiness, and few of them ever achieve it, or if they appear to have achieved it, they seldom keep it for long.

Diana, Princess of Wales, became the twentieth century's iconic figure in the search for happiness. In her life, all of the difficult aspects of happiness as a life's objective were played in a vivid parable more compelling than Hollywood could have possibly imagined, simply because it was real and not fiction. A beautiful child of privilege by the standards of the world, long before she met her prince she should have been happiness personified; and then as a royal princess, with all that goes with that title, she should have known even greater happiness. Then, when that happiness was exposed as fraudulent, she should have been happy in the pursuit of real happiness; and just when it appeared as if that real happiness was within her grasp—and hence in ours, as voyeuristic investors in her happiness—it was all taken away. Because it was taken away from us, her adoring public, we went into a mourning shock, certainly for her, but even more for ourselves.

In the interval of these years since the late summer of her death, little more can explain the irrational public paroxysms of grief that engulfed an otherwise rational and sensible people than the terrible sense of the illusion and fragility of what the world calls happiness. England had known public death and public grief before, with the death of Queen Victoria in 1901, which presaged the end of the world as most living English people knew it and was a cause for real and sustained grief, and the death of Churchill in 1965, which was certainly long anticipated at his great age and even by himself. Churchill had spent his declining years planning every detail of his last rites; yet he, unlike any other living person in modern history, had literally saved Great Britain from annihilation, and therefore both affection and gratitude warranted the staged public grief that was displayed when he died. Diana, though? What had she done to warrant the effusions of public grief that can only be described as a form of corporate morbid hysteria? True, she had touched AIDS victims, she had made the removal of land mines her special project, and she had grown assiduous in good works as a legacy of her time as a working member of the royal family. Diana had appeared to be a good and progressive single mother, the world's "soccer mom," as it were. These qualities alone, however, do not begin to explain the reaction that her unfortunate and premature death unleashed from the world.

With the almost strangely simultaneous death of Mother Teresa within the same news cycle, an unappealing but quite explicable comparison was immediately thrown up for the world's consideration. The world was not brought to a halt by the death of the tough old nun whose name had become synonymous with virtue and goodness, and although we felt as if we ought to see some moral equivalency in our grief, when all was said and done, we could not, for in the contest for our primal affections and basic self-interest happiness trumps goodness. Mother Teresa represented the "fragility of goodness," while Diana, Princess of Wales, represented the "fragility of happiness." The relationship between the two was never clearly made, a task, I suspect, that was too demanding for those whose job it was to read the news on the air and not to think about it; yet it is worthy of a speculation possible perhaps only now, in the time that separates us from the deaths of the two women.

Few people ever associated Mother Teresa with the conventional notion of happiness, largely because we could not imagine ourselves as happy in doing what she did. Goodness was her province, without contest. As for Diana, Princess of Wales, her happiness represented our happiness, for so many of those most devoted to her could easily imagine themselves happy in doing what made her happy. Who couldn't? In her constant pursuit of happiness, even in the failure of her happiness, she had legions of companions who could match her public failures against their private failures, her human battles against their eating disorders and self-esteem difficulties, her failed marriage and frustrated relationships against theirs. With each and all of those failures many millions of men and women could and did identify. When the fragility of her own happiness came to its ultimate end in death, with no opportunity for an improving second, third, or fourth chance, so died the hopes of so many of her devotees. Goodness was attached to her, and probably more so than was happiness to Mother Teresa, but it was not the death of goodness that was mourned by an emotionally paralyzed public in the streets of London on that late August day. It was the death of happiness—of hers, and of ours.

This excursus on happiness is meant to remind us of the dangers inherent in choosing it as a life's goal and of defining the meaning of one's life by the fragile definitions that each age brings to the concept of happiness; yet happiness has long been intimately associated with notions of what the good life ought to be. Any discussion of the good life, therefore, and especially such a discussion as we have undertaken here, must take into account happiness and its various definitions and appropriations. To do so places us in the company of the great traditions of ethics, values, and virtues that we have discussed here as part of our cultural, intellectual, and spiritual inheritance. Often without knowing it, those parents who utter the mantric wish of happiness for their children are tapping into this ancient tradition of the wished-for good life, the life about which Plato, Socrates, Aristotle, Augustine, Aquinas, and a whole host of classical and Christian thinkers wrote in some detail. The Beatitudes, some of the most well known and beloved words of Jesus, as recorded in St. Matthew's account of his Sermon on the Mount, have to do with happiness, for the most empathetic rendering of the Greek word from which the English word "beatitude" comes is "blessed," or, colloquially, "happy."

Taken in this light, the Beatitudes, as found in Matthew 5, with their seemingly impossible claims that the meek shall inherit the earth, the merciful shall obtain mercy, and the mourning shall be comforted, actually tell us that happiness, or blessedness, is, in part at least, a result, a consequence, or even a condition with which one would not ordinarily associate. It is that odd proximity between what we assume happiness or blessedness to be and the least of likely places in which we expect to find it that makes Jesus' comments in the Sermon on the Mount at one and the same time so arresting and so annoying.

Fifty years ago, Hugh Martin, in his little book on the Beatitudes, warned us that even the rendering "happy" may not do sufficient justice to Jesus' thought. Placing the Beatitudes within the context of answers to the question of what the good life is and how one should pursue it, Martin says that although "this word 'blessed' has become rather a sanctimonious, musty, remote word," the alternate term "happy," used by J. B. Phillips in his translation of the New Testament, perhaps "suggests a state too superficial and light-hearted to convey the idea."[2] Martin cites Thomas Carlyle's once famous distinction in *Sartor Resartus*, "There is in man a Higher than Love of Happiness: he can do without happiness and instead thereof find blessedness."[3] There are people, for example, who would appear to have no reason to be happy, whose circumstances are unfortunate, destructive, even perilous, and conventional pleasures and satisfactions appear to elude them. Jesus suggests the identity of some of those people as those who know how poorly off they are: the so-called poor in spirit; the humble-minded; the sorrowful; those who have nothing; those who mourn; and those who are persecuted, slandered, and otherwise maligned. How can such people be happy unless they are truly ignorant of which they lack?

The "problem" with happiness is that it seemingly depends upon what happens to us. Again, Hugh Martin suggests that "Blessedness is deeper, it is a matter of character, it can transmute what happens."[4] Martin and other New Testament scholars of his generation actually preferred the word "blessed" to "happy," because of the frivolous associations with the notions of ordinary happiness. As early as in his 1905 translation of the New Testament, R. F. Weymouth noted:

Blessedness is of course an infinitely higher and better thing than mere happiness. People who are blessed may outwardly be much to be pitied, but from the higher and truer standpoint they are to be admired, envied, congratulated and imitated.[5]

Perhaps we can sense the subtle distinction at work between happiness and blessedness when we recall the example set by the late Jacqueline Bouvier Kennedy Onassis at the time of the tragic death of her husband, President John F. Kennedy. I was in college in the fateful November of 1963, and November 22 was to my generation what December 7, 1941, was to our parents and September 11, 2001, will be to our children. It was not only a "day of infamy," as President Roosevelt described the attack on Pearl Harbor, but the moment of a colossal and collective loss of innocence that, like virginity, can be lost only once. Throughout those genuinely tragic days one image stood out and became the focal point of the national grief, and that was the image of the young widow and her two small children.

There she stood, a study in elegant, eloquent grief: no tears were shed in public, there was no emotional display, no therapeutic shuddering and shaking, no weeping and wailing. Many, I recall, thought this unnatural or even a little cold and calculating, but we had not yet reached the stage of public grief on demand and display that has since become the stock-in-trade of such people as Geraldo Rivera and Barbara Walters. With Mrs. Kennedy performing her grief for all of us, there was about her not merely the stoicism of the Roman matron or the typical *sangfroid* of the Eastern upper-class Wasp: there was in her a serenity, a calm in the midst of turmoil that had a calming effect on everybody else. Often the word "serenity" was employed to describe her public deportment in those difficult days, and not a few, including arch-Protestants and nonbelievers, attributed that show of inner strength to her undoubted conviction of belief as a devout Roman Catholic. Her aged mother-in-law, Rose Fitzgerald Kennedy, was seen as a Catholic martyr, disciplined in the faith and well practiced in the sorrowful mysteries with, alas, more to come; Jackie, young, beautiful, and the undisputed queen of the optimistic realm of Camelot, brought a strength to her dignity in grief that had to come from somewhere deep within her. Hers in that moment was a happiness, perhaps even that famous biblical peace that Jesus promises in John's gospel and that this world can neither give nor take away. In Jackie Kennedy in 1963 we saw what R. F. Weymouth in 1905 could not possibly have anticipated when he wrote of the blessed: "People who are blessed may be outwardly much to be pitied, but from the higher and truer standpoint they are to be admired, envied, congratulated and imitated."[6]

People admired that serenity, which stayed with her all the days of her life. Her celebrity was associated neither with a conspicuous goodness, such as that seen and admired in Mother Teresa, nor with the fragile happiness seen, emulated, and envied in Diana, Princess of Wales. When Jacqueline Kennedy Onassis died in New York with as much privacy and dignity as she had lived her life, many who felt they knew her and yet conceded that they did not nevertheless remarked over and over again on her inner strength and the way in which she chose to live her life, which had been a good life and happy, perhaps, but blessed, certainly. How did she do it? How could she do it? How can we? We'd all like to know.

The Happy Warrior

Jackie Kennedy was brought up as an informed and devout Roman Catholic, which means that she was brought up on the old *Baltimore Catechism*. In answer to the sixth question, "Why did God make you?" in Lesson 1, "On the End of Man," she would have replied with the required answer: "God made me to know Him, to love Him, and to serve Him in this world, and to be happy with Him forever in the next." Her catechist doubtless would have had her understand that in this life we are intended by God to know God, love God, and serve God. Knowledge, love, and service are our earthly work. God's purpose in our creation, however, is not simply for this world, for we are created to be happy with God forever in the next world. Happiness is not now, but later. At Question 8, the person is asked, "Why must we take more care of our soul than of our body?" and the required answer is: "We must take more care of our soul than of our body, because in losing our soul, we lose God and everlasting happiness." From the very structure of the catechism we learn that it is critical for the believer to understand that happiness is a consequence of knowing, loving, and serving God in this world, a consequence that cannot be assumed to be achieved in this life, but is guaranteed forever in the next life. If in this life one lavishes more care on the body than on the soul, then one risks losing the soul, and that means losing God and everlasting happiness.

To a Catholic this all makes sense, more or less, but to a Protestant, to a believer from another tradition, or to a nonbeliever, it is at best hard work. Anyone who has ever read Evelyn Waugh's classic apologetic for Roman Catholicism, *Brideshead Revisited,* or watched the lavish television adaptation of the book, which has become a staple of the Anglophile Public Broadcasting Service, will no doubt recall that the climax of the story, reached at long last with the ponderousness of a Russian novel, occurs in the deathbed scene of Lord Marchmain. A self-confessed "man of irregular life," the British aristocrat Lord Marchmain—played in the television series by Sir Laurence Olivier in what would be his last performance before his own death—has come home to Brideshead, his ancestral seat, to die.

As a young man he had wooed and won an attractive and devout Catholic woman, and in order to marry her he had converted to the Catholic faith in what was generally understood to be a conversion of convenience. Not for long did he keep either the faith or his marriage vows, decamping instead to Italy for a life of living in sin with an attractive Italian mistress. He remained undivorced and, doubtless, by his wife unforgiven. She has died before him, and the drama now centers on whether he will receive from the parish priest the last sacrament. His eldest daughter, herself lapsed but not thoroughly lost to the church, decides under intense emotional pressure to permit the priest to give the dying, and now nearly comatose, Lord Marchmain the rites, which, if properly given and properly received by some sign on the part of the dying man, would assure him of God's forgiveness and thereby secure for him forever both God and happiness in the world to come. The Protestant in the room, the story's narrator, wants to understand it all. He regards it all as so much stuff and nonsense, "mumbo jumbo," he calls it, and the scene therefore becomes a contest between understanding and reason, faith and happiness. The Catholics, not pretending in any way to theological sophistication, opt for faith and happiness. At the end of an earthly life of thwarted and illusory happiness, confronted now with the reality of sin and the inevitability of death, the Catholics rely upon the promise of God and of real and eternal happiness in the life to come. Nearer death than life, Lord Marchmain responds to the priest's ministrations with a heroic effort at making the sign of the cross, not long after which he expires. By the standards of the church and to some extent by his own admission, his had not been a good life; but because of words from the lips of the humble Catholic priest, his was now a good death, for which the faithful, in the midst of their grief and mourning, should be happy.

Jackie Kennedy would have known that the purpose of a good life was to achieve a good death in order to enjoy the really good life of eternal happiness with God. Rather than in fear of meaninglessness or extinction, those levels of doubt and despair that make of life a hostage to the fear of death, the one who lives in hope of more than this life alone, and who hopes to enjoy life with God forever, lives with equanimity and serenity, the kind of blessedness that inspires emulation, envy, and admiration. Many have known such a life, and many have elicited these qualities among those who knew them, but no one in the twentieth century more exemplified those qualities to a public both devout and impious than did Mrs. Onassis. Saints are expected to behave in that way, and hence there are no surprises in Mother Teresa;

but Mrs. Onassis was never thought of as a saint: she was an icon of modernity, not merely a symbol of tragedy. She was the very human vessel of these spiritual qualities, and that is what makes her so compelling, so interesting, and so hard to write off.

As a part of its Victorian cultural inheritance, an earlier generation would have known the great Romantic poet William Wordsworth's popular poem "The Character of the Happy Warrior." When, at the Democratic National Convention of 1924, the crippled Franklin Delano Roosevelt made the speech nominating the Roman Catholic, anti-prohibition, Tammany Hall–backed Governor Alfred E. Smith for the presidency with what will be forever known as the "Happy Warrior speech," everyone understood what he meant to say. Smith had known defeat and disappointment, yet had not only survived but triumphed in the rough-and-ready of electoral politics. Both he and Roosevelt knew that his were exactly the social and political qualities that were liabilities in the increasingly conservative and nativist political climate, where Catholics were by definition "foreign" and hence a threat to an isolationist public. Smith was defeated for the 1924 nomination, but his very contest for it was cast by Roosevelt in terms of the heroic struggle of the underdog, the happy warrior. In the opening lines of his poem, Wordsworth asks:

> *Who is the happy Warrior? Who is he*
> *That every man in arms should wish to be?*

The answer:

> *It is the generous Spirit, who, when brought*
> *Among the tasks of real life, hath wrought*
> *Upon the plan that pleased his boyish thought;*
> *Whose high endeavours are an inward light*
> *That makes the path before him always bright.*

Those "tasks of real life" are not easy to perform, nor is one assured of victory in performing them simply because one wishes or because the tasks are worthy. The happy warrior is the one

> *Who, doomed to go in company with Pain,*
> *And Fear, and Bloodshed, miserable train!*
> *Turns his necessity to glorious gain;*
> *In face of these doth exercise a power*
> *Which is our human nature's highest dower:*
> *Controls them and subdues, transmutes, bereaves*
> *Of their bad influence, and their good receives.*

This happy warrior knows both failure and success, and often more of frustration than of ease, but it is his character, his internal disposition, that can be relied upon to do the right thing with the hope, if not the expectation, of winning the day; but win or lose, he remains to do the right thing.

> *He labours good on good to fix, and owes*
> *To virtue every triumph that he knows . . .*
> *He rises by open means; and there will stand*
> *On honourable terms, or else retire,*
> *And in himself possess his own desire;*
> *Who comprehends his trust, and to the same*
> *Keeps faithful with a singleness of aim;*
> *And therefore does not stoop, nor lie in wait*
> *For wealth or honours, or for worldly state.*

This happy warrior is no mere philosopher or thinker on the sidelines whose chief vocation is contemplation. No, he is engaged, and when one is engaged in combat, for that is after all what warriors engage in, he not only contemplates failure and defeat; he is prepared to endure them.

> *But who, if he be called upon to face*
> *Some awful moment to which Heaven has joined*
> *Great issues, good or bad, for human kind,*
> *Is happy as lover; and attired*
> *With sudden brightness like a man inspired.*

Neither shape nor destiny, that is, neither the corporeal nor the spectral, can dismay him: he is not easily intimidated; nor is he betrayed by thought of tender happiness. He perseveres to the last, this happy warrior, "from well to better, daily self-surpast," and whether he prevails or fails,

> *Finds comfort in himself and in his cause;*
> *And, while the mortal mist is gathering, draws*
> *His breath in confidence of Heaven's applause:*
> *This is the happy Warrior; this is he*
> *That every man in arms should wish to be.*[7]

Roosevelt was no man of letters and Churchillian poetic diction was not his native speech, but he knew that in a popular world more literate than ours is now, Wordsworth's familiar figure of the happy warrior—one who prevails on the interior despite the outward circumstances of success or failure—would appeal to the emulative and the heroic where, in true Wordsworthian fashion, imagination always triumphs over the mere tyranny of fact. In preparing his speech, Roosevelt noted: "I tried the definite experiment this year of writing and delivering my speech wholly for the benefit of the radio audience and press rather than for any forensic effect it might have on the delegates."[8]

In this experiment he succeeded in capturing the imagination of the public. Smith was not nominated in 1924, but he was in 1928, when he then lost to Hoover. The real winner was Roosevelt himself, who in

1932 was the choice of the party over Smith, and of the nation over Hoover. Neither man ever forgave Roosevelt for succeeding.

The poem has to do with the elusive gratification of what the world calls happiness, and Wordsworth scholarship, a rather intense and highly specialized intellectual subculture, reminds us that it was with Samuel Coleridge that Wordsworth shared something of the notion that the means to happiness was not necessarily the satisfaction of material wants. In an early theological reflection, Coleridge noted of happiness:

> But we were not made to find Happiness in the complete gratification of our bodily wants—the mind must enlarge its sphere of activity, and progressive by nature, must never rest content. For this purpose our Almighty Parent hath given us Imagination that stimulates to the attainment of real excellence, by the contemplation of splendid possibilities, that still revivifies the dying motives within us, and fixing our eyes on the glittering Summits that rise one above the other in Alpine endlessness, still urges us up the ascent of being.[9]

Paths to Virtue

For many people, perhaps including the young Jacqueline Bouvier, and certainly the fictional Catholic Marchmain children, this relationship of imagination to happiness of the English Romantic poets would have been far too much of an abstraction, as it remains so for the poor high-school students and university undergraduates who may still be required to tease out the meanings of "The Prelude" and "Tintern Abbey." For those in pursuit of the happiness that comes from a good life there were the "virtues," lists with a pedigree from antiquity that had been sufficiently "Christianized" by Augustine and Aquinas to become an indispensable part of the church's practical guidance to goodness and happiness.

In the modern secular West we have become accustomed to thinking that it is only in the East that paths to virtue have been constructed. Certainly since the end of the war in Vietnam, and for some time before that, Eastern spirituality has enjoyed an increasing popularity in the West, which is seemingly exhausted by its own moral tradition. In the mall bookshops of America the wisdom literature of the Buddhist and Hindu traditions now takes up as much shelf space as the Bible; these Eastern books have generated a whole new category of shelving that happens to coincide with the most popular self-designation of people in search of books. You can still find Christian works under "Religion," a category I predict will grow smaller and smaller, but works to do with the Dalai Lama, who is possibly the most popular religious figure in the world today, are where the action is on the shelves, under the section marked "Spirituality."

Some years ago, while on the road promoting my book *The Good Book: Reading the Bible with Mind and Heart*, I found myself on a Friday evening in late spring in a very plush suburb of Atlanta, Georgia. I was to give a talk at a large Presbyterian church, but I was warned by my "literary host," the person who in each city of the tour had charge of me, that I should not be disappointed by an expectedly low turnout. "After all," she said, "it's Friday night, there is a home baseball game, and the Dalai Lama is in town." I could not have imagined a worse coincidence of competition, and so I expected a corporal's guard. As it turned out, we had a very large and lively crowd, which shows that there are more than enough people to go around in Atlanta on a Friday night. Several people, however, remarked to me before, during, and after my question period that they had come to hear me out of loyalty to the sponsoring church, and that they had enjoyed the evening despite the fact that they were more "spiritual" than "religious" and would have preferred to hear the Dalai Lama had they been able to get tickets. I was more annoyed than humbled, but I understood.

Augustine and Aquinas have been long dead, and when alive they could not have held a candle to the quiet charisma of the Dalai Lama. To struggle through Augustine's *Confessions*, much less through *The City of God*, or to try to make one's way through Aquinas's *Summa Theologica* without a host of interpreting nuns and Jesuits is indeed an exercise in terrific frustration. The Dalai Lama, on the other hand, as he is translated by such able English-writing scholars as Robert Thurman and Jeffrey Hopkins, is so accessible and sensible, and such a moral social witness in the bargain, that he is without peer as a teacher of wisdom and guide to the path of enlightenment. To many, he has a lock on the good life.

The Christian West, however, is not without its own ancient and viable resources, enumerations of virtue that, although they may sound abstract, are designed to be of daily practical use. As any nun or teaching brother has told many a skeptical Catholic boy or girl in parochial school, "They'll keep you out of hell, and get you into heaven."

Augustine argued that "the virtues are good in themselves and 'establish the order' which leads us to God."[10] The practice of virtue is the precondition for happiness because it permits us to do only that which is good, and happiness is a consequence of goodness. Another way of thinking about how this all works can perhaps be illustrated by the following schematic:

The Good Life:
- Objective = Goodness
- Result = Happiness
- Means = The Virtues
- Content or Manifestation = Faith, Hope, and Love

Happiness is a consequence of goodness, for to be happy is a result of being and of doing good; and thus to aspire to the good life is to aspire to goodness, from which proceeds happiness. The way to achieve this is by means of the virtues, which are gifts designed to help us achieve our end. The full manifestation of the good life is also its content: a life that expresses the supreme theological virtues of faith, hope, and love. The moral life, the good life, is the practical application of these gifts to that end.

The Four Cardinal Virtues

The principal discussion of the four cardinal, or principal, virtues that form the basis of the Roman Catholic moral life is derived from the writings of St. Thomas Aquinas, who, in the *Summa Theologica*, lists prudence, justice, temperance, and fortitude. These are qualities that help one to lead a Christian life. They are not ends in themselves, but they are the means to the highest end, which is the doing of and the living of the good life; and, what is more to the point of the human condition, they are discerned by reason—that is, a person using the quality of reason, which has been given by God, may determine which occasion requires which virtue. Just as an artisan knows which tool to use to create an appropriate effect or a doctor knows which prescription of procedure is appropriate to which medical condition, so the moral person who is equipped with reason and a desire for the good will know how to use the gifts of virtue. Such knowledge is essential to the everyday life of the person in pursuit of the good life, for at least two reasons.

The first reason is that proficiency in virtue, like proficiency on the piano, requires practice. Virtue is both an art and a discipline, but the art is compromised if the discipline is not made perfect in practice. One does not save the virtues for an extraordinary moment of need: in order for them to be available when they are truly needed, they must be practiced when it would seem that one could be doing something else. The musical analogy is not amiss here. Many of us of a certain age were required to take piano lessons, not so much because we came from musical families, although that was the case for me, but rather because a proficiency at the piano was regarded as a sign of cultural attainment and mental discipline. As with studying Latin in high school, piano lessons were undertaken not for their own sake, pleasurable as they may eventually be, but for the sake of much to be desired other qualities. Eye, ear, and hand coordination were among the benefits to be gained, as well as the possibility of providing quality entertainment for oneself and for others, but none of this would be possible without the drudgery of practice. One could not play tunes on the first try, for one first had to master many scales, flats, sharps, and accidentals before any display of talent would be agreeable to anyone listening.

In my case my mother was my piano teacher, and a very well qualified teacher she was, as she was a graduate of the New England Conservatory of Music. To learn to play the piano from your mother, however, is very much like being taught to drive by your father, and both are experiences that one never forgets and that one does not always enjoy. I was a difficult pupil because I had one talent that got in the way of my ability to learn other necessary things, and that was that I had a very good ear.

In a musician, a good ear is a good thing to have, and even the famously deaf Beethoven could not have done anything without his magnificent ear, because composition and performance are fundamentally works of the ear; but a good ear can also be a bad thing to have in one who does not have technical attainments. It can encourage shortcuts based on what one has heard, as opposed to on what one knows, and it can offer premature satisfactions and thus do away with the incentive to practice; and it can give one a sense of false security, which leads to the sin of pride. My mother loved the fact that I could reproduce almost anything I heard, saying that that was a gift; but, like most gifts, it could easily be abused. As it could inhibit the ability to actually know what one was doing, it could allow one to play, however imperfectly, something that one had never before read or practiced. My gift got in the way of my practice and I became a lazy pianist, leaving the hard work of practice to others less gifted than myself. As a result my mother gave up on me, saying that when I was ready to do the job properly, when I achieved sufficient motivation, I would return to the study of piano on my own and would do what it took to become proficient.

She was right. My limited talents took me only so far, and then when I wanted to know more, I had to learn the hard way. I began to play for Sunday school in our little church, then for the evening service, and later for other occasions, until my ambitions rose to meet the opportunities presented to me and made me acutely aware of my limitations and need for improvement. Practice was then no longer pointless, for it would take me where I wanted to go, and so practice became my joy, and even my passion. Over subsequent years my mother had the satisfaction of saying "I told you so," and I had the satisfaction of acquiring, the hard way, both a motivation and a skill. Before I entered the ministry I spent many happy years as a church organist, not a great one but a competent one, and I was always mindful of the practice it had taken for me to overcome my inherent musical liabilities and the temptations of my gifted ear.

It is within this context that I have always appreciated the story, apocryphal or not, of the great pianist Artur Rubinstein, who is said to have said, "When I skip practice one day, I know it; when I skip practice two days, the critics know it; and when I skip practice three days, everybody knows it." We know nothing of the musical ability of St. Thomas Aquinas, and there were no pianos in his day, but doubtless he, and the whole succession of moral instructors who stand in the great Thomistic tradition, understood and appreciated the metaphor of moral practice.

"Practice makes perfect" goes the aphorism, and we aspire to perfection, impossible as it may be, both in piano and in life. Practice is another word for the formation of good and useful habits. We heard of the utility of habit as perfecting moral practice in Aristotle, and the notion of the habitual practice of virtue is a fundamental aspect of Aquinas's moral philosophy. A virtue is in itself the habit of doing good, and a habit both supplements and overcomes, where necessary, our natural talents and propensities. The moral life consists in the forming of good habits and the prevention and correction of bad habits. Habits, of course, are related to self-discipline, but in their formative stages they are also dependent upon external forces. Random external forces contribute to the formation of habits that may be good or bad. The moral life—that is, the life that leads to the good life—cannot depend upon random chance and nature to provide those habits that lead to the good, and thus the formation of good habits is the most important responsibility that falls to those who have our best interests at heart.

The most important thing young parents can do is to form the habits of a lifetime in the little ones committed to their care. The moral education of the child begins at the first moment of awareness, in how the child is encouraged, loved, rewarded, and punished. The tough doctrine of original sin says that the child inherits the stain of the sins handed down the ages from our first parents, which were present in our birth parents. The child is not born into innocence, and yet the birth of a child is that transcendent moment when innocence is reborn in us all, if only for a moment. Every child is born into a moment of love at the moment of life and, from that moment of reception into the world, the real question is of the habits that will be formed in that child so that he or she may live as one who loves the good life.

Clergy friends of mine tell me that they can tell the character of a child when the child is presented for baptism, for the soul is already in the process of formation. Is the child good-tempered or bad-tempered, smiling or scowling, indulged by the parents or intimidating the parents? Perhaps this is crediting too much to external observations, but an old custom had it that a fussing baby at the christening meant an early and healthy struggle with Satan. Thus, I am told, some clergy pinch a too quiet baby to get a head start on the struggle! Just as certain yuppie mothers used to think that it was never too soon to prepare their children for admission to the day-care center of choice and played Mozart to them in utero, it is even more essential to commence the moral formation of the child from the moment of entry into the world, through the formation of good habits and the correction of bad ones. Initially, this will be more work for the parents than for the child, but it is the work of making a life that counts, not just the pleasure of having a child.

A habit is an essential ingredient in the formation of the life of virtue not only because "practice makes perfect," but because temptation and conflict are the stuff of daily human life: there is never a moment when these are not present, however latent or benign they or the person or the circumstance may appear to be. This is the second reason why St. Thomas urges practice of the virtues upon us: not simply to perfect the virtues themselves, but to make effective use of them in the discernment of evil and the prosecution of good. The practice of virtue is the daily work of the believer: it does not wait for a crisis, since to wait for a crisis is to create a crisis. The cardinal virtues are not made up by human philosophy as a consensus document for human practice. They are gifts of God, and they reflect what God is and what God values. Aquinas makes this point on the origin of the cardinal virtues by citing Augustine: "The soul needs to follow something in order to give birth to virtue. This something is God, and if we follow Him, we shall live the good life."[11]

In his discussion of the cardinal virtues, Aquinas argues that all other virtuous activities, patience, mercy, forgiveness, acts of charity, and acts of forbearance, to name a few, fall under one or another of the four cardinal virtues. For example, he says that any virtue that, on reasonable consideration, causes us to do good or to refrain from doing evil is the virtue of prudence. Every virtue that requires rectitude in behavior and due process in human encounter is the virtue of justice. Every virtue that restrains the passions is the virtue of temperance; and every virtue that strengthens the soul in the struggle with the passions is the virtue of fortitude. Prudence, for Aquinas is "the virtue which commands." Justice is "the virtue which is about due actions between equals"; temperance is the virtue "which suppresses desires for the pleasures of touch"; and fortitude is "the virtue which strengthens against dangers of death."[12]

This is heady stuff. Compared with such relatively simple moral road maps as the ever popular poem "Desiderata" and some of the list of aphorisms anthologized from the spiritual texts of the East, these Thomistic distinctions about the virtues move with the facility and velocity of a square wheel. They require some translation into modern moral English, and that is just what has been done for the fortunate young people of the Corpus Christi Parish School in Oklahoma City. Their teacher has put his summary of the cardinal virtues, consistent with Aquinas and the catechism.

Prudence

The first of the cardinal virtues is prudence, and of it the *Brief Catechism of Virtue* says:

> Prudence helps me decide what is good in every circumstance of my life. By prudence I choose to do good things and I do not do bad things. When I take the time to think of the consequences of my actions, I am prudent. When I don't do some things because of the bad consequences, that is prudence. Prudence is necessary for a happy and successful life. Prudence helps keep stress out of life.

It is not just the mention of "stress" that gives this a contemporary ring, but we certainly see that the notion of prudence has been liberated from its sanctimonious past and is flung fully into the center of modern life. Prudence involves the element of choice. Without choice we cannot imagine ourselves free, for the essence of freedom, as we have said before, is choice. Choice, however, is always exercised within the context of consequences, and for every choice there is a consequence. As my colleague Harvey Cox has famously said, "Not to choose is to choose." What prudence provides is not simply a rational analysis of choice and consequence, but an informed choice of the right and good thing. Although rationality is not mentioned in this particular definition, it is presupposed by prudence, for it is the wise use of the mind, the process of evaluation and assessment, that permits us to determine what the right and good thing is that should be done or the wrong or dangerous thing that should be avoided. Prudence is not simply "looking up the rules" in some form of moral bookkeeping or footnoting: it is the actual risk of engagement, with the unstable freedom of options, and the making of a choice consistent with the good to which one aspires.

Prudence sometimes suggests a lack of risk and imagination, an aversion to adventure, or a sense of moral or spiritual indecisiveness, and it is that that gives prudence a bad name, for we like nothing more than the freedom to take risks and to succeed at doing the unexpected. Prudence sounds too much like your maiden aunt or the overly cautious banker who lends money only to those who manifestly don't need it. It can often be an excuse for not doing anything, and that is perhaps its most ambiguous quality. Dr. Samuel Johnson observed that "Prudence is an attitude that keeps life safe, but does not often make it happy."

Yet prudence is understood as a positive enterprise as opposed to an exclusively negative one. "I choose to do good things, and I do not do bad things." The affirmation is meant to trump the negation. Thus, to make certain that our prudential behavior is a positive rather than merely a negative force, we are required always to remember that prudence is meant to enable good things. The prudent person is one who intentionally keeps close to the will of God. St. Basil, one of the Cappadocian fathers of the early church, put it this way: "Prudence must precede all our actions since, if prudence is lacking, there is nothing, however good it may seem, that is not turned into evil."[13]

Prudence can be an argument for the *status quo*, and it can also be an argument for radical change. Let us consider the famous case of Martin Luther King Jr. and the white ministers of Birmingham, Alabama.

When Prudence Acts

The confrontation in the streets of Birmingham, Alabama, between the forces of Martin Luther King and those of Public Safety Commissioner "Bull" Connor, in the spring of 1963, was played out live on worldwide television, and no longer could the American South's sin of segregation be regarded simply as a local matter. Dr. King and his followers were arrested and sent to jail; and the white ministers of Birmingham were troubled that King's tactics had led to this violence. As fellow Christians, they urged King to cease his provocative ways, which would only lead to more violence, and King, as a Christian, they argued, could hardly endorse that. They urged a counsel of prudence.

King's reply, smuggled out on toilet paper and other scraps, as he was denied writing tools by the authorities, became the famous "Letter from Birmingham Jail." The ministers had urged patience, and King began his reply:

> We have waited for more than three hundred forty years for our constitutional and God-given rights. The nations of Asia and Africa are moving with jet-like speed toward the goal of political independence, and we still creep at horse-and-buggy pace toward the gaining of a cup of coffee at a lunch counter. I guess it is easy

for those who have never felt the stinging darts of segregation to say "wait."[14]

The ministers argued that King's nonviolent movement promoted violence and that it was wrong. The "prudent" thing would have been to stop it. King replied:

> In your statement you asserted that our actions, even though peaceful, must be condemned because they precipitate violence. Isn't this like condemning the robbed man because his possession of money precipitated the evil act of robbery? . . . Isn't this like condemning Jesus because his unique God-consciousness and never-ceasing devotion to God's will precipitated the evil act of the Crucifixion?[15]

Prudence is not simply the taking account of the consequences of action and inaction: it is also the determining of which course is most in conformity with God's will for goodness, as determined by a reasonable person intent on doing good. For King, the only prudent course was to carry on: "If the inexpressible cruelties of slavery could not stop us, the opposition we now face will surely fail. We will win our freedom because the sacred heritage of our nation and the eternal will of God are embodied in our echoing demands."[16]

Sometimes prudence means "Carry on, come what may," for not to do so admits of a greater evil and perpetuates a great gulf of separation between God and the people who would follow God. Prudence is the agency that helps decide what to do in all circumstances, so that we may always choose the good, which does not always stand on the side of the *status quo.*

Prudence also, more often than not, is associated with the voice of conscience that tells us not to pursue a particular course of action—not because it is dangerous, but because it is wrong and will therefore do more harm than good. The prudent course for former president Bill Clinton was clear for all to see: he should not have pursued sexual relations with Monica Lewinsky in violation of his marriage vows and common sense, and he most certainly should not have lied about so doing. Casting prudence to the winds in the exercise of his appetites and failing to take into account the consequences for himself, Monica Lewinsky, his family, and the nation, he became the prime example of how the moral man in search of the good life ought not to behave. All of his public good works and moral ambition notwithstanding, history, alas, will forever mark him as an imprudent man who brought stress not only into his own life, but into our lives as well.

Justice

The second cardinal virtue is justice. The *Brief Catechism* says:

> Justice is a consistent decision to do what is good toward God and my neighbor. I respect the rights and duties of others. Justice brings harmony. Without justice, there is no peace. There are no rights without duties attached. If I wish to exercise my rights in justice I must also exercise my duties.

Aquinas defines justice as the virtue "which is about due actions between equals." Perhaps the most perfect expression of the rule of the virtue of justice is the famous "Golden Rule," which says that we are to do unto others as we would be done unto. The premise of this rule is that self-interest should guide our relations with others who, because we are all created by the same God and in the image of that God, are our equals. To offend someone is to offend God, and it is also to be offended ourselves. Thus justice is the exercise of the relationship of equity between equals.

The justice rubric, however, is not simply horizontal, but also vertical. Aquinas lived in a hierarchical society, as did Jesus, and as did most people before the age of American-style democracy. Justice was not only right behavior between equals; it was also right behavior between ranks, which in an earlier day we would have called "superiors" and "inferiors." Given the disproportionate distribution of power, those who had more of it were expected to be even more just in their relationship to their inferiors. It is in this context of expectation that the aphorism of behavior was articulated: "From those to whom much has been given, much is expected." In a medieval feudal society, where every person fell into an ordered ranking that spiraled up to God at the top, duties were specified both among and between the ranks. God's power was absolute, but it was mitigated by notions of mercy and the desire to inspire harmony and loyalty. Thus the king, who got his power from God, would recognize the relationship he owed to his inferior, the duke, and so on down the social chain.

To interrupt that ordered set of expectations, to fail in one's duty to fulfill responsibilities downward and upward and horizontally, was to create disorder; and where there was disorder and the absence of justice, there could be no peace. True peace can exist only in a situation where justice prevails.

One can argue that in a dictatorship with efficient and repressive military and police forces to silence dissent and root out troublemakers peace appears to obtain because there is no overt conflict. Between spasms of revolutionary outbursts in imperial Rome, or in czarist Russia, or in Afrikaaner South Africa in the twentieth century, one could say that peace obtained, but the mere absence of overt conflict was not peace, because there could be no peace in the absence of justice. The vacuum created by the absence of justice would always be filled by the potential for conflict, disharmony, and disease. From this comes the popular protest slogan of the twentieth century, "No Justice, No Peace."

In Hebrew scripture, peace is not simply the absence of war, strife, or
conflict; it is always connected with righteousness and justice. For
example, in Psalm 34:14, the one who would be righteous is urged to
"Depart from evil, and do good; seek peace, and pursue it." The Lord is
against evil, and the eyes of the Lord are toward the righteous, and his
ears toward their cry. In other words, the prerequisite of true peace is
righteousness, and those who would pursue peace must also pursue
righteousness. In Psalm 85:10, one of the loveliest images in all of scripture is offered in the image of righteousness and peace kissing each
other in fraternal affection. In the prophecy of Jeremiah the cry of an
easy peace without justice is condemned: "They have healed the hurt
. . . of my people slightly, saying, 'Peace, peace'; when there is no
peace" (Jeremiah 6:14, KJV). The desire for peace is understandable,
but the prophet insists that there can be no real peace as long as injustice prevails and righteousness is held hostage to civility.

For most twentieth-century Americans, the fictitious character of
lawyer Atticus Finch, in Harper Lee's Pulitzer prize–winning novel *To
Kill a Mockingbird*, is the figure of justice in the sense of this second
cardinal virtue. Harper Lee was a daughter of the South who created a
novelistic world that reflected the real world of the American South in
which she was reared, a South still deeply entrenched in its genteel
racist ways. In the midst of this idyllic land of gentle courtesy and slow
manners, where peace seemed to be the order of the day, and civility—
the courtly relationship between the classes and the races—served as
the fig leaf to cover the nakedness of a fundamentally unjust society,
the fundamental question was whether good justice would be found
here for a black man accused of a gross crime.

The novel was made incarnate in the movie version that featured the
incorruptible Gregory Peck as lawyer Atticus Finch, and it is Atticus
Finch who could easily have settled for peace, but who risks all for justice for the least of those among his townsmen. The question of equality before the law, as the prerequisite of true justice, challenges the

peace; and I would argue that there is no better moral tale in all of modern American literature—since Mark Twain's tales of Tom Sawyer and Huck Finn—that better illustrates the virtue of justice and the attainment of genuine peace. To enjoy the rights and benefits of peace one must exercise the duties and responsibilities of justice. The modern temptation is to accept a revision of the "Golden Rule," one that might say, "Do unto others before they do unto you," which to many might seem an appropriate accommodation to reality. The moral life says that this may accomplish a temporary satisfaction, and even the illusion of peace. Real and genuine peace, however, and not simply the absence of visible conflict, requires the priority of justice, the intentional decision to do what is right toward God and one's neighbor.

Temperance

If ever a word needed rescue from the captivity of its past association, "temperance" is it. When I was a young boy, a man came to our little church and, together with his wife, discussed with us the dangers of drink. Then the class separated, and the girls went off to a separate room with his wife while we sixth-grade boys remained with the husband. Standing there in our classroom, he proceeded to give us all the reasons why drink was wrong, but even more vivid than his explanation was his final demonstration of the effects that alcohol would have on our innards. On the table in front of him stood a large vat containing what he told us was clear liquid alcohol, and beside it lay an enormous beefsteak on the bone. This was not long after the war, and the sight of such a large piece of meat was still impressive to most of us. As he reached the climax of his talk, our speaker told us that we would soon see what alcohol would do to the beef, and that sin would do the same thing to our souls. He then picked up the beefsteak, dropped it into the vat of liquid, and in mere seconds before our horrified eyes the meat dissolved in a riotous fizz, leaving nothing behind but the naked bone. "Now, boys," he said, holding up some cards, "who'll sign the pledge?" Who wouldn't? I signed it immediately, and I kept the pledge all through high school and college and became a notorious prig for so doing. I broke the pledge only in the first of my days in divinity school, when I discovered that the sweet, cold punch I was consuming at the dean's garden party for new students was so filled with wine and spirits that a stevedore would not be ashamed to be seen drinking it.

Temperance in my youth was a misnomer for abstinence—not from sex, as is now the case, but from drink. The Women's Christian Temperance Union, colloquially the WCTU, was still a force to be reckoned with in local politics, and our pastor annually preached a sermon encouraging the adults to vote "Dry" in the annual town elections.

Temperance seemed anything but moderate, and moderation would seem to be an ambiguous virtue, for why would one want to be moderate or temperate in good things? Barry Goldwater's 1964 acceptance speech of the Republican nomination for the presidency challenged the prevailing notion of moderation, and he defended himself and his party against the charges of extremism when, in the last two sentences of his speech, he said:

> I would remind you that extremism in the defense of liberty is no vice! And let me remind you also that moderation in the pursuit of justice is no virtue![17]

So much for temperance. Yet the *Brief Catechism of Virtue* defines this third cardinal virtue as: "the virtue of balance and moderation. It is the mastery of my will over my urges. If I have the desire to do what is wrong, I resist it. I can and do govern myself."

Aquinas calls temperance the virtue that governs the passions. When we are excited by the passions to do something we know to be unreasonable and we know that those passions should be curbed and restrained, then the practice, the habit, of temperance becomes the means by which we moderate those passions so that they do not control us, but we them. The reason temperance became so intimately associated with drink is that drink, as a stimulant, loosens our natural inhibitions. The very reason people drink, as the temperance people so often put it, is the very reason they should not. We drink to loosen our defenses, we drink to escape our familiar restraints, we drink in order to become more agreeable to others, whom we might ignore when sober.

Temperance, according to Aquinas, has to do with the cultivation of that rectitude that controls the appetites. What might be good and pleasing to us in small doses, when taken in excess, can prove dangerous. The occasional glass of wine when taken in moderation, "for thy stomach's sake," as St. Paul commends, is good. Our maiden aunts of a generation ago used to take their surreptitious sips of brandy "for medicinal purposes," but when such little habits develop into the excesses of alcoholism and binge drinking, then we are in trouble. Temperance is something of the habit of the Aristotelian mean between two extremes, indulgence and abstinence, and it was the person of moderate habits whom Aristotle upheld as his exemplary person. Temperance is meant to be an exercise in self-governance, not in self-perfection, and the temperate person is the one who strives for a balanced life and tries to maintain an equilibrium in the midst of temptations to do otherwise. Such is the moral ambition of one of the greatest of all English prayers, composed in the seventeenth century by the English Catholic John Austin:

Fix thou our steps, O Lord, that we stagger not at the uneven motions of the world, but go steadily on our way, neither censuring our journey by the weather we meet, nor turning aside for anything that may befall us. Amen.[18]

Here the world is assumed to be driven by uneven motions and, ordinarily, normal people will stagger at them, being thrown to and fro like a drunken man out of control and at the mercy of the elements and circumstances. The virtuous person is one who, knowing this, maintains a steady, temperate disposition in which control and destiny are not lost. It is commonplace to think of the moral life, the good life, as a context between two extremes, a cosmic battle between consummate good and consummate evil where big battles and big decisions are the order of the day. The harder fact of life is that most of us contend with less than a cosmic struggle where the extremes of our resources are summoned into play. For most of us it is a sufficient moral struggle to maintain our balance and keep our sense of proportion. Temperance, rather than a negation of the contests of life, is perhaps better represented by the starter's instructions to those about to run a long-distance race: "Ready! Steady! Go!"

Self-government ultimately is what it is all about, and that involves both self-knowledge, knowing our weaknesses and our strengths and having an honest estimation of each, and self-discipline, which allows us to know what our resources are and how, when, and how much to expend them. Such moderation can sound priggish and dull, like prudence, for example, and we might be tempted to the cynic's cry at Aristotle's "golden mean": "Moderation in all things, especially moderation."

In a world that believes that "nothing succeeds like excess," how can we afford to make room for the virtue of temperance? In the hours and days in the immediate aftermath of the terrorist attacks of September 11, 2001, there was an enormous temptation to panic. The world was coming to an end, we thought, and Armageddon had, at last, arrived; there was a terrorist around every corner. The very goal of the terrorists was to incite panic, which would do even more damage than had their lethal plane bombs, for in panic we become our own self-immolating weapons. The heroes of the day in such circumstances are those who do not panic, who somehow are able to call upon inner resources that have perhaps lain in reserve, waiting for the moment of greatest need.

Panic, after all, is the overestimation of the problem and the underestimation of the resources. The habit of temperance allows one the necessity of self-governance, that is, of self-control in the moments when that control is most needed.

In this regard, I think of that ordinary, brave citizen Todd M. Beamer, on one of the hijacked planes, who, once he took full account of the situation, decided to act. According to nearly every account of the sequence of actions on that plane in Pennsylvania, Mr. Beamer first called his wife on his cell phone and apprised her of the situation. Then, we are told, he "eyeballed" the situation on board and realized what was at stake, and then enlisted the support of some of his fellow hostages. Then, we understand, he said the Lord's Prayer; and, finally, in the language of the "can-do" culture, he said, "Let's roll!" What followed none of us will ever fully know, but we do know that his actions and those of his colleagues, the result of a temperate assessment of an impossible situation, served to deflect the plane from its intended deadly mission, and that at the cost of his own life Todd Beamer saved the lives of many.

Todd Beamer's actions, I argue, were the actions of a temperate man, and that on balance he took the most reasonable course available to him. As one of my favorite students is fond of saying, "When you're damned if you do and damned if you don't, always do." With Mr. Beamer forever locked in our memory, we should remember that another word for courage is fortitude.

Fortitude

Fortitude presupposes a conquest over the temptation to evil and fear and is the defensive quality against the seemingly overwhelming forces that intimidate and tempt one to concede to apparently superior forces. Fortitude is not stoical indifference, a "charge of the light brigade" mentality that confuses heroic foolhardiness with moral courage. Fortitude, as the Thomistic moral syllabus understands it, is the ability to stand in hope against the overwhelming pressures, tragedies, and fears of the world and, most especially, against the fear of death and the reality of mortality.

John Henry Cardinal Newman, in one of his "Four Prayers to St. Philip," asks for "The gift of Fortitude that with bravery and stubbornness I may battle with my foe." The "foe" is anyone and anything that diverts us from God, not necessarily some jack-booted bully or cowboy in a black hat. The "foe" in Genesis is given the persona of the serpent, which is described as "subtle," that is, able to insinuate himself into the most reasonable and acceptable reaches of life. Thus the virtue of fortitude requires a certain sensibility, an awareness of the places in which we are vulnerable to the blandishments and temptations of somebody not only more powerful than we are, but also much smarter. The fundamental trouble with the virtuous, as all of literature records, is the almost ineradicable instinct to underestimate the powers of the foe and overestimate the capacities of the righteous.

A False Peace

Of all the tragic figures of the twentieth century, the most tragic, in my opinion, is British prime minister Neville Chamberlain. He was not a wicked man or even a stupid man, and his service to the British people was considerable and significant, but we remember him for one awful and terribly public moment when, trusting in his own righteousness and that of his cause and thoroughly underestimating the perfidy of the German with whom he was dealing, he declared, after Munich, that he had secured with Herr Hitler "peace in our time." Anxious to avoid a second world war, for which England was woefully underprepared, he waged a campaign of appeasement with Hitler and Mussolini. The best face to be put on his policies was that he was trying to buy time for Britain to rearm sufficiently to meet the new military threats of Germany and its Italian ally, but the general sense of Chamberlain was that he was prepared to buy peace at any price, he lacked a sufficient understanding of the reality of evil in Hitler, and he was ruled more by fear of conflict than by fear of conquest. History has recorded him among those who were prepared, in Jeremiah's words, to cry "Peace, peace" where there was no peace. He thought himself a realist, and he is a perfect example of the absence of fortitude. Fortitude conquers fear, and, in Aquinas's words, "strengthens against dangers of death." Chamberlain foresaw another generation slaughtered in the trenches, as in World War I, and because his fear of another conflict inhibited his vision, he could not see that an even greater conflict awaited his people, with consequences far grimmer even than those of the first war. Thus, he was intimidated by the past, seduced by the present, and heedless of the future.

Fortitude, then, is designed to help us to see clearly and unflinchingly the situation in which we find ourselves: it is a counsel of realism, and fortitude enables us, that is, fortifies us, in all necessary strength to contend against that which threatens our perseverance in the good. Fortitude supplies us for the combat that allows our inner strength to contest and ultimately to prevail over outward turmoil. As a virtue, then, fortitude is indispensable in the daily conflicts of life, for without it we are a race of moral quitters. With it, we are, in St. Paul's memorably heroic words, "more than conquerors through him who loved us" (Romans 8:37).

Fortitude is that moral quality that allows us to persevere when others would easily give up or give in; it is the fuel of the long-distance moral runner who, despite inner fatigue and the apparent outward success of others, nevertheless keeps on keeping on. It is thus perhaps the most enabling and valuable of all the virtues.

Profile in Fortitude

When, from 1968 to 1970, I was a young instructor at Tuskegee Institute, now Tuskegee University, in Alabama, the famous school founded in 1881 by Booker T. Washington, I encountered one whom I even then understood to be a profile in fortitude. Tall, lean, taciturn, with the combined noble physiognomy of the Native American and the African American, Charles G. Gomillion, professor of sociology, was already a legend in his own time. There was something austere, even aloof about him, and while he was not much for small talk or idle chatter, even in my tender years of inexperience among my people in the Deep South I knew that Dr. Gomillion was a force with whom to be reckoned. He moved about the academic corridors with the authority of a Roman senator, and people got out of his way and paid him modest deference. He was neither imperious nor pretentious, but one sensed that he had made a career of not suffering fools gladly, whether white or black; and that in every sense of the cliché he was very much his own man.

Gomillion was famous for his participation as litigant in what was a landmark U.S. Supreme Court case, *Gomillion* v. *Lightfoot*,[19] which in 1960 had been argued before the high court and decided in favor of the litigants. In that year, black citizens of the city of Tuskegee in Alabama sued in a federal district court in Alabama for a declaratory judgment that an act of the Alabama legislature altering the boundaries of the city of Tuskegee was unconstitutional, in that it would alter the shape of the city from a square to an irregular twenty-eight-sided figure, the result of which would be to disenfranchise all but four of the four hundred registered black voters without eliminating a single white voter. The effect was to deprive the black voters of the suffrage on the basis of race, contrary to the provisions of the Fifteenth Amendment to the United States Constitution. Gomillion was president of the Tuskegee Civic Association, and Lightfoot was mayor of Tuskegee. It was a classic instance of political gerrymandering to achieve a racial purpose, which was the effective disenfranchisement of the black voters of the city of Tuskegee, many of whom were faculty, staff, and alumni of Tuskegee Institute. The Court decided in favor of Gomillion and his fellow petitioners, in a decision delivered by Mr. Justice Felix Frankfurter on November 14, 1960, in which he noted:

> It is difficult to appreciate what stands in the way of adjudging a statute having this inevitable effect invalid in light of the principles by which this Court must judge, and uniformly has judged, statutes that, howsoever speciously defined, obviously discriminate against the colored citizens. The [Fifteenth] Amendment nullifies sophisticated as well as simple-minded modes of discrimination. (*Lane* v. *Wilson*).

The judgment in favor of the Negro citizens of the city of Tuskegee was significant, and *Gomillion* v. *Lightfoot* takes its place alongside *Brown* v. *Board of Education* and other historic cases in the history of civil rights law. What was most interesting was the unlikely character of the person who gave his name to the petitioner's suit. Dr. Gomillion, born in 1900 and thus sixty years old at the time of the suit, was no radical or agitator in the conventional sense of the term. He was, in the black youth language of the time, "old timey." Dr. King and all of his associates were young enough to be Gomillion's children, and most of the Tuskegee students were young enough to be his grandchildren. There was nothing flashy or oratorical about him. He was as far from the prototype of a civil rights leader as you could get. He wasted neither time nor words, he was neither preacher nor lawyer, and yet, as a contemporary of his whom I knew well said, "In his quiet way, he just would never give up."

There was about Dr. Gomillion a certain rectitude, perhaps even an intimidating moral certainty, a combination of the best qualities of

A. Philip Randolph and Roy Wilkins. A sociologist by training and an academic by disposition, he was not given to extravagant gestures, but he had grown up in the Old South and his natural dignity had been forged upon the anvil of overt and covert discrimination. It had not broken him, but had made him stronger and thus unwilling to give in to the overwhelming cultural and political forces that would condemn him and his people to permanent second-class status. So he chose to fight and to enable others to fight in a coalition that was not easy to maintain. Some were afraid of taking on the establishment, and others felt that Gomillion and his plodding ways belonged to another generation, but in the end it was his conscientious, persistent leadership that not only won the day, but provided the foundation for the final dramatic assault upon the old ways of the segregated South.

When in the fall of 1968 I came to Tuskegee, Gomillion was still going about his duties as professor of sociology, and in the corridors of Huntington Hall, the main teaching building, I would pass him and we would exchange solemn nods. There was no reason for him to know me, for I was but a lowly instructor, but I am grateful that I knew him however slightly, and that I was able to put a face and a figure, and even a carefully modulated voice, to a legend in civil rights legal history. He was a legend because he never gave up, he had the gift of fortitude and stood up for what was good and true, and his fortitude conquered fear.

In the final three chapters of this book we will discuss the three great theological virtues of faith, hope, and love as both the content and the manifestation, or expression, of the good life lived here and now.

CHAPTER 9

FAITH

SUBSTANCE AND EVIDENCE

It is cynicism and fear that freeze life;
it is faith that thaws it out, releases it, and sets it free.

HARRY EMERSON FOSDICK

In the first part of this book, we discussed the search for the good life as the yearning for something more: a cause worth living and dying for, a noble destination. We affirmed the notion that, despite all evidence to the contrary, human beings desire a life that is worthy of sacrifice, are prepared to take on great things, and wish to be both wise and good. If the cliché is true that life is a journey, then most people see the good life as both a process and a destination. It takes a good life to achieve the good life, and thus, in the words of T. S. Eliot, "The end is where we start from."

In the second part of the book, we considered what would be essential to take on our journey and what it would be wise to pack. Thus we discovered failure and success, discipline and freedom, and the creative tensions of their relationships as vital to our own formation as pilgrims in search of the good life. These concepts, fundamental to our human nature, and each in its own way demanding something significant from our inner resources as we encounter the experience of living, form a part of our moral equipment.

In this third and final part of the book, with our destination clearly in view and with some useful moral luggage, as it were, we now consider the ways, means, and ends of our journey toward the good life, which include the four cardinal virtues of prudence, justice, temperance, and fortitude. The three theological, or "great," virtues of faith, hope, and love are the content and expression of the good life. No life can be called good that does not exhibit in some way these qualities that we call the great virtues, for not only are they the means to the formation of communities of moral worth, but because they are gifts of God to help us toward more godly living, they become an expression of our relationship to God and to one another and of God's relationship with us all. Whereas the other virtues enjoy their special relationships with us as means of living the life that is good and worthy in an imperfect world, these three "great," or "theological," virtues enjoy their particular esteem because they are both the content of the good life and, as gifts of God, the expression of the good life lived. Just as an idea contains a content that requires an expression or manifestation to give it life, so the good life, as an idea of goodness, has as its content the great, theological virtues of faith, hope, and love, a content expressed by the exercise of these virtues in the world. Thus, faith, hope, and love become both the expression and the objective of the good life.

St. Paul gives us the three great virtues in 1 Corinthians 13, where he speaks of faith, hope, and love, with the greatest of these being love. In Christian theology these three virtues were called "theological" because it was believed that they were not natural to us, but were conferred as gifts of God through Christian baptism. Thus, their special status derived both from their divine origin and from their utility in helping to make the human life expressive of the divine purpose within and beyond it. If the cardinal virtues, the works of prudence, justice, temperance, and fortitude, are habits of *action*, then the theological virtues are habits of *being*, of being loving, hopeful, and faithful. One might argue that doing is the means to being, and that the quality of being is expressed by what one does.

For Paul, these three theological virtues of faith, hope, and love are those "higher gifts" of which he speaks at the close of 1 Corinthians 12. They are the means to that "still more excellent way," which he promises to demonstrate to the Corinthians when he writes "But earnestly desire the higher gifts. And I will show you a still more excellent way" (1 Corinthians 12:31). This invitation follows his extensive discussion of the varieties of spiritual gifts and services, in which he is keen to point out that the same spirit is capable of gifting different people in different ways, but all for the same purpose and from the same source. In 1 Corinthians 12:7, he notes that "To each is given the manifestation of the Spirit for the common good." Then this diversity of gifts is listed: to one is given through the Spirit the utterance of wisdom; to another, the utterance of knowledge; to another, the gift of faith; to another, the gift of healing; to another, the working of miracles; to another, prophecy; to another, the ability to distinguish between spirits; to another, various kinds of tongues; and to another, the interpretation of tongues. All of these gifts come from the same Spirit. All people do not have all of these gifts; their distribution is at the will of the Spirit. This diversity of gifts reflects the diversity of the Christian community, and thus no one should feel either inferior to or superior to another because of the different gifts and talents each has been given. Paul drives home the point with his extended metaphor of the body and its various functions, which contribute to the whole, and to a whole greater than the sum of its parts:

> *For just as the body is one and has many members, and all*
> *the members of the body, though many, are one body, so it is*
> *with Christ. For by one Spirit we were all baptized into one*
> *body—Jews or Greeks, slaves or free—and all were made to*
> *drink of one Spirit.*
>
> I CORINTHIANS 12:12–13

He wants the Corinthians to understand that the diversity of gifts reflects both the diversity of the community and the diversity of needs and opportunities; yet even more than this, he wants them to understand that this diversity comes from and serves the unity of the whole body of the community, reflecting therefore the unity of God. A single believer does not contain everything the whole community requires; nor can an individual on his or her own have or do everything essential to the spiritual welfare of the community. Paul's is a vivid invitation to see oneself as part of something greater and better than oneself, although it is not meant to diminish the significance of one's own particular part or role, for without it the whole would clearly be impaired. The eye, for example, is critical to the power of the whole person, but the whole person cannot be reduced to the eye or to the function of sight. The dignity of the eye, or of the ear, or of any other bodily part or function is in relationship to its own unique function and to its participation in the whole enterprise. Both the particular part and the whole of which it is a part are the gifts of the one Spirit:

> *If the whole body were an ear, where would be the sense of*
> *smell? But as it is, God arranged the organs in the body, each*
> *one of them, as he chose. If all were a single organ, where*
> *would the body be? As it is, there are many parts, yet one*
> *body.*

> I CORINTHIANS 12:17–20

Then Paul leaves the metaphor for the practical application to the working needs of the community and the role of the individual talents within it. As the body of Christ and as individual members of it, they are to exercise their God-given gifts as God has appointed: "First, apostles, second prophets, third teachers, then workers of miracles, then healers, helpers, administrators, speakers in various kinds of tongues" (1 Corinthians 12:28).

Each one has the gift of a responsibility and the ability to carry it out. The one who has been assigned to prophecy will be given the talent to prophesy; the teacher, the ability to teach; the administrator, the facility for administration; and so forth. This is an affirmation of order and planning: God does not just hope that things will turn out all right; God provides those persons with the talent to see that it does, for the benefit of the whole. This passage comes strongly to mind whenever people ask if they will be able to perform the tasks that fall to them. At ordinations, for example, I usually remind those for whom, as their former teacher, I have been invited to preach to remember that they have not been chosen because they are talented, but, rather, that because they have been chosen, God will give them talent, that is, enable them to do what they have been called to do.

This discussion about talent and opportunity, gifts and the occasion for their use is all very good, and people need to be affirmed in their particular work as part of the whole, but that particular job and this particular talent are not all there is to it: there is a great deal more. This is the point where Paul asks these gifted people to "earnestly desire the higher gifts. And I will show you a still more excellent way."

Although this discussion of talents and opportunities is fruitful at times of baccalaureate and commencement ceremonies, more often than not I have used it in College in my opening sermons and talks to freshmen. In the case of the newest members of an American academic community such as Harvard, I know that they know that I know just how able and talented they are. Our average entering class has board scores off the charts, is filled with class presidents, salutatorians, valedictorians, and National Honor Society superachievers. The records are impressive and they should be, particularly since most of the students have been pressured for success from the womb. In day care, nursery school, kindergarten, and primary school, they have been subjected to one goal, and one goal only: college, and the best one they can get into and, ideally, one as good as or better than the ones their parents attended. The conspiracy of competition that ambitious parents impose upon their young is a national scandal that produces the overtalented and emotionally underdeveloped young prodigies who flood our campuses in the fall. Every mother is a "theater mom," every father is "Leopold," the dreadful father of the boy-genius Mozart; and the worst of it all is that they succeed in their campaign for what they call "excellence" and are "rewarded" by places like Harvard and Yale and Princeton. Our admissions officers decry the culture of breathless competition, the fanatically driven parents, the stressed-out kids, the "system" that produces worn-out and exhausted teenagers who, like the sorcerer's apprentice, simply cannot stop doing what they have always done.

Many years ago, I gave a commencement talk at a posh girls' school in Manhattan. I took as my text not this most useful passage from St. Paul, but the very colorful words of Jesus in the Sermon on the Mount, where he says, "Consider the lilies of the field, how they grow; they toil not, neither do they spin: . . . yet . . . even Solomon in all his glory was not arrayed like one of these" (Matthew 6:28–29, KJV). I thought it an apt sentiment, and with gusto I delivered my talk against anxiety, urging these brightest of the bright to slow down and smell the flowers, indeed, "to consider the lilies." I was pleased with my talk, and so were most of the girls and their parents, judging by the applause and general conversation. Thus, I was unprepared for one lean Wall Street–type father who approached me not with the expected compliment, but with a serious bone to pick. "My girl got into this school on anxiety, she is graduating on anxiety, and she has been admitted to Radcliffe on anxiety. If she had taken your advice, she wouldn't be here to hear it." On and on he went about the gospel of constructive stress, productive anxiety, and the benefits of the eighteen-hour day for the firm and for the character. His argument reminded me of what a colleague of mine once said when we were discussing the suicides of several foreign graduate students in the chemistry program: "They just couldn't take the pressure. Talent, after all, is perfected in tension."

Talented people, gifted people, are the people of whom St. Paul is speaking. He does not denigrate their talent but honors both it and those who have it as indispensable parts one of another and of the greater whole. Mindful, however, of what is good about it all, he argues that it is not good enough, and thus he invites them not simply to consider, but to earnestly desire, what he calls "the higher gifts," and he promises to show them "a still more excellent way."

Those "higher gifts" and that "still more excellent way" are the subject of Paul's next chapter, perhaps the most famous chapter in all of the Bible and, next to the Twenty-third Psalm, the most familiar and beloved verses of scripture. This is the chapter on love, in 1 Corinthians 13, with its lyrical beginning, "Though I speak with the tongues of men and of angels" (KJV). Although dreadfully declaimed at far too many weddings and printed on too many tacky greeting cards, 1 Corinthians still has not lost its power over the hearts and imaginations of those who read and hear it. Most people know and care nothing of the theological context of the Corinthian church; they probably have not read Chapter 11, and have no idea that Chapter 12 is not simply a bit of beautiful prose, but the development of a very sophisticated argument about gifts and their use. Chapter 13, however, is not just about love, although love is the qualifying gift by which all other gifts and opportunities are interpreted. In the final verse of the chapter, love is described as the greatest of the three great gifts, and that serves to remind us that there are three great gifts, three higher gifts, which, taken together, give the greatest sense of the whole to the believer, who in this world can see only in part, as in a distorted mirror of the sort found in carnival fun houses, in which what you see is real but not really real, for all the proportions are wrong. The way to see things whole, the way to live wholly and not in part, the way for past and present and future to make some semblance of sense for those who have to keep these dimensions together, is through the more excellent way and the higher gifts of faith, hope, and love.

Although love is recorded as superior, these three gifts are meant to be seen together in a cooperative relationship with one another. They become the summary of the good life itself, as is said in the Holy Eucharist: "The gifts of God for the people of God." As we have noted before, they are gifts that come to supply what we lack. Faith is the gift that displaces our natural doubt, fear, and skepticism; hope confounds our hopelessness and innate despair; and love replaces the anxiety that produces both hate and fear and the sense that we are not simply unloving, but unlovely and therefore unlovable. If, then, as the church has historically taught, we want to live not only a good life but the best possible life, we will have to do so in the context of, and under the tutelage of, these three most excellent gifts of faith, hope, and love.

When St. Augustine was asked to write a short and useful summary of the faith for his friend Laurence, by use of the Lord's Prayer and the creed he produced a commentary on faith, hope, and love. Laurence had said that he wanted a small book he could hold in his hands, a slender book that the Greeks would call an *enchiridion*, which is the title by which Augustine's little treatise has long been known. Properly, it should be called "Augustine's Catechism on Faith, Hope, and Love." Although the work is small by Augustinian standards and yet fills the bill for the learned Laurence, it does take up all three gifts both in their interrelationship and separately, although more space is devoted to faith than to either hope or love. Some speculate that because faith is the most teachable of the qualities, Augustine devoted more time to it; nevertheless, Augustine is concerned to show the relationship between the three qualities. Citing Paul's words in Galatians 5:6, on "faith working through love," Augustine says: "So love cannot exist without hope nor hope without love, nor can either exist without faith."[1]

In that "still more excellent way" that is in essence the good life, the three great gifts of the theological virtues of faith, hope, and love are considered both in their distinctions and in their relationship. In what follows I will try to do the same, devoting what remains of this chapter to faith, and taking up hope and love in the final two chapters. Although we can take the benefit of Augustine's use of the creed as the foundation for his discussion of faith, for the creed was to him both the symbol and the substance of what a Christian was to believe, I will use faith in a slightly more elastic sense, addressing certain of its conundrums and opportunities more closely related to what William James, notoriously noncreedal, called "the will to believe."

The Need to Believe

In the last quarter of the nineteenth century, in a land and a time famous for its preachers, Phillips Brooks of Boston was among the most famous of the famous. We remember him today as the author of the beloved Christmas carol "O Little Town of Bethlehem" and, at least in Boston and in the Episcopal Church, as rector of Trinity Church, Copley Square, which is itself perhaps the most acclaimed bit of nineteenth-century ecclesiastical architecture in the world. Brooks, with his architect friend Henry Hobson Richardson, designed the building, and for that alone he would be famous. In his lifetime, however, he enjoyed an incredible charisma as a preacher of what Theodore Roosevelt would later call "muscular Christianity." While Henry Ward Beecher was famous for appealing to the ladies, Phillips Brooks was a man's kind of preacher who appealed neither to spirituality nor to a desiccated intellect, but to the men and boys of what would later be called the "establishment," the kind of men who would run the financial and legal professions, who themselves had gone to Harvard and who sent their sons there, and who maintained the fabric of bourgeois society. Brooks was neither an ascetic priest nor a social reformer; it was his eminent sensibility that appeared to appeal to the people who year after year filled the pews of Trinity Church. He was himself among the "landmarks" that visitors to Boston were advised to see.

Understandably, Brooks was equally popular on the college circuit, where, under the regimen of required chapel, there never could be enough preachers of reputation to supply the insatiable needs of college and preparatory-school pulpits. A graduate of Harvard College, where he had not distinguished himself as a scholar, he was one of its most popular sons in the pulpit of Appleton Chapel. Even when compulsory chapel was in 1886 abandoned at Harvard for the voluntary system, in a move largely spearheaded by Brooks himself as an influential member of the Board of Preachers, he remained, perhaps for that reform alone, the most popular of all the preachers. He is said to have pushed the reluctant President Charles William Eliot to finally initiate the reform of the chapel requirement by observing that his preaching at Harvard was very much like his preaching at the Massachusetts State Penitentiary at Charlestown, except that at the prison, Brooks noted, the guards wore guns.

One of Brooks's most famous sermons, doubtless preached at Harvard and at other schools and colleges on the circuit, was entitled "The Candle of the Lord." In looking out over his congregation of young men of the ruling class, he said:

What shall we make of some man rich in attainments and in generous desires, well-educated, well-behaved, who has trained himself to be a light and help to other men, and who, now that his training is complete, stands in the midst of his fellow men completely dark and helpless? These men are unlighted candles. . . . They are the spirit of man, elaborated, cultivated, finished to its very finest, but lacking the least touch of God. So dark in this world is a long row of cultivated men . . . to whom there has come no fire of devotion, who stand in awe and reverence before no wisdom greater than their own.[2]

One can almost hear him saying, "What a waste! Here is all this human potential, waiting but impotent because there is no divine spark, nothing of God to set them ablaze for good, either for themselves or for others." What a damning thing it is to be accused of standing "in awe and reverence before no greater wisdom than their own." Brooks may well have seemed the self-satisfied high priest of the *status quo*, preaching to a culture that was as much a "can-do" and "self-oriented" culture as our own, but it is clear that he was not content to allow these students or their parents to see themselves as unmoved movers. What was needed was a spark to turn these "unlighted candles" into something ablaze, for in the dark there is nothing more useless than an unlighted candle. His text, "The spirit of man is the candle of the Lord, searching all the inward parts of the belly," came from Proverbs 20:27 (KJV), but he could have as easily taken as his own the words of Jesus from the close of the Sermon on the Mount, "Let your light so shine before men, that they may see your good works, and glorify your Father which is in heaven" (Matthew 5:16, KJV). Changing the metaphor to a Pauline one, but addressing the same point of the actualization of human possibility by the power of the divine, he could have said, "Awake thou that sleepest, and arise from the dead, and Christ shall give thee light" (Ephesians 5:14, KJV).

I, too, have looked out over many a congregation similar to those to whom Phillips Brooks preached, and I have had much the same feeling: what an amazing thing it would be if these young men and women could realize the spiritual potential for good that was already in them, waiting simply for a spark of the divine to cause them to burst into flame, and give power and light to a dark and needy world. Certainly, most of them are prepared to serve others, although usually by leading them somewhere, for nobody to whom I preach initially aspires to be a follower. People who go to college at enormous expense have been trained to expect themselves to be leaders, and most would rather be bad leaders than good followers, or, to use familiar but politically incorrect expressions, to be "all chiefs and no Indians," or, as they say in Texas, "all hat and no cattle."

That, I would say, was largely the situation when I began in my ministry now more than thirty years ago. Despite the troubled decade of the 1960s, or perhaps even because of it, the young were still very much filled with an egotistical self-confidence. They may not have been as well behaved as the young people to whom Brooks had preached three or four generations earlier, but they could still be described as "rich in attainments and in generous desires, well-educated," and trained "to be a light and help to other men." The source of the social revolution of the 1960s and early 1970s was not too little belief on the part of these college students, for they believed too much, and they believed too much in their own singular cultural ability to bring in the Age of Aquarius by sheer will and love power. Distrustful of institutions, of adults, and "in awe and reverence before no wisdom greater than their own," they were stuck with little more than the banality of their own self-indulgence. This, after all, was the generation of *Hair, Jesus Christ, Superstar*, and *The Greening of America*, each of which in retrospect is something of a cultural embarrassment, somewhat like looking at pictures of your parents in bell-bottoms, platform shoes, and love beads.

Fortunately, the young people who inherited this landscape were smart enough to realize that they wanted and deserved something more than this. In politics they turned increasingly conservative; in religion they turned increasingly evangelical and even fundamentalist; and in academics, to the consternation of those now running their colleges and universities, they began to ask questions about "the true, the good, and the beautiful," and were not in any way nearly as offended by Alan Bloom's *The Closing of the American Mind* as were their tutors, instructors, and professors, most of whom were happily and defiantly standing "in awe and reverence before no wisdom greater than their own."

The young had not lost belief; nor had they dismissed it as irrelevant. More teachers than students embraced the brave new world of deconstructionism and the ennui of cultural relativism. In fact, more and more of the young were beginning to ask for something beyond themselves that would be worthy of their belief and the last full measure of devotion. "God talk" became increasingly the subject of conversation, not in the sense of a religious revival or a recovery of an old paradigm, but more of the "What if?" and "Why not?" variety in a tentative exploring of the possibilities of belief, a gentle probing of the hint of the divine, a quiet, almost clandestine, suspicion that there must be some secret source of meaning, purpose, and service beyond the currently acceptable social models of reform and self-esteem into which they would like to tap.

One would expect this of the increasing number of students who, at Harvard and other elite schools, as a result of a deliberate effort at wholesale meritocratic revision of the admissions criteria, were coming from increasingly diverse backgrounds. Often, in this period, when we think of "meritocratic admissions" and the "culture of diversity," we understand these words, smugly, as code for some racial affirmative action by which we incorporate the rising number of persons of color into the academic mainstream. Although I am no sociologist and defer mostly to those who are better number-crunchers than I am, I argue, on the basis of observation at Harvard and elsewhere over these thirty years, that the chief beneficiaries of these changed and anti-elite admissions policies have been the children of the largely white non-Eastern American middle class, students who in another day would never have considered applying to the elite Eastern colleges and universities or been considered by them. Not all of the people now coming into the bloodstream of higher education were necessarily prepared to leave their values questions at home or to reject the faith and piety of Mom and Dad, if Mom and Dad had any to reject. Add to this the new constituency of those who come from truly secular homes, for whom religious belief remains a thing to be discovered when in college and safely away from the environment of such homes, and you have a recipe for what could be called, at the end of the 1970s, the "recovery of belief."

Most of us who were religious professionals on college campuses at the beginning of the 1970s were under the baleful influence of the diminishing religious expectations anticipated by the theories of secularization, of which my colleague Harvey Cox was the prophet in his 1965 trend-describing book *The Secular City*. Cox and I both arrived at Harvard Divinity School in the fall of that year, he as the newest and brightest star on the faculty and I as a first-year student. Because we were both American Baptists, I suspect, I was assigned to him as a student advisee, but since he was so popular and in demand around the world because of the nerve that his book had struck, I saw little of him. We divinity students in those days were far too busy learning Greek and Hebrew and sitting at the feet of our demanding professors to speculate much on the fact that we were preparing for service in the Christian Church, an institution that would likely either not be there or would be changed beyond all recognition by the time we were ready to take our places in it. *The Secular City* was but the first trump that led to such other titles as *The Uncomfortable Pew, The Suburban Captivity of the Churches*, and ultimately to *The Death of God*. God's demise was officially confirmed not by the so-called death-of-God theologians, who gave a name to this theological windstorm, but by *Time* magazine, that weather vane of American culture, which featured "The Death of God" as its Good Friday cover story.

In June 1968, I was ordained to the ministry, a few days after I had taken my theological degree from Harvard Divinity School. I remember one of my college friends saying to me at the party following my ordination service, "I hope you are prepared to do something else, as in a short time I don't think there will be much ministry for you." I think it was meant as friendly counsel, a word to the wise. Fortunately for me, I thought, I was not going into the church, but off to teach history at Tuskegee Institute in Alabama, where there would always be a need for teachers and I would not be caught in the vocational "downsizing"—a word not yet concocted—that would eventually eliminate the ministry into which I had just been ordained.

So, when I arrived back at Harvard in 1970 to take up a post as assistant in the University church, even though I was grateful for the job, I asked my senior, Charles Price, then Preacher to the University, why, with so little to do, he needed an assistant. He replied simply that it was a lonely job and he craved company in it; and I joined him gladly. I suspect we were silently agreed that we would go down with the ship, for, thinking that we were at the end of an era, neither of us could imagine that we were actually at the beginning of a long cycle of renewal and discovery.

The signs, however, were there. One of the few public lectures I remember from that period was given by Professor B. Davie Napier, the very popular dean of Stanford Chapel, who came to Harvard at Dr. Price's invitation to give the William Belden Noble Lectures. He called his rather poorly attended series "To Unbelieving Believers," and I remember thinking that it was wishful thinking. I remember as well that the new president of Harvard, Derek Bok, himself a Stanford man, was obliged to introduce the lecturer, and later confessed himself mildly embarrassed by the pieties uttered in the face of secular reality.

This disapprobation notwithstanding, in retrospect I think Napier was on to something. He understood that an appeal to a pre-modern, pre-secular faith was not likely to succeed on the kind of campus that he and I served, yet he was also aware that we were serving an increasingly sophisticated and spiritually dissatisfied constituency of people who were neither easily persuaded by the old pieties nor easily seduced by the secularities widely presumed to be replacing them.

It would, however, not be a theologian or even a preacher who would describe the banalities of modernity and predict the future shape of the return of the sacred. It would be the eminent secular scholar Daniel Bell, professor of sociology at Harvard, who, in his 1977 seminal article "The Return of the Sacred: The Argument About the Future of Religion," would explain how we had arrived at what might be called the paralysis and death of disbelief, and who would venture an opinion as to what might rise to replace disbelief. Curiously, while the clergy and much of the religious establishment were still dealing with the implications of a theory of secularization that helped to provide useful explanations of the decreasing appeal of "mainline" American religion, sociologists such as Bell were responding to what they perceived in the culture as a new religious sensibility.

By 1977, Daniel Bell's credentials as a prophet of social change had long been secure. In 1973, for example, he published *The Coming of Post-Industrial Society: A Venture in Social Forecasting.* In his review of the book, upon its republication in 1999, entitled "Why Daniel Bell Keeps Getting It Right," Daniel Lind, in the *Los Angeles Times Book Review* of August 15, 1999, wrote:

> Today it has become commonplace to observe that we live in a post-industrial society in which the old ideologies of left and right are moribund. None of this was obvious in 1973, when Daniel Bell published *The Coming of Post-Industrial Society: A Venture in Social Forecasting.* Reissued by Basic Books, with a new 30,000-word foreword by the author, *The Coming of Post-Industrial Society* is that rarest of things, a book the passage of time has made more timely, and cries out for a fresh consideration on the eve of the 21st century.

Now that we are into the twenty-first century, the same can be said of Bell's 1977 article "The Return of the Sacred." In describing our cultural discontents and our rediscovered and never fully suppressed need to believe, few have gotten it more right more often than has Daniel Bell. He begins his essay with this historical analysis:

> From the end of the eighteenth to the middle of the nineteenth century almost every Enlightenment thinker expected religion to disappear in the twentieth century. The belief was based on the

power of reason. Religion was associated with superstition, fetishism, unprovable beliefs, a form of fear which used as a protection against other fears—a form of security one might associate with the behavior of children—and which they believed in fact had arisen in the "childhood" of the human race.[3]

The future held the unbinding of Promethean man who would "leap from the kingdom of necessity to the kingdom of freedom." From the end of the nineteenth century to the middle of the twentieth century, Bell went on to observe, most sociological thinkers "expected religion to disappear by the onset of the twenty-first century."

It did not disappear, however, a fact that on the surface of the culture was difficult to discern. That religion was a premodern phenomenon that simply could not survive the demands and delights of modernity had so long been the conventional wisdom of those who defined the conventional wisdom, that the death of religion as a credible force, at least in Western society, had become entrenched as an article of faith in the secular credo. The so-called American religious revival of the 1950s in the age of Norman Vincent Peale, Billy Graham, and Bishop Fulton J. Sheen was seen by theologian Paul Tillich as fundamentally shallow; and by the late 1960s it was seen by many mainline Protestant thinkers as a "false dawn." By the early 1970s, as Bell was formulating his ideas on the postindustrial society and life after the death of the age of ideology, pundits were describing "mainline" religion as "sideline" religion, and the trinity of rationalism, materialism, and individualism would be declared on their way to inevitable victory. Religion, in its defensive mode and quite prepared to believe the accounts of its own imminent demise, sought to make itself more relevant to the age that presumably was about to destroy it. It wanted to become more rather than less rational, it took the material world more rather than less seriously, and above all it wished to see itself and to be seen by others as with the times, whatever they were, rather than as against them. Transcendence was suspect, authority distrusted, and the mystical made sensible. Otherworldliness, long a central concept in the religious imagination, was considered morally irresponsible, and personal piety a form of self-indulgence.

Within this context of urgent self-reappraisal, many of the churches sought their earthly salvation in liturgical revision, stimulated by the reforming zeal of Pope John XXIII and Vatican II. The language of "Thee" and "Thou" became the language of "you," and in the Episcopal Church, as one of my parishioners once harshly put it, the seventeenth-century *Book of Common Prayer* became the "book of options." For many people religion was no longer a discipline or a way of life, but rather the subject of its own discourse: inward, self-absorbed, and anxious. This was the period of the famous fork-in-the-road joke about religion: at a fork in the road when one sign points to "Heaven" and the other to "A Discussion About Heaven," most people will follow the second sign.

The anxieties about religion by the religious were not only a response to an internal loss of confidence, but also a response to the apparent triumphalism of a self-confident secular culture that said, in effect, "Either join us or be left behind." Beneath the apparent malaise of the religious and the braggadocio of the secular, however, lurked a profound cultural insecurity and dissatisfaction that only a little provocation might bring to the surface. Bell cites the countercultural historian Theodore Roszak on this period: "America in the mid-seventies . . . is launched on 'the biggest introspective binge any society in history has undergone.'"[4]

In the wake of religion, modernity had produced what Bell called "alternatives" to religion. Freed from the restraints of traditional religious belief, the nineteenth and twentieth centuries produced substitutes for the modalities of religious belief; and the failure of two of these substitutes, aestheticism and political religions, "opened up the beginnings of various searches for new religious answers." These "new searches," Bell argued, are the result of the exhaustion of modernity's ambition to replace God and religion:

I believe that the "ground impulses" behind aestheticism and political religions are exhausted. These were the impulses to abolish God and assume that Man could take over the powers he had ascribed to God and now sought to claim for himself. This is the common bond between Marx and Nietzsche and the link between the aesthetic and political movements of modernity.[5]

Bell enunciated his "theory of exhaustion" in 1977. At the 1978 Harvard Commencement, Aleksandr Solzhenitsyn, the then extremely fashionable Russian exile, would confound his audience by speaking of the moral and spiritual "exhaustion of the West," a phrase that was, for those of that self-satisfied audience who "got it," not so much prophetic as it was annoying.

At the level of social structure and culture, Bell observed, "the world has been secularized and profaned," and in the place of these failed and "exhausted" ideologies, which had attracted the secular and intimidated the religious for so long, would arise a "return of the sacred, the rise of new religious modes." Of that Bell had no doubt. What will these "new religions" be like?

If there are to be new religions—and I think they will arise—they, contrary to previous experience, will return to the past, to seek tradition and to search for those threads which can give a person a set of ties that place him in the continuity of the dead and the living and those still to be born. Unlike romanticism, it will not be a turn to nature, and unlike modernity, it will not be the involuted self; it will be the resurrection of memory.[6]

I did not know Professor Bell when in 1970 I went to Harvard, and this remarkable essay of 1977 would be written three years after I had been given charge of The Memorial Church. Only many years later would I discover that this prescient sociologist was explaining the reality of my own experience. It was my sense that, despite the immediate pressures to conform to the secularizing trends of mainstream Christianity in the mid-1970s, the action, as it were, was in rediscovery and recovery of a faith and a liturgical style that was not dependent upon the politically and liturgically correct demands of the day. It was my view that faith in its best sense was more an act of remembrance than of anticipation, and that what we remembered and how we remembered it liberated us from the tyranny of the moment and its almost instinctive submission to the culture of modernity. For the university's church, therefore, I cultivated an essentially conservative liturgical posture that I hoped would be hospitable to an evangelical understanding of the gospel of Jesus Christ—good news for the secular and the confused. At some considerable cost, I resisted the demand that our worship and work define themselves in terms of the relentless demands of secular modernity, which landed me in trouble with the rising tide of feminism, the liturgical renewalists, and with those who felt attention to doctrine and the continuity of the faith a capitulation to a despised Christian particularism that to many, both religious and secular, seemed inappropriate in a great secular and pluralist university. At the same time, I felt that the particularly Christian, indeed Protestant, identity of the church should not be compromised in favor of some neutral "house of good works," but should be the unassimilated lump in the midst of a University that would just as soon wish it were not there. This position naturally won me enemies in many quarters. Finally I argued that the church need neither apologize for its particular profile at the center of the University nor shrink from its role as resident alien critic of so much of what the modern university was becoming. When I was "inducted"—Harvard's peculiar phrase for "installed"—into my office in 1974, I was advised by my friends that I was inheriting an anachronism, and that therefore I should keep a low profile lest, if noticed, the church and I antagonize those who suffered our existence only because we seemed so harmless. My office, which had once been styled with the grandilo-

quent nineteenth-century title of "Preacher to the University," was now
demoted and parochialized merely to "Minister in The Memorial
Church." Literally, I was put in my place by an unknowing and quies-
cent establishment for whom "religion at Harvard" was an embarrass-
ing oxymoron.

That intentional humiliation notwithstanding, I found myself in the
middle of a phenomenon to which I could not give voice, but one that
Daniel Bell would shortly describe with prophetic clarity. He suggested
that what he called the "new religions" would be of three kinds, the first
of which he called "moralizing religion": "Its roots and strength are in
a fundamentalist faith, evangelical and scourging, emphasizing sin and
the turning away from the Whore of Babylon."[7]

Anticipating what was to many the surprising rise of fundamentalism and the conservative, evangelical appeal in modern American
religion, Bell suggested that this movement was the result of the "exhaustion of modernism and the emptiness of contemporary culture."[8]
Those who would be sympathetic to these more conservative trends in
American religion, Bell observed, were usually to be found among
"farmers, lower middle-class, small-town artisans, and the like," the
very cultural constituency long underrepresented in the elite institutions of higher education, who increasingly were the beneficiaries of
those institutions' aggressive ambitions for cultural diversity in admissions. These people brought their evangelical cultures with them, and
they were not prepared to be morphed into the cultured despisers of
religion.

What Bell calls the recovery of tradition, Bell suggested would find
"its adherents in the intellectual and professional classes." The characteristic of this element would be, in his word, "redemptive," represent-
ing both a "retreat from the excesses of modernity" and the growth of
"mediating institutions," in reaction against central government, large
and inefficient bureaucracies, and what he calls "the megastructures of
organization." The distrust of federalism, the decline in denominational

loyalty, the distrust of the public school and the increasing popularity of home schooling, and the impetus toward volunteerism, all formed a new basis for caring and support. Bell does not mention them, but he certainly anticipated them.

The third form of this religious renewal of which he speaks "will be a return to some mythic and mystical modes of thought. The world has become too scientific and drab. Men want a sense of wonder and mystery."[9] I remember being astonished by the popularity among student evangelicals of the more fantastical works of C. S. Lewis and J. R. R. Tolkien. I understood the intellectual and dogmatic appeal of Lewis, who made belief respectable among easily intimidated evangelicals, but his *Narnia Chronicles* and the Hobbit cycle of his fellow "inkling" made no sense to me at the time. The Harry Potter series was yet to be conceived. I was, however, fascinated by the large percentage of "hard science" concentrators at Harvard, the chemists, physicists, biologists, astronomers, and mathematicians, who were professed members of the most evangelical of the undergraduate religious groups, and who saw no conflict between the demands of their intellectual disciplines and their premodern theologies. Interestingly enough, they seemed to find no conflict between religion and science, and they lived comfortably if not always compatibly in both worlds. What Bell calls the "mythic modes" come from the "pre-scientific and pre-conceptual roots" of our past and will transform them. These modes seem at first glance strangely non-Western in conception, but what was striking to Bell in 1977, and in retrospect incredibly prescient as we look back on the nearly quarter of a century since the publication of his 1977 essay, is that the West has with ever-increasing scrutiny been looking toward the East ever since: "What is striking—in the serious realm of philosophers, poets, physicists and artists—is that the journey [toward the East] now is being undertaken."[10]

What is clearly at work here is not the invention of something new, but the recovery, at least in part, of something long lost and now, in its rediscovery, adapted to the old needs of a new age. Bell said that "The thread of culture—and religion—is memory;" and I have long said that faith is more remembrance than mere anticipation. A sociologist doubtless would not wish to be anticipated by a mere poet, and yet T. S. Eliot, that desiccated Anglican confection so annoying to the secular American conceits of the mid-twentieth century, famously said in "Little Gidding," written some thirty years before Bell's essay:

> *We shall not cease from exploration,*
> *And the end of all our exploring*
> *Will be to arrive where we started,*
> *And know the place for the first time.*[11]

Bell understood that we stand at the end of a long era and also at the beginning of something new: "The exhaustion of modernism, the aridity of communist life, the tedium of the unrestrained self, and the meaninglessness of the monolithic political chants, all indicate that a long era is coming to a close."[12] What will take the place of these exhausted convictions he does not know for certain, but as he believes that the "existential questions of culture are inescapable," he concludes: "I feel that some new efforts to regain a sense of the sacred point to the direction in which our culture—or its most sentient representatives—will move."[13]

Looking back over the period from 1977 to these opening years of the twenty-first century, even the most cautious of us would have to concede that what Daniel Bell anticipated has largely come to pass. Again, in the words of Phillips Brooks a century ago: "So dark in this world is a long row of cultivated men . . . to whom there has come no fire of devotion, who stand in awe and reverence before no wisdom greater than their own."

The disquietude of modernity has not cast us into a perdition of nihilism, the despair out of which the mid-twentieth-century secular intellectuals found it impossible to emerge. Faith has acquired a new and urgent credibility that invites a reconsideration of that which not so long ago seemed permanently unavailable to us. A return to faith seemed as impossible as the return of Adam and Eve to the Garden of Eden. We remember that upon their expulsion from that place, God "placed at the east of the garden of Eden cherubim, and a flaming sword which turned every way, to keep the way of the tree of life" (Genesis 3:24, KJV).

It has been the very "success" of modernity that has cultivated a longing for a wisdom greater than our own, and it is of this that the *Boston Globe* columnist David Warsh, writing in May 2000, spoke when he wrote of what he called:

> the maldistribution of spiritual assets. A sense of purpose, family ways, and the ability to resist hedonism are the sorts of resources that today are in short supply. The common denominator among the faiths is a determination to make the attributes of good character more widely available to all, to deepen social capital.[14]

Faith is not some abstract theological construct confined to an ancient formulary of the Christian faith. It is the way by which people make sense of a world that alone, on its own terms, makes no sense. Faith, in this sense, in the words of Paul's Letter to the Hebrews, makes us conscious of things we cannot see (11:1).

Surrounded, as we have been for so long, by the things we can see, the things we wish to possess, and the things that possess us, we are not surprised to discover the profound sense of dissatisfaction that haunts us. This may not be a revival of religion in the classic American sense of revival, despite the claims of some that we are passing through one of our periodic American "great awakenings," but the barrenness of life in the midst of a culture of prosperity suggests that we may have discovered the truth of E. F. Schumacher's provocative view that "the modern experiment to live without religion has failed." In *A Guide for the Perplexed*, he has written:

> It may conceivably be possible to live without churches; but it is not possible to live without religion, that is, without systematic work to keep in contact with and develop towards Higher Levels than those of "ordinary life," with all its pleasure and pain, sensation and gratification, refinement of crudity—whatever it may be.[15]

Faith Under Fire

Faith in "modern man's omnipotence" has produced a crisis of belief in modernity's ability to deliver the goods of peace and happiness. At the end of World War I, Europe lay in ruins, and the flowers of Western civilization, the great cultures of Germany, France, and England, were enfeebled and bankrupt, done in by their own hands. The brightest and best of civilized minds cultivated a technology and science whose harvest was havoc and despair, and beneath the roar of the "Roaring Twenties" could be heard the psychic heresy attributed to Alfred North Whitehead, that "all our progress is but improved means to unimproved ends." Perhaps not since 410, when the Romans wondered how so great a civilization as theirs could have been laid low by the sack and capture of Rome at the hands of Alaric and the Goths and Slavs, had there been so self-conscious a loss of cultural confidence. Responding to this psychological shock, the Romans had blamed the Christians for seducing the people away from their duties toward their gods, who ordinarily would have protected them from such humiliation.

It was in response to this scapegoating of the Christians that St. Augustine wrote his epic book *The City of God*. To him, the Romans had misplaced their faith in the false gods so celebrated by the pagans, who could neither deliver prosperity nor deliver them from adversity.

The only hope, argued Augustine, was a faith in the Christian God, who tested and formed his people by adversity in this life, the earthly city, in order to prepare them to live fully and faithfully in the life to come, the heavenly city, or the city of God. Twentieth-century Western civilization might not yet be ready to place its entire faith in the city of God despite Augustine's long entreaty to do so, but its faith in its own earthly city was deeply shattered and would undergo even more devastating challenges as the century wore on. Faith, as Augustine would point out over and over again, was forged not out of prosperity, but out of adversity. That was a hard lesson to take in the fifth century, and even harder in the twentieth century, where the most powerful and successful worldly cultures were accustomed to bingeing on prosperity, victory, and revenge.

One who knew and experienced the faith that is forged out of adversity was the German theologian and preacher Helmut Thielicke, who, in the immediate aftermath of Germany's defeat, published in 1948 an essay he called "The Reality of the Demonic." It has a compelling history. In 1941, Thielicke, who had already gained a reputation as a Christian threat to National Socialism, was forbidden by the Nazis to speak or travel without strict supervision. He was deprived of his professorship, forbidden to publish, and placed under house arrest in a small city in the interior of the country. He was, however, permitted to give one public lecture a week in the cathedral at Stuttgart, where it was thought that he could do little harm and perhaps calm the fears of the German inhabitants, to whom the reality of the war was being brought home by Allied bombing raids. How would he use his limited and closely watched opportunity? He wrote:

> The Nazi tyranny has not only pitched us into a ghastly war which every day is destroying our men, our brothers, and sons on the battlefields; it is not only exercising the most monstrous reign of terror within the country, but it has also attacked and desecrated

everything that is holy to us. It has introduced pagan gods and is bent upon using them to drive out Jesus Christ. It interprets all of life, it interprets birth, death, history, and eternity in a way that is different from what we learned as Christians and also found to be true and reliable. This has brought bewilderment and confusion to many people, and besides, this godless interpretation of life has made an impression upon not a few.[16]

He determined that the only form of opposition available to him was to incite the people to a remembrance of the faith they had once known in Jesus Christ: "I wanted to help them to see their life and the course of history from the standpoint of Christ"; and so he decided to use his permitted public weekly lecture to instruct the people in Luther's small catechism. This he did from 1941 to 1944, while Germany was literally tumbling down around him.

His audience each week comprised nearly three thousand people: "Workers and businessmen, students and professors, soldiers and generals, Nazi functionaries (naturally, in civilian clothes!) and Jews, Dutch compulsory laborers (they had been deported to Germany and I gathered them together secretly), and sometimes whole classes from the schools."[17] Even during the air raids and the bombing of the cathedral itself, the lectures continued, moving from safe place to safe place. The local newspapers, increasingly fearful of the Nazis, eventually declined to advertise the lectures, allowing only a small notice, which read "Thursday, 8:P.M.T." Thielicke described what he was doing as "Teaching theology in the face of death": "There the only thing that was of any help at all was the gospel itself. Everything else simply dissolved into thin air. We were living only upon the substance of our faith."[18]

It might not seem "heroic" for a Christian theology professor to lecture on theology in the middle of the war, for as he noted, "It is, after all, quite possible to calmly philosophize about good and evil. The demonic, however, is that which is utterly menacing." He described living in Germany in this period as living in times out of joint, for even though the external "order" created and imposed by dictatorship prevailed, demons had been let loose and the constraints of conscience had been abandoned, which led to chaos and disorientation. Enlightened cultures, accustomed to consigning the demonic to some precritical age, are left defenseless when the reality of the demon appears in their midst. How can you protect against something you no longer believe exists? The denial of the reality of the demonic is the first victory the demonic obtains over its victims.

The weakness of the modern mind, Thielicke argues, is that it becomes blind to demons and is therefore incapable of recognizing one of the fundamental factors in history and incapable of discerning history as a whole. "Anybody who would understand history must be in possession of the category of the demonic."[19] The demonic, first of all, is not an exterior force alien to humankind. "We must not look outward but inward into our own heart," he argues, "if we would fully understand what Luther called 'the Old Adam,' who is actively at work in us, like an enemy agent in the interior of a country, giving information by radio to the hostile power and directing it to the weak spots in the front."[20] Under any circumstances this is a telling metaphor, but it is all the more so considering that it was written by a German theologian in German and addressed in 1943 to German Christians under fire.

Philosophers and theologians like to argue about the origins of evil. Where does it come from? How does it enter the world? Thielicke reminds us that the Bible spends no time on such explanations. In the Bible, evil is simply "there": "The Bible faces this brutal and physical fact that the enemy has broken into the land. I stand in utmost peril. This is not the place for me to philosophize; here I must fall to and fight. This is an emergency that leaves me no time for reflection."[21]

Perhaps such urgent teaching could be promulgated only within the crucible of a cruel and brutal war, but the concepts precede that particular context, a fact not lost upon those who have understood the good life as fundamentally one of opposition to a perverted and partial truth. To seek after goodness and virtue in this world is an act of defiance against the powers and principalities both within and without, in which the faith is unleashed under adversity, first by remembering it as the evidence of things not seen, and then as a rebuke to the things that are.

Faith as Experience

Not long ago, the *New York Times* carried notice of the death of the Reverend Ernest Gordon, who from 1955 to 1981 was dean of Princeton Chapel. Although I, alas, never met Dr. Gordon, I certainly knew a great deal about him and admired his long ministry at Princeton. Often he would send Princeton students to me when they came for graduate work at Harvard or to live in the Boston area, and I always encouraged Harvard people in the vicinity of Princeton to sit at the feet of Dr. Gordon. He was a tall, imposing Scot, with that magnificent Scottish accent with which God would speak were he trying to sound like Sean Connery. Gordon preached in the days of compulsory chapel at Princeton and gave good value to those who had to hear him, and even after compulsory chapel was abandoned in the late 1960s, he never lacked for a large and enthusiastic congregation.

Part of this had to do with the fact that he was a genuine celebrity, a survivor of one of the worst of the Japanese prison camps in World War II. The story of his imprisonment, of how he found his faith under the worst of human conditions and of his ability to forgive those who had tortured and nearly killed him, was first told in his 1962 book, *Through the Valley of the Kwai*. A movie based on his life and book, titled *To End All Wars*, is scheduled for release in the spring of 2002.

Of the brutality of Dr. Gordon's captivity, he said, "We were treated worse than animals. The conditions were worse than you could imagine."

Bayonettings, beatings, and beheadings were routine, and the horrific treatment of prisoners of war at the hands of the Japanese, who were notoriously barbaric, could not be exaggerated. Enduring all of this, he and the other prisoners were forced to watch the public executions, by beheading, of men who had made unsuccessful escape attempts. Dr. Gordon's account of one of these beheadings was printed in his obituary:

> As he was marched before a Japanese officer for beheading, the soldier seemed unafraid, even cheerful. He was allowed to read briefly from a Bible. "Cheer up," he said, seeing the distress in his comrades' faces. "It isn't as bad as all that. I'll be all right . . ." He knelt, bared his neck, and the samurai sword flashed in the sun.[22]

He often said that it was in that hellish environment, where he lived from his capture in 1942 until the end of the war in 1945, that he had found his salvation: "Faith thrives when there is no hope but God. It is luxury and success that makes men greedy." Hate and the thirst for revenge were what kept many a man alive: "We hated the Japanese and we would willingly have killed them, torn them apart, if they had fallen into our hands." It was not revenge or hatred or violence that ruled the day, however, for in that place of utter hopelessness faith was formed. In the very last days of the war when, on June 24, 1945, Allied bombing at last destroyed the infamous bridge on the River Kwai, Gordon saw a group of badly wounded Japanese soldiers while he and the other prisoners were being transferred to the hills outside Bangkok. Seeing their suffering, he could not hate them. Were he to let himself be consumed by hate, he thought, he would be wasting the life that had been spared him, and he would be untrue to the faith that had sustained him. When the war ended and he was liberated, Gordon determined to study for the ministry. Ordained in the Church of Scotland in 1950, he soon came to the United States; and in 1955 he began his remarkable career at Princeton.

Here was a man who, when he preached about faith, knew what he was talking about. He was, as St. Paul said in another connection, his own credential, and it was the power of his witness to faith, and not simply his celebrity status as a survivor of wartime horror, that made his preaching so powerful. Dr. Gordon's faith had been forged in the crucible of adversity: he was himself the evidence of things not seen.

Substance and Evidence

The great Canadian literary critic Northrop Frye spent the academic year 1974–75 in residence at Harvard as the Charles Eliot Norton Professor of Poetry, the highest humanistic distinction the University has to offer. In addition to his formal public lectures before capacity audiences, he gave an enormously popular undergraduate lecture course on the Bible. Despite the fact that he enjoyed near iconic stature, he appeared to be anything but charismatic, as he was shy and socially uneasy with students, he made little small talk, and even his silences were intimidating. Although he had been ordained in 1936 as a minister in the United Church of Canada and was given to some preaching, it was primarily as a critic of English literature that he was known throughout the literary world. His theological credentials surely played little if any part in Harvard's invitation to the prestigious Norton professorship, and to some people they may have proven a disqualification. How could someone who "believed" in the Bible lecture on it with objectivity?

I decided to ask him to preach in The Memorial Church, and to my great delight he agreed to do so. He was to preach in November, and for all of the Sundays of the fall term preceding his date in our pulpit, with a combination of pleasure and intimidation I saw him sitting with Mrs. Frye in our pews and taking his part in the services. On Sunday, November 17, 1974, he preached a sermon titled "Substance and

Evidence," taking as his text the famous first verse of Hebrews 11: "Faith is the substance of things hoped for, the evidence of things not seen" (KJV). A capacity congregation had come to hear him, including many of my colleagues in the English department who were not ordinarily seen in church, except when attending the memorial services of their colleagues.

I remember wondering what he was going to do with that old chestnut of a text. He began by reminding us that faith, hope, and love are the classical theological virtues, but that their importance consists in the fact that they are not qualities natural to the human condition:

> We're not born loving: we're born sentimental and gregarious, and vociferously demanding to be loved. We're not born with hope: we're born with an instinct for survival; and we're certainly not born with faith: we're born credulous, gullible, and superstitious.[23]

We all from time to time have a need to believe in something beyond the world of our senses. This need to believe is not necessarily religious, for it can be a belief in a political or social theory, and we "take things on faith" often because we are passive in accepting the authority of the conviction. Faith is easily confused with credulity, and credulity is often induced by an unquestioning loyalty to ideology, which it is more trouble to doubt than to believe. Religion is not the only place where this happens. Frye cites left-wingers who had so much faith in the ideals of Soviet Russia that they steadily maintained there was no terrorism in Stalin's regime, or that if there was, it was a necessity for the best. He cites right-wingers who refused to believe that Joseph McCarthy ever victimized an innocent person, or if he did, that was a necessity for the best. "This kind of faith," he argued, "is not a virtue; it's a mental disease."[24]

Faith, for Frye, is the actualization of what we hope for: "Faith is the realization, the bringing into being, of what we do achieve." This is how he reads the King James Version of Hebrews 11:1, "Faith is the substance of things hoped for, the evidence of things not seen." Nor is it to be equated with mere opinion, what we think about something. "If I'm right, then faith is not anything we say or believe, or that we think we believe, or that we believe we believe. *What we really believe is what our actions show that we believe.*"[25] When we realize that faith is not what we believe but what we do, then we have to take some account of our actions. Given what we profess, we may just have to change how we live, and that may mean that faith, in this sense of doing, is costly and risky. If our faith demands high ideals, values, and beliefs that we respect and want for ourselves, then we will have to live into our beliefs, or live up to our faith. Faith is thus neither an abstraction nor a consent to a formula of convictions. Faith is the expression of a vision that we then act out. In order for doctors to be good doctors, for example, they must have not only the knowledge of medicine, but a vision of good health. What they do reflects that vision: they do not have faith "in medicine"; rather, their practice of medicine *is* the expression of their faith.

Faith is also the evidence of things not seen. For Frye, the best way to think about this is the way he believes the author of Hebrews uses the word "evidence." "They think of it [evidence] . . . as something they can't see but know to exist," like air. We can't see air, but we know it is there and that it is the medium for the visible world. If we could see the air, it would be as mist or fog, and it would thus obscure what we ordinarily can see. The works of faith are visible because the source of faith is invisible. Reminding us that the Hebrew word for "vanity" means "fog," "vapor," or "mist," Frye argues that we are meant to see clearly through the fog. Faith is thus not the opposite of works, rendering moot that old and difficult debate as to which is better, faith or works. Faith is works that are beliefs in action, for as a person believes, so does he or she act. The believer makes the God who cannot be seen in the world real in the world by the visibility of the acts of God done by those who believe, who have faith in God. Faith, then, is God's love actualized in the acts of those who have faith in the love of God. "The love of God," he concludes, "is the revelation to man that he can, if he tries, find something at the centre of his life that is not only immortal but invulnerable."[26]

The argument was dense and unaccompanied by the usual preacherly rhetoric of aphorisms and soothing stories to make it go down more easily. Frye was, after all, dealing with the nuances of texts in a university community where he assumed that such austere precision would be appreciated. Much of the sermon, I fear, was lost in the single hearing. Only upon reading it did I come away with the refreshing realization that faith was not simply believing in the impossible, but translating the impossible love of God into our actions: "Our faith is what we do to help bring this vision into the world."[27]

The Faith of Others

I remember few sermons from my days as a student in the Harvard Divinity School, which is understandable for two reasons: it is nearly forty years ago that I listened to them, and the standard of faculty preaching was not memorable. Over the years, however, I have remembered one sermon, preached in 1965 or 1966 by Gordon D. Kaufman, a Mennonite and a professor of theology known for his academic rigor. He took as his text Luke 5:17–26, which is the account of the paralytic man brought by his friends to Jesus, with the most dramatic part of the healing story the resourcefulness of the friends. There were so many people present in the house where Jesus was preaching that the friends could not get in, and so they climbed up onto the roof, removed some tiles, and through the resulting hole lowered their friend on his pallet right to Jesus' feet—thus going straight from the periphery of the crowd to its center and doubtless interrupting the proceedings. If they had wanted to attract Jesus' attention, they had found the most effective way to do it, and Jesus, when he saw their faith, said to the paralytic, "Man, your sins are forgiven you" (Luke 5:20). The Pharisees and scribes then argue about the authority by which Jesus could forgive sins, and Jesus settles the argument by both forgiving the man's sins and healing his illness, with the famous words, "Rise, take up your bed and go home." The paralytic did so and went home, leaving the crowd amazed and saying, "We have seen strange things today" (Luke 5:26).

All of this is a reasonably conventional reading. What Professor Kaufman wanted us to note was the fact that Jesus acted because he was impressed with the faith of the paralytic's friends who had brought him for healing: "When he saw their faith . . ." Nothing is mentioned of the faith of the paralytic himself. It was the persistent faith of his friends, a persistence expressed by their having carried him around on his couch and not been put off by crowds, and by the ingenuity of their approach through the roof. They believed enough in the power of Jesus to act upon their faith in a vivid and persistent way, and because of this expression of their faith, good things happened to the paralytic, for he was both forgiven and healed. Faith here was sacramental, the outward and visible sign of an inward and spiritual grace, the expression of a conviction. The point the professor was trying to make was that our faith may make a difference for good in the life of someone else. Had the friends simply believed that Jesus could heal, had they just hoped for the healing of their friend, nothing would have happened; but they acted upon their convictions, translated their faith into deeds, and made real the vision. As Northrop Frye would say: "What we really believe is what our actions show that we believe."

In the *Enchiridion*, Augustine's little handbook on faith, hope, and love, he says that the objects of these three theological virtues are "What we should believe," "What we should hope for;" and "What we should love." Now to hope, and finally to love, we turn in pursuit of the good life.

CHAPTER 10

HOPE

UNREASONABLE AND INDISPENSABLE

*For we are saved by hope: but hope that is seen is not hope; for
what a man seeth, why doth he yet hope for?*
ROMANS 8:24 (KJV)

*As long as matters are really hopeful, hope is a mere flattery
or platitude; it is only when everything is hopeless that hope
begins to be a strength at all. Like all the Christian virtues, it
is as unreasonable as it is indispensable.*
G. K. CHESTERTON

Profiles in Hope

Mother Teresa, Daddy King, Nelson Mandela, Desmond Tutu, Billy
Graham: what have they in common? They are moral celebrities, profiles in hope, and their very names are synonymous with all that is
hopeful and good in the world. In an age of pygmies, they stand out as
giants. College students are easily written off as cynical, indifferent, not
easily impressed, moved only by glamour, politics, and money; yet I
have seen Harvard students turn out in vast numbers to be in the presence of such people, who are by their work, witness, and person, in St.
Paul's words, "ensigns of hope."

About a decade ago, Mother Teresa was the chosen speaker at a
Class Day celebration at Harvard, which is usually a riot of frivolity,

self-congratulation, and self-indulgence on the day before Commencement, when thousands of students, parents, and friends assemble on a June afternoon in front of The Memorial Church to be entertained by the speaker. The Class Committee has in recent years gone out of its way to try to attract outstanding name-recognition speakers so that the students will not have to explain to Mom and Dad who the speaker is. In the days before the late 1960s, the Class Day speaker was usually the class's favorite Harvard figure who was invited to give a fond farewell; but ever since the "troubles," the general consensus has been that the last thing Harvard students want is a last word from a professor. So, since then the search has gone out for the biggest name that prestige can buy, as the speaker is neither paid nor presented an honorary degree. When the late Barbara Jordan of Texas, protégé of Lyndon B. Johnson and famous for her diapason-like voice—which she used to good advantage in the Watergate hearings, at the height of her fame— was invited to Class Day, at first she accepted, for the invitation was, after all, from Harvard. When she learned that this was an invitation to Class Day, however, and not to Commencement, she declined and waited for the better offer, which subsequently came. It was said that in the year Mother Teresa was chosen, she was actually second choice to the perennial favorite, Woody Allen, who, as regularly as he is invited, declines to accept.

Before she was to address the class, I spent a few minutes with Mother Teresa. Though gracious, she had little to say, or at least not to me, and I learned that small talk was not one of her specialties. When I asked her, "Where have you just been?" she replied, "I do not know." When I asked about her next stop, she replied again, "I do not know." When I commented on the many students who were eager to work with her in Calcutta, she said nothing at all. Realizing that I had made a statement and not asked a question, I reformulated it as a question and asked, "Does it not please you that so many Harvard students are eager to work with you?" and she replied, "It pleases Jesus." I thought that was a good point at which to stop, and for the next ten minutes not another word was exchanged between us. When at last the university marshal arrived to escort Mother Teresa to the platform and whispered to me, "I bet this has been a very meaningful encounter," I responded, "It was unbelievable."

When she appeared on the platform before the howling throng, however, she was at no loss for words. She told them that what the world needed was the love of God, and then she told them that in order for them to better do what God wanted from them, they should be chaste. Now, chastity was not a subject of frequent discourse in Harvard Yard in those days, and most people at first thought that she was speaking of some form of pursuit. Only as Mother Teresa went on, growing more and more impassioned, did it become clear that she was indeed speaking of chastity, purity, and abstinence, of sublimating the flesh for the spirit.

Many people were not sure how to respond to that, although a lot of parents were pleasantly surprised. Catholics were reminded that although she was a "living saint," the almost universal title accorded her, she was also a real nun, and that that was the way real nuns still think and talk. One does not "boo" a living saint even when she speaks of disagreeable moral absolutes and, as one of my secular colleagues was quick to notice, "she certainly got their attention." Rather than the usual professional athlete, corporate motivational speaker, or media darling of politics or entertainment, here was a tough old nun whose sole credential in life was that for Christ's sake she took care of the dying on the streets of Calcutta. In the middle of hopelessness she was a living, breathing, working sign of hope.

When Daddy King came to Harvard, it was to speak in The Memorial Church during the annual university commemoration of his son's birthday, and I was honored to be his host. We had met only once before, in Atlanta, when I was invited to preach the baccalaureate sermon at Spelman College and he was the guest of honor. "I'll have to have you down here to preach, son," he had said with the air of the patriarch that he was; "I'm not without influence around here, you know." My invitation to him came before he could follow through on his to me, and our church was filled to capacity with people come to hear the great man. Here he was, the father of the father of the civil rights movement, large in voice and frame, less nuanced than his son, a Baptist preacher's preacher who had married the boss's daughter and inherited his great pulpit. Now, however, he was up in years and we all knew the burdens he bore, with one son assassinated, another son dead by an untimely accident, and his wife murdered before his eyes by a deranged gunman while she was playing the organ in church.

As he entered the pulpit, the congregation rose as one and burst into an applause that lasted for minutes and that in vain he tried to quell. Finally he succeeded, and he began his sermon by saying, "I don't deserve it, but I won't refuse it because I know why you're doing it." Then he said, "I have no bitterness in my heart." He recited each of the terrible things that had happened to him, and after each, like a mantra, he would say, "but I have no bitterness in my heart." He preached an old-fashioned gospel of love and forgiveness that day, something he must have said a thousand times in his long ministry and something familiar to us all, and yet it was if he and we were speaking and hearing for the first time "The old, old story of unseen things above / of Jesus and his glory / of Jesus and his love." The young people for whom the younger King was a historical figure located somewhere between Abraham Lincoln and Elvis Presley listened to the elder King, this man who knew the segregated South and an indifferent nation, and who had suffered the trials of Job; and they heard him say over and over again, "I have no bitterness in my heart." This was not simply a "forgive and for-get" gesture, for how could a rational man do either? Here was a preacher of hope, preaching the good news that there is more to bad times than bad times: here was hope in hope, as unreasonable as it was indispensable, and the young people heard him gladly.

Desmond Tutu came to us on his way to receive his Nobel Prize in Oslo. A special noonday service had been arranged on a Monday, and a crowd of epic proportions had been on hand for hours before the service was scheduled to begin. Every politician in three counties made a claim for the occasion and it was a media frenzy, but we determined that priority would go to students, and they turned out in large numbers to see this archbishop. He was late, of course, and that only added to the high level of expectation. When he finally did enter the church, he was greeted with the roar of a Worldwide Wrestling Federation crowd on steroids. It was almost impossible to restore order. Tutu was Tutu, however, and he began to speak, compelling the crowd to listen. He asked them what they thought was the most important thing to be done for his people in South Africa. Now this was at the height of the anti-apartheid movement, when sanctions and boycotts were a big deal and the institutional tool of choice was divestment. Harvard was not in the divestment mode, having adopted its own convoluted—some would say self-interested—approach to the problems of being a moral investor, and many had hoped that Tutu would humiliate Harvard by calling for divestment in its own church. He did not, but he did whip the crowd into a rhetorical frenzy by repeating the question: "What is the greatest thing you can do for us?" Finally, he gave the answer: "Pray for us!" What an anticlimax. This was as secular and politically savvy a crowd as could be gathered under the roof of the church at one time, and, to put it mildly, they were not "into" prayer as a method of political coercion.

They couldn't cheer and they dared not "boo," so they sat with mouths agape while Archbishop Tutu taught them that prayer, especially for one's enemies, was the most powerful weapon in the world, and that prayer for one's friends was not a bad thing either. He said that, surrounded as he was every day by symbols of hatred and oppression and people of conspicuous ill will, it was reassuring to him to realize that somewhere, indeed everywhere around the world, an invisible army of the faithful were praying for him: this, he told us, kept both himself and his people going. It slowly dawned on this audience, as it must have slowly dawned upon those who heard Jesus, that this was no ordinary dispenser of good cheer and righteous strategy: here was a man of action, but the substance of his action was prayer. Here was a man fighting a hopeless situation with the only weapon that ultimately wins over hopelessness, which is hope, as unreasonable as it is indispensable.

A footnote: at the end of the long and enthusiastic service, Tutu and I withdrew into the vestry. The archbishop, who had all of his Episcopal regalia on, was drenched in perspiration by the might of his exertions. "Can we now get out of these things?" he asked; and I, eager to please and without a second's hesitation, said, "Yes, Bishop, by all means, let us now divest." There was a split second of charged silence, and then in that voice of high-pitched glee he said, "You said it, not me, my brother!"

When some years later, on Friday, September 18, 1998, President Nelson Mandela came to town, the moral and political victory of South Africa was a well-established fact. He came to the University at the invitation of President Neil Rudenstine, and he was to be honored with an outdoor convocation assembled for the purpose of conferring upon him an honorary degree. Such occasions are rare in Harvard's long history; only George Washington, the Marquis de Lafayette, Winston Churchill, and a handful of others have been similarly honored over the course of more than three hundred fifty years. The ceremony was to take place on a day in September before classes had begun in the fall term, and a Commencement-sized crowd filled the great outdoor Tercentenary Theater in front of The Memorial Church.

The occasion went off without a hitch. The audience was ecstatic and Mandela magnanimous; and there was an electricity in the air that had never been felt before and that was not likely to be felt, or seen, again. In the aftermath and the inevitable "postgame analysis," the students in particular, again usually cynical and with short attention spans for even the greatest of occasions, kept remarking on what it was that had made them feel so elated and so good. Certainly the charisma of the man had played a part—he was "the only real hero in the world today," one student said—and certainly the heroic nature of the struggle and the final death of apartheid without a shot being fired were part of the collective consciousness that lingered for days over Cambridge.

There was more to it than that, however, for there was something about having nearly thirty thousand people gathered in one place, filled with emotion, and moved to high purpose in the presence of one who had given his life in the pursuit of a hope that, to most, for too long had seemed hopeless. Mandela was not an explicitly religious figure: he preached no sermon and he made no moral claims, but he didn't have to, for he made the ordinary and the politically extraordinary seem holy, even sacred. We saw transcendence in him, and it was powerful because it was not a matter of piety, which would have allowed the secular to write it off.

In the intervening time since that extraordinary moment, I have had time to think further about what made that occasion singular. The best sense of it came from a student who had graduated the previous June and at the time of Mandela's September visit was a new student in one of the graduate schools. He said it best: "It wasn't about us, and it wasn't even about him: it was about what he believed in that had saved his life, and saved his country." It was indeed about that persistent, elusive virtue we call hope, as unreasonable as it is indispensable.

Twice in my time I have had the pleasure of hosting Billy Graham as a preacher in The Memorial Church. In 1982, I invited him to preach and conduct a mission at Harvard, which at that time was not the usual thing to do, as Harvard has never really been able to shake the sobriquet "godless Harvard," which had been flung at it in 1886, doubtless by Yale graduates when Harvard was the first of the Ivy League colleges to abandon compulsory attendance at chapel. Billy Graham, the world's most conspicuous Christian preacher, and Harvard, a lion's den for believers, would not seem to be an ideal match. Many Christian evan-gelicals advised Dr. Graham not to come, and many of my colleagues criticized me sharply for having invited him. Everyone, it seemed, would have something to lose if he came. My view was that if Harvard could not stand to hear what Billy Graham had to say in its own church, then it deserved to fall. I also felt that if Billy Graham could get a fair hearing in the Soviet Union, Latin America, and Yankee Stadium, then he ought to get a fair hearing in Harvard Yard.

He came, and he preached on "Peace in a Nuclear Age." He had just come back from the Soviet Union, and many expected him to give an account of the policy discussions he had had there. The Kennedy School of Government was especially interested in this dimension of the visit, as it was a fact that Graham had spent more personal time than any other citizen with American presidents since Eisenhower. Again we had an enormous crowd, and although he did preach about "Peace in a Nuclear Age," it was not about the sort of peace that was brokered in the corridors of power or called for by the Birkenstock crowd. His peace was the peace "that passeth all understanding." He was talking about Christ's peace, and that in an age of uncertainty and dangerous power one could survive spiritually because of the power of the spiri-tual. Some critics were disappointed. "Just more religion," one of them said; but others, particularly the students, were deeply moved.

After one of his sessions, Billy Graham took questions from the floor, and many of them were hostile and rude. One student asked him why he had not used his influence with Johnson and Nixon to end the Vietnam War sooner: Where was "truth to power" when we needed it? Graham disarmed his audience by confessing to the sin of not having been a better friend, in the sense of Christian candor, to those two men, who had needed to hear the gospel from him. He then went further and confessed to the sin of procrastination in the early days of the struggle for civil rights. He said that he had no trouble confessing to these sins of omission and of commission, because he believed in the redemptive love of a savior, Jesus Christ, who, in the spirit in which he received the penitent thief on the cross, would receive him as well. That was his witness, his testimony before God. That was not what many in the audience had been expecting: guilt, yes; contrition, maybe; but redemption and glorification? Well, that was something new.

On Sunday, September 16, 1999, seventeen years later, Dr. Graham came back to Harvard again, to preach in The Memorial Church. There was no controversy this time, only the great expectation of seeing the one whom *Time* magazine had called "The Lion in Winter." He and I were both older, and Billy was suffering with the advanced stages of Parkinson's disease. Of this visible affliction he said, "It doesn't kill you, but sometimes you wish it would." To be certain of a place in the pews, students in great numbers had camped out all night on the entrance porches of the church, and by half past nine in the morning every seat had been taken for the eleven o'clock service. Again, while we could have filled the church twice over with the great and the good from all over New England, we had determined to give priority to students. Graham was both surprised and delighted by his reception, and in his self-deprecating way he suggested that it must have been somebody else whom the students had waited all night to hear.

It was Billy Graham, and nobody else, however, who was the man of the hour. He looked tired, his body did not seem entirely under his control, the lion's mane of golden hair was now white, and in repose he showed the scars and wounds of fifty years on the front lines for Christ. When he began to speak, however, the years seemed to roll away, that liquid magic in his voice began to flow, and his eyes sparkled as of old. His opening words were, "I know I am going to die soon, but that doesn't scare me. Does it scare you?" Then he preached the confident gospel he has shared with the world for a half century. What made him confident was his confidence in the promises of God: that was his sure conviction, and on such foundation was based the only hope worth having, as unreasonable as it was indispensable. We had come to hear and to see something of his hope, and our hope was that we might acquire a little of that hope for ourselves. A characteristic of a Billy Graham meeting is the invitation to accept Christ, to "make a decision for Christ," and I think we all understand that this is neither simply a decision for Christ nor simply an invitation to make a decision, but an invitation to hope, and a decision for hope when all around and within seems hopeless. It is this hope that causes people to give their lives. It is this hope that makes people sleep outdoors all night so that they can be invited by hope to hope in the morning.

An Infused Virtue

None of those speakers had been brought to Cambridge to speak to students about hope, but hope was the substance of their messages and it was so, and known to be so, because they each spoke out of a context of hopelessness. They lived out and through impossible conditions, unreasonable conditions, and reminded us that hopelessness is the context of hope. Starving, dying people by the millions on the streets of Calcutta; racial inhumanity and animosity in South Africa; death, sin, and fear still ruling rampant in the world—to the naked eye and the vulnerable soul these are conditions of hopelessness, studied, analyzed, and fought, but not yet overcome by anything except that persistent and elusive virtue called hope. What is it about hope that allows us to see and to endure the worst that can be seen and endured, and yet, in St. Paul's words, "having done all, to stand" (Ephesians 6:13)?

St. Thomas Aquinas writes, "The object of hope is a future good, difficult but possible to obtain"; and in its relation to faith, he writes of hope:

Hope cannot lead to faith absolutely. For one cannot hope to obtain eternal happiness, unless one believes this possible, since hope does not tend to the impossible, as was stated above. It is, however, possible for one to be led by hope to persevere in faith, or to hold firmly to faith; and it is in this sense that hope is said to lead to faith.[1]

That future good for St. Thomas and the Scholastic theologians is God: the knowledge and experience of God. What we hope for is God. It is as St. Augustine's prayer puts it, "Thou hast made us for thyself, and our hearts are restless until they find their rest in thee." In our creation we are present with God. This is the whole story of Adam and Eve: proximity to God, participation even in the good, which is neither past nor future, but present. The tragedy of the "fall" is that we lose that proximity to the good, to God, and it is now in our past; but we never lose our desire for that good, for God, the fulfillment of which is now of necessity a future good. It is possible to obtain the intimacy and proximity that we lost, but it is difficult. The desire for the future good is placed within us by God: our taste for God, as it were, is placed in God, who alone can satisfy it. God gives us the three theological virtues of faith, hope, and love as means to help us in the difficult but possible task of achieving that future good. These virtues are gifts of God, and are infused into us because we do not possess these qualities in our natural state: we are not naturally believing, we are not naturally hopeful, and we are not naturally loving.

Hope is often referred to as an "elusive virtue." We do not "do" hope as they "do" lunch in California. We can speak of "works" of faith and "works" of love, but it is not so easy to speak of "works" of hope. There can be and have been constructed "rules" of faith and "rules" of love, but it is difficult to conceive of "rules" of hope or a "process" of hope. Hope is not a habit in the sense that discipline, temperance, and fortitude are habits perfected by practice. Hope is something that we do "do," however, for in one sense it enables us, by holding on to a small vision of the great good, to aspire to the difficult but possibly greatest good.

Hope is further elusive in that it is the lack of that future good, the object of hope, that encourages us to persist in hope. The prisoner hopes for freedom and is stimulated in that hope by the very absence of the thing hoped for. The poor widow hopes for relief and perseveres in her hope in direct proportion to the degree to which she is oppressed and constrained. Hope, therefore, is essentially linked to a future condition, a situation yet to be achieved, a desire yet to be fulfilled; and to be without hope is essentially to be without a future. In Dante's great *Divine Comedy,* which is a geography of desires, Paradise is the place where hope is fulfilled, the difficult but possible future good finally and fully achieved. In Paradise there is no more desire, no more longing, for all that one could desire or want is now supplied. We may call it fulfillment, we may call it achievement, we may call it restoration, we may call it reunion: the nature of Paradise is that all passions are spent; there is no work, hence there is no rest, as in the sense of cessation of work, for rest here properly means full and blissful accomplishment. This notion of Paradise as the fulfillment of hope is found in one of the *Book of Common Prayer*'s loveliest collects, in which the faithful say:

> O God, who hast prepared for them that love Thee such good things as pass our understanding: pour into our hearts such love towards Thee, that we, loving Thee above all things, may obtain Thy promises, which exceed all that we can desire.

The source of that ultimate good is God, who has "prepared for them that love Thee" things so good that we cannot understand them; they are beyond our capacity. These future divine goods, the goods of Paradise, are contained in promises that exceed our imagination, that is, our capacity to envision, or our desires, that is, our ability to long for that which we want more than anything else. We do not even know what to hope for, and such hope as we have is exceeded by the blessings of God. Dante and Aquinas understand that Paradise is not the place in which all our fantasies and desires are supplied. They understand Paradise to consist of the satisfaction of only one desire: society with God. That is what the church calls "the blessed hope."

In Dante's *Purgatorio,* hope is still present. The people have not yet achieved the state of blessed hope, but they have not yet forever lost the capacity for hope. Thus, in that Scholastic logic, which marks Aquinas and Dante, they may yet hope for hope. Over the doorway to the Inferno, however, Dante has written those famous words: "Abandon Hope All Ye Who Enter Here." The people can never aspire to see God, and in fact it was their lack of the vision of God that had got them consigned there in the first place. They cannot hope to get out, because hope has as its object "a future good, difficult but possible to obtain." In the case of the damned, the notion of the future good has been perverted, and as hope consists only in the hope of that good which is God, hope itself is gone. The inscription does not mean "Don't hope of getting out of here." It is more like airport security, where, as you pass through the metal detectors, you must leave your hope, along with your keys and other metal objects, on the far side. Unlike airport security, in the Inferno you will not be given back your hope on the other side, for not only is your hope taken from you, but as you descend into the lower depths even the memory of your hope evaporates.

It is interesting that Dante says "Abandon Hope" upon entrance into the fatal and desperate last place, and not "Abandon Faith" or "Abandon Love." He does so, good Thomist that he is, because hope is the theological virtue most intimately associated with the future; it allows one to endure terrible things for the promise of better things and, ultimately, for the greatest thing to come. When you think of it, if ever anybody needed hope, in the sense of actualizing beyond one's circumstances, it would be a person in Hell or the Inferno. To deprive a person of hope — that is, to deprive someone of even the possibility of the future or to consign someone in the present only, always to bear the burden of the past — is the ultimate punishment. Dante wants his readers to understand the point that when hope is gone and there is no possibility of its return, then one is worse than dead.

The Positive Virtue

Hope may be an elusive virtue, but it is also a positive, persistent virtue, for its very existence makes it possible to endure what to those without hope would appear to be hopelessness itself. The positive direction of hope is always forward, and thus hope always hallows, or makes holy, the future. That is the direction of religious people, and the irony of much of religion is that it so often seems backward-looking rather than forward-looking. Hymns like "Give Me That Old-Time Religion" and the very notion of "revival" almost always suggest that things were better off long ago and far away than they are now and that our best hope is in going back to some imagined past perfection.

This religious retrospective probably has as much to do with the notion of "paradise lost" as with anything else. If we could only know "paradise regained," then all would be well and we could, so to speak, put the genie back in the bottle, the apple back on the tree, and Adam and Eve back on the job. The children of Israel, for example, freed from slavery in Egypt, are led by Moses in the wilderness, trekking toward the Promised Land. They should have been happy, delighted with being free at last, and looking forward to a new world order, but early in the book of Exodus we find them whining for the past where, at least in Egypt, they had had the security of bondage and the certainty of three square meals a day, more or less. They actually longed for the fleshpots of Egypt, and they complain bitterly about their forced march into the future. As religious people, it seems, they were always looking backward, always driving by their rearview mirrors.

Modern religious people are the same. We are learning more and more about the appeal of Islamic fundamentalism. An essence of that appeal is not simply antimodernity, a phenomenon almost universally associated with the modern West. There is also the notion that Islamic purity essentially resides in the past in a period nearer to the Prophet, is simpler in its demands, and is therefore more attainable and hence more pleasing to Allah. Thus fundamentalist movement is almost always in reverse, and hope, such as it is, is the achievement of that backward vision, the recovery and restoration of what was and what has since been lost.

Christian fundamentalism, particularly in North America, partakes of much of the same motive: "Let's get back to the good old ways and the good old days." There is a sense of disenfranchisement in funda-mentalist circles, a sense that the clarity of an earlier and more homo-geneous day has been obscured or even nullified by the complexities of the moment. Thus, the only way forward is not forward but backward, and as far back and as fast as possible; and claims to be the most authen-tic "primitive" or "biblical" community are to be taken seriously as proofs of orthodoxy and legitimacy. Unlike many of the great traditions of Jewish scriptural interpretation, where the text has value not only in itself but in the accumulations of meanings that have arisen around it over the centuries, the fundamentalist attitude toward scripture is eager to clear the text of all but its "original" meaning. Any ideas since those of the authors of the text are suspect and must be resisted. Hence, the exegetical energy is always in recovery mode, and any other mode is dis-regarded as inventive, either "adding to" or "taking from"; either way, one is corrupting the purity, and hence the authority, of the original.

This regressive impulse in the interpretation of scripture and in the imaging of the life of a religious community is also seen in the con-struction of the notion of the good life. My colleague and teacher Krister Stendahl always used to warn us against the temptations to play "Bibleland" in our efforts to take seriously New Testament Christianity. By that I think he meant that we should understand that our sacred Christian past was once the Christian future, and that to reconstruct that past, socially, morally, or biblically, except by the historical archae-ologists among us, was essentially to miss the point.

In much of the virtue literature of recent years, one can see this temptation playing itself out in the well-meaning effort to recover some of the ground we have lost as our culture becomes coarser and more self-destructive. If we could only get people to behave the way they used to, we think, then all would be well. Certainly, almost any alter-native to the culture of rudeness, crudeness, and selfishness is wel-come. The cult movie *The Stepford Wives* was produced as a moral parody against the mindless conformism of suburban America in the 1950s, and when I was watching it on television with some friends not too long ago, one of them said, I think in sardonic jest, "Today, it doesn't look quite so bad." Of course it does, but we knew what he meant, for so far and so fast have we moved from even the most con-ventional mores of civility and conformity that in our present deca-dence a little conformity can go a long way toward looking respectable.

Most advocates of the "return to values" for the young imagine a world of Beaver Cleavers, of small suburban boys struggling with moral dilemmas and getting into scrapes not because they are bad, but because they are not yet well enough strengthened to be and to do good. In their case, there is always a wise and good Mom and Dad on hand to help and explain. These advocates do not seem to realize that there are far more Eddie Haskells in the world than Beaver Cleavers; and what was it about that lovely, tree-lined neighborhood that pro-duced both a Beaver and an Eddie?

All of this, including this book, is meant to remind us that the only hope we have ever had has always been out in front of us, leading and guiding us to a place where neither we nor anyone else has ever been before. The good life is not to be found wrapped up and waiting for us like the Dead Sea Scrolls or some ancient artifacts from a culture that once flourished but is now long gone. Not at all. The good life, whose object, like that of hope, is a future good, difficult but possible to obtain, enables us to live now that which we seek. The direction is always forward. We can be instructed by the past, and remembrance is one of the most powerful engines that drives us forward, but forward is the direction in which the engine will move us.

This was early impressed upon me when, as a young boy, I observed the solemn celebration of the Lord's Supper in our little Baptist church in Plymouth. The Communion service was held on the first Sunday of the month and, in earlier days, was preceded by the covenant or prayer meeting of which I have earlier spoken. It was a simple service: the table was laid with a fair linen cloth, and the silver tray that contained the little glasses of Welch's grape juice glistened in the morning light. On either side of that silver centerpiece were two silver trays with carefully cubed white bread, covered with starched linen napkins. The minister stood behind the table, the deacons to his right and left. The service consisted in the communal eating of the bread and the drinking of the cup. That was impressive. What was even more impressive were St. Paul's sober Words of Institution: "For as often as ye eat this bread, and drink this cup, ye do shew the Lord's death till he come" (1 Corinthians 11:26, KJV).

Now, the memorial feature of the Communion had long been made clear to us. We understood that we did this because Jesus had commanded us to do it "in memory of me." Thus, in our Spartan, biblical way, we tried to replicate that simple final meal. Not for us the excesses of the Roman Mass with its talk of sacrifice or the elaborate liturgies of the Episcopalians and the Lutherans. We were even suspicious of the Methodists, otherwise kindred spirits with us, because they knelt to receive a common cup. We knew we were remembering, or, as our pastor always reminded us, "putting back together," for that is what it means to remember.

The part that impressed me most was the forward-looking part where the pastor repeated Paul's words, that we were to "eat this bread, and drink this cup," showing the Lord's death, "till he come." Even as a young boy I understood that that was no historical moment to be recaptured. "Till he come" was about the future, the indefinite tomorrow "when Jesus comes." It was in those words, describing our central Christian act, that I realized that ours was meant to be a faith for the future and not just of the past. Now was never to be good enough, and the past could never be where we were meant to be: we were meant for the future, a time that is not yet and is yet to be. In our little Communion we have often sung, in the words of the old hymn, "A foretaste of glory divine." The only way to get there is by hope, for hope hallows the future and moves us from here to there.

Hope in Time of Abandonment

One of the many criticisms uttered against Jürgen Moltmann's "theology of hope" was that it cultivated a lot of futuristic happy talk that ignored present realities and past experience and postponed everything to an escapist time of fulfillment. "Hope gives hope a bad name," pronounced one wag. Hope does have a wimpy reputation, and as we have less and less confidence in the future, much less the one who holds the future, we have watched the declining value of the power of hope. Bill Clinton campaigned as the "man from Hope." Was hope in his case simply code for ambition? When we say "I hope things turn out well," the implication is that we are not certain that they will and that whether they do or not is beyond our control.

Consider further the total destruction of the word "hopefully." We know what people mean when they say, "Hopefully, we won't be audited." Their meaning is: "It is to be hoped that we won't be audited" or "Let us hope that we won't be audited." The grammarians have lost the war that tells us that this is a misuse of an adverb. "Hopefully" properly means "full of hope" and usually requires a proper noun to modify: that is the point Miss Thistlebottom made over and over again in eighth-grade English. Thus, properly used, we can say, "I hopefully [that is, 'full of hope'] look forward to the dance" or "She hopefully [that is, 'full of hope'] opened the mail." What we mustn't say is, "Hopefully, Pat Buchanan will not run again for president." Pat, you see, is hardly "full of hope," and what we really want to say is, "It is to be hoped that he won't try again."

Some say our grammatical looseness is a form of democratizing speech, but I doubt that. It is largely ignorance of correct usage and a bad habit that makes us think that the adverbial form sounds more literate. There would be no problem if we followed the usage of an older generation, which routinely peppered phrases about the uncertain future action with "D.V.," shorthand for the Latin phrase *Deo Volonte*, or "If God wills it." Often in clerical correspondence of two generations ago you would find "I'll preach in Chicago next Sunday, D.V." or "D.V., I'll finish this book on time," and so forth. What has happened here is that our mangled human-driven "hopefully" is neither good grammar nor good hope, and it tends to weaken everything it touches. We are not, however, in these secular times, prepared to ascribe the resolution of uncertainty to the will of God, and so we are left with an abuse of hope.

Hope is meant to be a word of strength and not of weakness, of anticipation and not of hesitation. In no other way could hope serve people when they have been abandoned by everyone and everything. Hope in time of abandonment is the theme of what is known as the Negro national anthem, "Lift Ev'ry Voice and Sing," written in 1900 by James Weldon Johnson. In a letter to his friend Vernon Jordan, Bill Clinton described himself as the only white man in America who knew all the words to "Lift Ev'ry Voice and Sing,"[2] which remark confirms the view of Toni Morrison that Clinton was our first black president. Once a year or so the song is sung by diverse and well-meaning audiences on Martin Luther King Jr. Day in January, but as many testify in the book published to commemorate the one-hundredth anniversary of the song in

2000, you had to grow up singing it; as the Negro national anthem, it was a phenomenon of the first half of the twentieth century and devoted almost exclusively to black people. In my youth I never heard "We Shall Overcome," and to this day to me it is an anthem of integration and the civil rights movement. "Lift Ev'ry Voice and Sing," however, with its Victorian ambition to high purpose both in text and in tune, was ours and, until fairly recently, ours alone.

In 1935, James Weldon Johnson described how he came to write the song with which he is forever associated:

> A group of young men in Jacksonville, Florida, arranged to celebrate Lincoln's birthday in 1900. My brother, J. Rosamond Johnson, and I decided to write a song to be sung at the exercise. I wrote the words and he wrote the music. Our New York publisher, Edward B. Marks, made mimeographed copies for us and the song was taught to and sung by a chorus of five hundred colored school children.[3]

The Johnsons went on to other things, but by the 1930s the song had entered into general use in the black community, often being pasted into the back of hymnals, and used most regularly in the increasingly popular Negro History Week that had begun to be celebrated in the 1920s in the February week of Abraham Lincoln's birthday. The text is both provocative and optimistic, and the social context even more remarkable, the best and worst of times for black people in America. Slavery had yielded to racial segregation in the South and to simmering racial antagonisms elsewhere. A strong black middle class was emerging, but the very promise of success for black America was perceived then, as now, to be a threat to white America; and within black America, given the long and painful experience of our presence here, we would be better off somewhere else, as Marcus Garvey would propose with his "Back to Africa Movement." Or should we cast our lot in the land for which our father sighed, and make a go of it in America? Those were among the issues swirling about the question of race and black citizenship in 1900, when "Lift Ev'ry Voice and Sing" was written.

Thus, Johnson's words both confront and inspire. In the first verse the note of optimism and affirmation is rung:

> *Lift ev'ry voice and sing,*
> *Till earth and heaven ring,*
> *Ring with the harmonies of Liberty . . .*

The American dream of liberty is ours, and we want everybody to know it. We have reason to rejoice, for we are here now as freeborn men and women, and we want our thanksgiving for that fact to rise as high as heaven on the wings of our song. Faith and hope are a part of this experience: ". . . full of the faith that the dark past has taught us." Even in the bad days of our time here, those times of slavery and those times since when our dreams have been deferred or openly denied, even then we have not lost our faith. Nor have we lost hope, for the present is full of hope. Because of it we are at the dawn not only of a new century, but of new prospects:

> *Facing the rising sun*
> *Of our new day begun,*
> *Let us march on till victory is won.*

To have reached dawn, that is, to have survived the dark night, is no small accomplishment, but the beginning of the day. "Facing the rising sun," means that there is work to be done. Often this first verse was the only verse sung at the start of the school day in the black schools of America. With a reading from the Bible, the pledge of allegiance to the flag, and such other opening acts as the principal or teacher deemed necessary, the school day would then begin with the singing of "Lift

Ev'ry Voice." Ironically, black America had a national anthem before white America, because "The Star-Spangled Banner" did not come into general use until the depression in the 1930s. "Lift Ev'ry Voice" was an exercise in nation building within a nation that was problematic for the Negro.

The second verse is the account of hope in abandonment that was meant to be a lyric exercise in black history and the liberating power of hope. It was a favorite borrowing from the experience of Israel, God's chosen people, who too had been liberated from slavery, and who also had suffered much in their wanderings to the place for which their "fathers sighed." All of this for black America occurred "in the days when hope unborn had died" that was the experience of the stony road and the chast'ning rod, the experience of slavery and the lash. Hope had been stillborn, killed in the womb, born dead, the worst thing that can happen to hope, and yet it is out of this hopelessness, this sense of abandonment, even betrayal, that motivating hope arises. In the face of the death of hope:

> *Yet, with a steady beat,*
> *Have not our weary feet*
> *Come to the place for which our fathers sighed?*

This is the path of tears and of blood, of the gloomy past that in 1900 would have been raw in the memories of the youngest and oldest. To write these words could be considered incendiary. The great white fear in America has always been the fear of a just revenge and retribution on the part of black people, the terrible sense of a justice waiting to happen, for white America knows how complicit it has been in the destruction of black people; and if black people are reminded by other black people of how badly they have been treated by white people, and not just by Southerners, then a revolutionary revenge worthy of the French or Russian Revolution would drench the land in blood. This has always been white America's fear: a call for justice is a call for judgment and, indeed, for punishment, and so for middle-class black children at the turn of the century and at the height of this paranoia, to sing of the "stony road," the "chast'ning rod," the way of tears and the "blood of the slaughtered" seemingly was to provide a "Marseillaise" with which to enflame the populace.

American Negroes, however, aspired to be the new Israel, not radicalized French peasantry. They were not prepared to declare war, but victory. The God of the weary years and the silent tears was now the God who would lead them into the light. Light was the metaphor of the twentieth century, the century of electricity and hence of promise and power, the American century. While we would not forget the dark days where God had met us, nor be seduced by such secular success as was sure to come our way, "drunk with the wine of the world," we would reaffirm under God our loyalty to God and, what was more, our loyalty to our "native land." The "native land" here is not Africa, which a heightened sense of Afrocentricity might have suggested. The native land is America, the land where we were born, and where we constituted a long and legitimate part of the native-born population, a distinction all the more important and significant in the America of 1900 as the country was beginning to be overwhelmed by white European immigration. James Weldon Johnson wants black people to remember and affirm that we are natives, not foreigners, that we belong here by right, that we have earned our way, and that we should defer to nobody either in loyalty or in possession of the land.

Hope, then, is not passive and wistful, but energizing and empowering, and out of stillborn hope has come the object of hope: a future good that is difficult but possible to obtain.

The Anatomy of Hope

Looking at the experience of black Americans, of ancient Israel, and of early Puritan America, we can see certain familiar constituent elements of hope that help us to understand how it works. Hope invariably involves a sense of promise and a sense of future. The promise is by nature about the future, for a promise is the assurance of a postponed gratification, and therefore promise and future are intimately related in the matter of hope. One has confidence in the promise because one trusts the one who makes the promise; and one desires the fulfillment of the promise, and thus desire is an enabling expression of hope. Desire is not in and of itself bad, although it has a bad reputation because it is so often confused with lust and with lusting for the wrong things. Moral theologians always encourage us to pray for right desires, to long for the right and the good. If we desire the right things, the good things, then we are motivated, literally moved, to find the right way to fulfill our desire and thus to accomplish the object of that future good, which is difficult but possible to obtain.

Hope is the elusive virtue because we are not certain into what we should put our hope. For the Christian believer, however, hope is particular and specific. The *Baltimore Catechism* tells us:

> Hope is the theological virtue by which we desire the kingdom of heaven and eternal life as our happiness, placing our trust in Christ's promises and relying not on our own strength, but on the help of the grace of the Holy Spirit.

We do not simply "hope for the best." We hope that we may obtain the promises of God, which will deliver happiness to us. If we are what we hope for, that is, if we orchestrate our lives and desires to fulfill our hopes, then if we hope for goodness we will be good, if we hope for godliness we will desire all that is godly. The desire for the future good, difficult as it may be, makes possible the way in which we conduct and construct our lives between the wish and the fulfillment. We do not do this on our own. Christian hope is not simply personal satisfaction, but the work of a community. On our own we cannot possibly hope to fulfill our hopes. We need one another and the strength of an ongoing tradition, and, as the Catechism points out, we need the help of the grace of the Holy Spirit. Hope is a cooperative, communal venture.

Jesse Jackson never did a better thing than when he spent years visiting the schoolrooms of America filled with dis-spirited black youth and sold them his mantra "Keep Hope Alive." He knew that hopelessness was the ground of despair, and that despair was an antivirtue that led to destruction and, ultimately, to death. The absence of hope was death, and for there to be life and not merely existence, hope had to be present as a force for both present and future. This was no easy thing to achieve in an age of instant gratification, when people would rather have anything now rather than wait for something good later.

Black Christians have always been accused of having a religion of too much tomorrow and not enough today: "Pie in the sky, by and by." The infamous Reverend Ike, famous for his assurance of spiritual access to material success, used to say, "I want my pie right here and now, with ice cream on it." He and many others struck the theme that God wants us successful, and visibly so, here and now. Something of the amazing popularity of *The Prayer of Jabez* has to do with the notion that people ought not to have to live on the speculation of a future hope. Theologies of hope that are only about tomorrow and not about today are increasingly suspect, and, in the minds of many, rightly so.

Not everybody, however, can be successful here and now, or all of the time. Mountaintop experiences are wonderful, but most of us spend most of our time in the valley, and the air on the mountaintop is notoriously thin; few human beings thrive up there, and the only thing one does once up there is figure how to get back down. The Bible tells us that "where there is no vision the people perish," which we can translate in a slightly different but empathetic way to say "where there is no hope the people perish." The secret of the good life as exemplified in those personalities of hope with which we began this chapter consists not in their power or success, but in the indisputable and visible fact that they were possessed of hope, and that their lives were lived in the service of a future good, difficult but possible to obtain.

Heroes were invented so that we might have examples by which to model our own lives. They were placed on plinths and pedestals not to remove them from us or to keep them at a distance, but that more of us might see and emulate them. Heroes are profiles in hope, meant to encourage, stimulate, and enable us. In Hebrews 11, the chapter that begins with the great definition of faith as the evidence of things not seen, the substance of things hoped for, there follows a list of names of biblical men and women whose lives are the very evidence and substance of faith and whose examples are meant to give us hope:

> *These all died in faith, not having received the promises, but having seen them afar off, and were persuaded of them, and embraced them, and confessed that they were strangers and pilgrims on the earth.*
>
> HEBREWS 11:13, KJV

What makes them interesting to us, heroic even, is the fact that while in life they did not achieve what they set out to achieve. It was the hope of that achievement, the sure conviction of the promises, that made it possible for them to do all they did. The theory is that if they could do it, so can and should we.

Once upon a time we found the company of heroes and heroines congenial and inspiring, and we found no shame in admiration, for we were encouraged by the examples of others. The Greeks once said that a people are known by the heroes they crown: observe those whom we admire and learn what we think is admirable. Somehow, however, we have the notion that the heroic and the democratic are mutually exclusive, and that to hold someone else in high esteem is to diminish our own self-worth. So, with a systematic fury, in the last century we set about removing heroes and replacing them with celebrities. The difference between heroes and celebrities is that, on one hand, heroes have qualities we recognize as intrinsically good, and we celebrate our heroes for those good qualities and seek to emulate them. Celebrities, on the other hand, may or may not be good, but we create celebrities and we unmake them as well, and hence the so-called power is with us and not with them. When we expect our celebrities—the creatures of our own hands—to behave like heroes on the basis of their own intrinsic worth and they are unable to do so, how we then despise them and tear them down. Who really cares what Madonna thinks about foreign policy? Who cares about Brad Pitt's views on the economy? What Hollywood teenage stars would you like your children to turn into as adults? What made Donald Trump think we could take him seriously for anything more than he is?

In the search for the good life, more and more people are less and less interested in abstract virtues and qualities and more and more are interested in moral models, in people whose lives portray the values to which we aspire. Having spent a half century tearing down our idols, we are now in the serious business of trying to find models worthy of our hope and emulation. Perhaps the twenty-first century will witness the recovery of the heroic and the renewal of the exemplary.

Where Shall We Put His Statue?

If we want to look for hope alive in human form, we will look, as G. K. Chesterton suggested, where everything is hopeless, for it is only there that "hope begins to be a strength at all. Like all the Christian virtues, it is as unreasonable as it is indispensable."[4] The greatest hopelessness of modern times was Nazi Germany, and so it is there that we must look for a modern exemplum of hope equal to those portrayed in Hebrews 11. That inquiry leads us to one person alone, the solitary Christian, Dietrich Bonhoeffer.

Not too many years ago, in a conversation with a major donor from whom I was soliciting a large gift for The Memorial Church, the subject of Bonhoeffer came up. My donor was from an aristocratic German family on his father's side, with equally strong and well-placed English connections, and as a result coming of age in the mid-1940s was a miserable experience for him. As he put it, "I was in the middle of a family culture war," and he had the psychological bruises to prove it. Although he was devoted to international business, his great moral avocation in life was the life and work of Dietrich Bonhoeffer, whom he regarded as the moral hero of the twentieth century. "Don't you think we ought to have a statue to him at Harvard?" he asked. Naturally, with a large gift in sight, I was inclined to agree, but we were both realists and good friends, and we knew how difficult such an achievement would be in a university that had recently declined to honor its own graduates who had died on the Confederate side of the Civil War. We moved beyond this topic, and he gave us the gift, but his last words on the subject went something like this: "Harvard students need a model for the good life, and Bonhoeffer is as good as it gets."

I had read a little book of Bonhoeffer's while in college, along with works of Barth and of Bultmann, the three "B's" in favor in our undergraduate religion department, and I knew that Bonhoeffer had stood up to Hitler on Christian principles and had been killed by the Nazis in the last days of the war. More than that I did not know; and then, while I was contemplating this chapter on hope and the heroic, I received a Christmas card from old friends in which, with the sobering events of September 11 in mind, they had adapted excerpts from a poem Bonhoeffer had written on December 28, 1944, and enclosed with a birthday letter to his mother. This is the original poem.

POWERS OF GOOD

With every power for good to stay and guide me,
Comforted and inspired beyond all fear,
I'll live these days with you in thought beside me,
And pass, with you, into the coming year.

The old year still torments our hearts, unhastening;
The long days of sorrow, for some, endure;
Father, grant to the souls thou hast been chastening,
That thou hast promised, the healing and the cure.

Should it be ours to drain the cup of grieving
Even to the dregs of pain, at thy command,
We will not falter, thankfully receiving
All that is given by thy loving hand.

But should it be thy will once more to release us
To life's enjoyment and its good sunshine,
That which we've learned from sorrow shall increase us,
And all our life be dedicate as thine.

Today, let candles shed their radiant greeting;
Lo, on our darkness are they not thy light
Leading us, haply, to our longed-for meeting?
Thou canst illumine even our darkest night.

While now the silence deepens for our hearkening,
Grant we may hear they children's voices raise
From all the unseen world around us darkening
Their universal paean, in thy praise.

While all the powers of good aid and attend us,
Boldly we'll face the future, come what it may.
At even and at morn God will befriend us,
And, oh, most surely on each newborn day![5]

The man who wrote did not describe himself as a poet, and in a postscript to another poem, "Stations on the Road to Freedom," he says, "I can see this morning that I shall again have to revise them completely. Still, I'm sending them to you as they are, in the rough. I'm certainly no poet!"[6] Of the "Powers of Good" poem he says nothing. He does not need to. It speaks for itself. By New Year 1945, Bonhoeffer had been in prison since his arrest in April 1943, and the war would be over and Germany defeated within a few months; but before that, Bonhoeffer would be hanged in the last spasm of Nazi horror. He had been arrested for being a meddlesome clerical thorn in the side of the Nazis, having been particularly outspoken on the sin of anti-Semitism; and he was executed when it was discovered subsequent to his arrest that he had been associated with the so-called Officers' Plot, which resulted in the failed attempt of July 20, 1944, to assassinate Adolf Hitler.

Bonhoeffer came from a distinguished family of clergymen and academics and, enjoying the best of German education, he prepared himself for a profession as a clergyman and theologian. He spent time traveling widely, he was a graduate student at New York's Union Theological Seminary, and he was a pastor in London. In 1931 he became a professor of theology in Berlin, and in 1935 head of the theological school of the Confessing Church at Finkenwalde. The seminary continued underground after it had been closed by the Gestapo in 1937. In 1939, he returned to the United States, where he was urged to remain, but he was determined to share in the trials of his people and returned to Germany, where he continued his opposition to the Nazis. He was forbidden by the government to preach, write, or teach, but he did so anyway, underground. These activities caused his 1943 arrest.

Bonhoeffer not only saw the demonic of which Thielicke speaks; he experienced it. First he experienced it in the rise of the Nazis to power in the 1930s, when he saw the human face of evil and what it was doing to his people, his country, and his church. Second, he experienced the demonic through the horrors of his own imprisonment, the accounts of which in his *Letters and Papers from Prison* are chilling; and when we consider that his correspondence was subjected to the most rigorous of censorship, we can only begin to imagine what terrible things he had to endure.

Some might be tempted to think that his faith would protect him from the evils of the day, but nothing could be further from the truth: it was precisely Bonhoeffer's reading of his own faith that had got him into trouble with the powers that be. German pastors since Luther had had a large tradition of quietism, and "Let God do it" was a policy of nonintervention in social and political affairs. Bonhoeffer first resisted and then confronted this historic position in light of the Nazi threat to Christian values. *The Cost of Discipleship*, perhaps his most famous theological work, warns against the temptation of an easy, or "cheap," grace, a faith without cost or consequence in this life. As Geffrey Kelly writes:

> For Bonhoeffer, the "cost of discipleship" was one's own life. Death to self-interest, to sin, and to the drive for security is costly. Yet, if one's life is to be patterned after the example of Jesus Christ, it is the only way for the disciple to share fully in Christ's ministry of forgiveness and in the fellowship of Christian faith. Such is the power of Christ that even the apparent weakness of human suffering can be turned to the advantage of the gospel, and the reconciliation of people in love and freedom is made possible.[7]

Bonhoeffer's hope was not based on the notion of humanity's coming to its senses; nor did he necessarily believe in the theory of a great human deliverer, a prophetlike figure who would bring justice and recompense. Bonhoeffer's hope was placed in what Calvinist theologians called "the sovereignty of God in history." Of this he writes:

> I believe that God can and will bring good out of evil, even out of the greatest evil. For that purpose he needs men who make the best use of everything. I believe that God will give us all the strength we need to help is to resist in all time of distress. But he never gives it in advance, lest we should rely on ourselves and not on him alone. A faith such as this should allay all our fears for the future.[8]

Living in the midst of the greatest evil, Bonhoeffer did not regret his return to Germany in 1939, although had he stayed in the United States and joined Paul Tillich at Union Theological Seminary in New York, he might well have accomplished more than he could possibly have achieved from a prison cell. Writing to his friend Eberhard Bethge from Tegel Prison just before Christmas 1942, he said that he expected to be released into the army in January or February. That would have been a form of execution, for in all probability Bonhoeffer, like other imprisoned intellectuals and clergy, would have been drafted into the army and sent to the Russian front, where he would have become cannon fodder. That assessment was to prove optimistic, however, for he remained in prison. He had no doubts about the rightness of his decision to return to Germany:

> Now I want to assure you that I haven't for a moment regretted coming back in 1939—nor any of the consequences, either. I knew quite well what I was doing, and I acted with a clear conscience. . . . And I regard my time being kept here (do you remember that I prophesied to you last March about what the year would bring?) as being involved in Germany's fate, as I was

resolved to be. . . . All we can do is to live in assurance and faith—
you out there with the soldiers, and I in my cell . . . [9]

Daily, Bonhoeffer was paying the cost of discipleship. In prison his sufferings are magnified by his inability to relieve the sufferings of others,
and his account of the daily brutalities of prison life, the indignities and
humiliations that the staff heaped upon the prisoners, has since
become the stock-in-trade of what we crudely call "Holocaust movies."
What they portray is hardly *Hogan's Heroes*, and one wonders if the per-
petrators of such domestic horrors could ever really be rehabilitated.
Yet Bonhoeffer refuses to resign to fear, and instead invokes every
power for good "to stay and guide me." He is "comforted and inspired
beyond all fear," and thus has room and time to think of his family.
Torments are real, and the time of torment does not hasten along. Only
with God is granted the healing and the cure, and should God choose
to release him and the others from this terror, "to life's enjoyment and
its good sunshine," he hopes that the pleasure of the good times will not
erase what has been learned for good in the bad times. He makes the
Epiphany point: there can be no light without darkness. From this sentiment, not unique to Bonhoeffer but especially poignant in the darkest
and coldest time of the year in a place of hopeless confinement, Martin
Luther King Jr. later would remind us that dark cannot drive out dark,
only light can, and hate cannot drive out hate, only love can.

Even in prison, and perhaps because he is in prison, Bonhoeffer is
able to boldly face the future, attended by "all the powers of good" that
aid and attend him; and whatever the future may bring, and we who
know the end of the story know that it brought death within the sound
of the Allied victory, he is prepared to face it boldly:

At even and at morn God will befriend us,
And, oh, most surely on each newborn day!

Bonhoeffer was executed in the concentration camp at Flossenburg on April 9, 1945, seven days shy of his fortieth birthday. The war would be over in six weeks—

> *As long as matters are really hopeful, hope is a mere flattery or platitude; it is only when everything is hopeless that hope begins to be a strength at all. Like all the Christian virtues, it is as unreasonable as it is indispensable.*
>
> G. K. CHESTERTON

CHAPTER 11

LOVE

BEING AND DOING

God does not love us because we are valuable.
We are valuable because God loves us.
ARCHBISHOP FULTON J. SHEEN

We cannot do great things,
but we can do small things with great love.
MOTHER TERESA

To love God is to love oneself truly; to help another person to
love God is to love another person; to be helped by another
person to love God is to be loved.
SØREN KIERKEGAARD

He who does not love does not know God; for God is love.
I JOHN 4:8

In 1996, I wrote *The Good Book: Reading the Bible with Mind and Heart*. It is a fortunate thing for an author, especially a clerical one, when his book attracts some public notice, and I was then grateful, and I remain so, for the largely favorable attention my book attracted. Many interesting people came my way, and I was invited to do many interesting things, frankly enjoying the success, even the notoriety, and the added pleasure of reaching an audience beyond the appreciative but limited range of my Sunday sermons and academic lectures. I even took a perverse delight in something of the condescending approbation of my theological colleagues in the Faculty of Divinity, one of whom, upon hearing of my good sales numbers, said, "You've certainly done well with that basic little book of yours." The remark, cloaked in collegial *bonhomie*, was borne on the wings of the familiar academic suspicion that a popular book, that is, one that wins readers and makes money, especially on the subject of religion, could not in the end be very sound. I took the remark as a compliment, which, of course, it was not intended to be.

That a book would generate years of enormous correspondence I had not had the slightest idea, for in a lifetime of reading books I had only once taken the trouble to write to an author. When I first came to Harvard, in 1970, the leading humanist in the Faculty of Arts and Sciences was the Johnson scholar, Walter Jackson Bate. His classes were legendary, and he himself was the portrait of the disheveled scholar who had given his life to his subject and therefore life to his subject, the polymath Samuel "Dictionary" Johnson. Jack, as Bate was known to one and all, had written what was then regarded as the best biography of Johnson since Boswell, and he enjoyed an enormous celebrity; I read the book not because I was keen on Dr. Johnson, but because I adored Jack Bate. As I came toward the close of its nearly six hundred pages, I began to ration my reading, as I did not wish to finish it too soon, but in almost a passion I consumed the last chapters and discovered that, when I finally did put it down, the morning sun was rising. I had read through the night, something I had not done since I was a student, because I had lost all sense of time and was completely enveloped in the world and the words that Jack had created. Both exhausted and exhilarated, I immediately tossed off a note of gushing appreciation to Walter Jackson Bate, thanking him for what he had done for me. He wrote back in his own hand on a half sheet of typing paper, saying that mine was one of the letters he would keep.

On my work, *The Good Book*, I received a lot of letters, most of them a delight to receive, and in dark days I read them over again. For every ten letters of this sort, however, there would be one that I rather wished had not come, not because I was afraid of criticism, although as with most people I don't relish it, and I took the correction of errors to heart. I was instructed by many people who knew more than I did, and there were some letters with wisdom I wished had been available to me before I had even set pen to paper.

Then there were letters of anger and violence, which, if I had allowed them to, would have cast a pall over all the nice and good things that the vast majority of the letters had said. For the most part those came from people who took me to task for my chapter on homosexuality and the position I had taken that this last permitted prejudice did violence to the scriptures, to the church, and to the Christian faith. I had known perfectly well that to venture anywhere near this social minefield would excite anxiety and anger, and I was not unwilling to stand by my convictions that homophobia should be exposed for the sin that it is, but I was surprised, although I should not have been, by the vehemence of my fellow Christians on this subject and the intensity of the personal animosity they were pleased to direct toward me and my views. As I told a secular friend of mine, the worst letters I got were from people of self-described Christian conviction who wrote to defend the "faith" against my pernicious views, and who nearly always signed their letters, when they did so at all, with such complimentary endings as "In the love of Christ," "In Christian love," or "For the love of Christ and the Church." Such letters as these reminded me of the aphorism that says that we have just enough religion to know how to hate, but not enough to know how to love.

The experience helped me to better understand a strange encounter I had some years ago with an old theological hero of mine, the famous Bishop of Woolwich, John Arthur Thomas Robinson. In 1963, Bishop Robinson wrote a modest little book, entitled *Honest to God*, that would become an explosive tract for the times. Not having set out to rock the foundations of the Anglican Church, he had as his purpose to put into plain English both the honest doubts of the ordinary secular people he encountered in the gritty streets of his London diocese and the basic truths of the Christian faith, in an effort to make sense of it in the modern world. I was a sophomore at Bates College then, and my professor in Religion 101 had assigned *Honest to God*. It was easy to read, as it was a short, pithy book devoid of most theological jargon, yet written by a man of deep learning and piety. Robinson was already well known as one of the leading New Testament scholars of his generation, and, as only the English would say, he was a churchman "with the mark of preferment on him." It was reassuring to me and to many of my generation that a man of Robinson's stature could address the religious doubts of a college sophomore with a candor that enhanced rather than diminished the ultimate claims of faith. In some sense I owed my rescue from a "religion of doubt" to the facile pen of John A. T. Robinson, although, needless to say, I never wrote to him.

Many years later, while I was on sabbatical leave at the University of Cambridge, where Robinson had been for some years the Dean of Chapel at Trinity College, I determined to tell him what his book had meant to me. I wrote him a short note, and by return mail he invited me to dine with him the very next night in Hall at Trinity. It was a memorable evening, for on that afternoon Buckingham Palace had announced the engagement of His Royal Highness, the Prince of Wales, a graduate of Trinity, to the Lady Diana Spencer, and in celebration of this indirect honor to Trinity, the Fellows at dinner, where I was among the guests, sent for a bottle of vintage port with which to toast the royal good news. After these festivities the bishop and I retired to his rooms, and I proceeded to gush about *Honest to God*. He did not respond as I had expected, and for a very long time he didn't respond at all, and simply gazing into the middle distance. I was not even sure that he had heard me, and foolishly I talked on until, with more sadness than irritation, he said, "I wish I had never written that damned book." He was not repudiating a word he had said, but what he had intended for good had become in a sense the curse of his life. "I shall always be known as 'Honest-to-God Robinson,'" he said, certain that all else would be forgotten; and by "all else," he referred to his considerable scholarship, his years as a noted preacher and theologian, and his work as a pastor of indefatigable energy and effectiveness. The controversy surrounding that book had taken its toll on him, and much of that had been exacted by Christians, his "fellow believers." My effusions therefore were consolation too little and too late, so it seemed, although soon the thunderclouds lifted and we went on to discuss marvelous things, and his company over the ensuing months was one of the delights of my time at Cambridge.

What is it about Christians who, despite professing themselves followers of Jesus Christ—himself "The King of Love"—are yet capable of monstrous acts of hatred, intolerance, and even violence, all in the name of love? The evil in manifestly evil people can be attributed, as it usually is, to an absence of love and a subordination to Satan. They are said to lack the fundamental quality of love that marks those who know God, love God, are loved by God, and hence should love all of God's people. This, perhaps, we can understand in the perversions of a Hitler, a Stalin, or a Pol Pot and the evil ascribed to Osama bin Laden, the genocidalists of Bosnia and Rwanda, and the abuses of the so-called heathen, wherever they are to be found across the pages of history and in the contemporary world. How, though, does one explain the perversions of good people—Christian believers—who in the name of love do hateful things? In the covenanted community of my little Baptist Church, when people say, "I tell you this in love," there usually follows something hateful, spiteful, and fundamentally destructive.

At the risk of confirming the impression of myself as an Episcopal name-dropper, I turn to another old friend, Richard Holloway, who, as bishop of Edinburgh in the last decades of the twentieth century, made a career of offending the faithful by his forthright positions on such unpopular causes as homosexuality. I first came to know Richard when he was rector of Boston's Church of the Advent, a tony Anglo-Catholic parish on Beacon Hill famed for the quality of its sherry in the after-church coffee hours and for the finery of its ecclesiastical haberdashery. His preaching there set the parish on its ear, but that was as nothing compared to his Scottish episcopate. Unlike Bishop Robinson, he relished the fray, and in more than twenty books in almost as many years, he made many Christians angry. In his latest book, *Doubts and Loves: What Is Left of Christianity?* published in 2001, he tells of his motivation in writing yet another book when in well-earned retirement he should be collecting stamps or tending to his roses. It was while attending the 1998 Lambeth Conference, the decennial conclave of the world's Anglican bishops gathered under the patronage of the Archbishop of Canterbury, that he witnessed a strange encounter between Christian believers, many of whom were his fellow bishops, and the unbelieving young people on the campus of the University of Kent, where the conference was held.

As usual, the bishops were roiled about sex, and in particular about the vexed subject of homosexuality. The rising tide of evangelical influence in the Anglican church—a coalition of American conservatives who funded the antihomosexual lobby with American money and political savvy, and Anglican bishops, largely from Asia and Africa, whose biblical morality provided the zeal against any hint of compromise in what they understood to be the church's historic position on sexuality—sought to draw a line in the sand against any further erosion of traditional teaching. Holloway described the confrontation as the most traumatic experience of his life. "Looking back," he said, "I can now see that something profound happened to me during those hours that has radically shifted my attitude to Christianity":

The shift started one lunch time during the conference, which was held on the campus of the University of Kent. Anticipating the debate, a group of Christians mounted a demonstration, holding up banners of the sort that gay and lesbian people are familiar with: *No sodomite can enter the kingdom of heaven. Abandon your evil practices or God will smite you.* My wife got hold of their leaflets and threw them in the nearest bin; but the thing that both heartened and saddened me was the action of a group of students who politely told the demonstrators how offensive and out of place their attitudes were in a university that prized human rights and personal freedom. They were answered with texts from the Bible.

Puzzled, the students tried again to explain to the demonstrators how abusive and insulting their presence was. Again they were answered from the Bible. Finally, the students shrugged their shoulders and wandered off. I don't know what these students' beliefs were, but I am fairly certain that their encounter with Christianity that day scandalised them. They had met blind prejudice and ugly hatred paraded in the name of Jesus, and they had rejected them.[1]

In America, alas, we are all too used to such confrontations in the name of the Christian gospel of love. Fred Phelps, a Baptist preacher from Kansas, has made a career of picketing, with such signs as "God Hates Fags," along with members of his congregation—who are largely members of his own family—the funerals of gay men dead of AIDS. His most notorious picketing of this sort occurred at the funeral services of Matthew Shepherd, who died not of AIDS but at the hands of straight white men who tortured and killed him because he was gay. Less offensive but equally intimidating confrontations are routine in the debates within such mainline American denominations as the Episcopal, Presbyterian, United Methodist, and many of the Baptist Churches, although no one of these Christian communions would argue perhaps as blatantly as Fred Phelps that their opposition to homosexuality is grounded in hatred. On the contrary, the weapon of choice in what so many regard as a "holy war" is love, and the threadbare rubric that gives protective cover to this moral aggression is "Hate the sin, but love the sinner." Alas, it is usually the "sinner," however, who feels the brunt of the hate that is unctuously delivered in "love."

One of the new books of 2002 is Philip Dray's *At the Hands of Persons Unknown: The Lynching of Black America.* It is a terrifying subject, not simply for the monstrous violence imposed by one group of humans upon another, but as well for the fact that the violence was carried out by a culture that prided itself on its Christian civility and gentility. Although lynching was the peculiar instrument of racial control maintained by white Southern Christian Americans, it was a part of the frontier "justice" that was peculiar to America, which otherwise understood itself to lead the world in the values and virtues of Western civilization. Toward the end of the nineteenth and throughout the first half of the twentieth century, lynching increasingly became an activity confined to the Southern states of the old Confederacy, but, as the review headline in the *New York Times* of January 21, 2002, notes, it became "a devastating stain upon the hands of a nation."

The religious dimension of lynching in the culture of Southern America is all too clear. Dray, citing my colleague Orlando Patterson, notes:

After the trauma of Appomatox, the Southern community had to be restored in the most extreme compact of blood, and its God propitiated in the most extreme form of sacrifice known to man. . . . It takes little imagination, and almost no feeling for the workings of the religious mind, to understand how, as the flames devoured the flesh and soul of each Afro-American victim, every participant in these heinous rituals of human sacrifice must have felt the deepest and most gratifying sense of expiation and atonement.[2]

Walter White, who was for many years the executive secretary of the NAACP, and thus very much involved in its anti-lynching crusade, in 1929 wrote concerning the unambiguous Christian origins of lynching:

> It is exceedingly doubtful if lynching could possibly exist under any other religion than Christianity. . . . No person who is familiar with the Bible-beating, acrobatic, fanatical preachers of hell-fire in the South, and who has seen the orgies of emotion created by them, can doubt for a moment that dangerous passions are released which contribute to emotional instability and play a part in lynching.[3]

Although lynching was hardly the exclusive province of the infamous Ku Klux Klan, the Klan did not hesitate to appropriate the already well-established Southern habit of racial vigilantism to its own purposes. Seeing itself as a Christian organization for the maintenance of Southern cultural and religious values, a symbol of the deadly combination of violent patriotism and piety, the Klan attracted as boosters and supporters many Southern clergy. "Jesus Christ himself, it was said, would have been a Klansman."[4]

Neither Dray nor I argue that the Christian South engaged itself in lynching as a form of Christian love. Surely it was a terrible acting-out of a perverse form of cultural paranoia, destroying the feared and despised black man, whose very existence as free and black reminded white Southerners of their own awful defeat at the hands of the feared and despised North in the all too well remembered Civil War. Interesting and compelling as that idea is, however, what interests me is that nowhere in the ample record of this violence is there any notion that this behavior is in any way inconsistent with the gospel of love that lay at the heart of the Christian faith in Jesus Christ, a faith to which Southern white America was conspicuously and self-consciously attached. Indeed, it was always the boast of the Christian South that it was by far a more church-going and Christian place than any other part of America; it is too easy to attribute this phenomenon to a fundamental evil in the Southern Christian.

A comparison with Nazi Germany is perhaps helpful here, for although it was a Christian culture of a particular Lutheran sort that provided the seed-bed for German anti-Semitism, a controversial thesis advanced by Professor Daniel Jonah Goldhagen in his book *Hitler's Willing Executioners*, no one would describe Germany as a hot-bed of Christian zealotry, nor the most conspicuous Nazis as practicing Christians. Indeed, one could argue that in the Wagnerian myths that figured so hugely in the Nazi imagination, it was a pre-Christian Aryan paganism with no pretensions to Christian civilization at all that was the fundamental religious impulse. Both Dietrich Bonhoeffer and Helmut Thielicke, among other contemporary Christian critics of the Nazis, saw National Socialism not as a heretical form of Christianity, but as an anti-Christian appeal to all those forces that centuries of Christian teaching and preaching had sought to suppress.

In Southern Christian America, however, the contest was not between a culture of lynching and a culture of Christ: the culture of lynching was incorporated into the culture of Christ, was not seen at all incompatible with it, and seemingly caused no significant complaint of moral schizophrenia or anxiety. The terrifying analysis is that, although in Nazi Germany one could argue, as many have, that the Holocaust, the rational and systematic extermination of Jews by means of dreadful ovens and camps, was an aberration lasting little more than a decade, lynching in the Christian South was a consistent part of the Christian culture, aided and abetted by it, that lasted with little interference and few significant protests for well over half of the twentieth century. How does one begin to explain this pathology that stems from a religion based on Christian love? How does one explain the highest good of the good life, which is love, when love appears to be so profoundly compromised by those who profess it?

In his 1995 book *The Death of Satan: How Americans Have Lost the Sense of Evil*, historian Andrew Delbanco unearths a modest theological anecdote about Franklin Delano Roosevelt that may help us to formulate an answer. Frances Perkins was FDR's Secretary of Labor, and in her memoirs Delbanco found an account of FDR's first encounter with the thought of the then relatively still obscure nineteenth-century Danish philosopher Søren Kierkegaard. According to Miss Perkins, in 1944 Roosevelt's young minister at Hyde Park recommended to FDR the mystery novels of Dorothy Sayers, and said that she was much influenced by the thought of Kierkegaard. Apparently the president had never heard of him, whom many have called the "other gloomy Dane," and the young minister explained, insofar as he could, the essence of his thought. The president asked questions, took down the names of book titles, and, in Miss Perkins's words, "listened more than he talked." Miss Perkins goes on to describe an encounter with the president some weeks later, when he asked if she had ever read Kierkegaard. She had not. "Well, you ought to read him," Roosevelt said. "It will teach you something." Miss Perkins continues her account of his conversation:

> It will teach you about the Nazis. Kierkegaard explains the Nazis to me as nothing else ever has. I have never been able to make out why people who are so obviously human beings could behave like that. They are human, yet they behave like demons. Kierkegaard gives you an understanding of what it is in man that makes it possible for these Germans to be so evil.[5]

It is a pity we do not know which books of Kierkegaard's so instructed Franklin Delano Roosevelt, but we can congratulate his young pastor for being so ahead of the curve in 1944 as to recommend the thought of a Danish philosopher not much then in the public realm to his theologically untutored but very famous and powerful parishioner. I am indebted to Kierkegaard for his hefty book *Works of Love*, which has for me liberated this third and highest of the theological virtues from the realms of theological abstraction and erotic sentimentality.

> To the Christian love is the works of love. To say that love is a feeling or anything of the kind is an un-Christian conception of love. That is the aesthetic definition and therefore fits the erotic and everything of that nature. But to the Christian love is the works of love. Christ's love was not an inner feeling, a full heart and what not, it was the work of love which was his life.[6]

Since I was ordained to the Christian ministry in 1968, I cannot begin to calculate the number of weddings I have performed. Some have been large, fashionable affairs, others very intimate with only myself and the bride and groom present, and once I took part in a splendid wedding in Winchester Cathedral in England, in the presence of Her Majesty, the Queen. Many years ago I married two old Harvard friends whose service became "The Wedding of the Year" in a local Boston magazine, in part because the groom was a spry ninety and the bride a fetching sixty. Experience has taught me to expect anything at weddings, and it doesn't surprise me that Jesus' first miracle, as recorded in the Gospel of John, took place at a wedding where the wine had run out; it is nothing short of a miracle that most weddings go as well as they do.

Over the years I have had a running battle with couples who wish to have portions of St. Paul's famous chapter on love, 1 Corinthians 13, read as part of the wedding service, not because I have anything against St. Paul, Corinthians, or love, but because I feel it my duty to remind the couple that the love of which the apostle speaks and the love they propose to pledge to one another are not the same thing. Paul did not have marriage in mind when he wrote those words, and he certainly did not have in mind the sort of romantic love we most associate with the wedding industry. This popularity of 1 Corinthians 13 at weddings is a fairly modern one, not much older than fifty years. Before then, the English translation of the Bible most commonly used was the King James Version of 1611, in which 1 Corinthians had the word "charity" in place of what in the Revised Standard Version of 1952 was rendered as "love." As an example of the law of unintended consequences, that modern translation, which determined to liberate Paul's thought from captivity to older notions of philanthropy and social welfare with which "charity" was associated by substituting "love," made Paul's essay on theological virtues a how-to manual for newlyweds and as ubiquitous at modern weddings as "Here Comes the Bride" and the poetry of Kahlil Gibran's *The Prophet*.

"But it sounds so nice, so right," they all say, and that makes it all the more difficult to explain to them that Paul is speaking of a love that is more difficult and demanding than even the love that they are now prepared to pledge to one another. The love of which he speaks here is not that inner feeling and full heart; nor is it the erotic contemplation that is at the secret heart of most weddings. It is not even about love between or for Christians; rather, it is a kind of love that characterizes what Christians do as opposed to how Christians feel. I then thoroughly confuse them by rehearsing the old aphorism that distinguishes the modern American love marriage and the arranged marriages of older cultures. In America, we are told, you marry the girl you love, while in India you love the girl you marry. Ironically, the Indian proposition is nearer to the substance of what Paul is speaking about than the conventional Western notion. It is not that Paul is in favor of arranged marriages, for although he said that it is better to marry than to burn with lust, he does not seem very keen on marriage at all. Rather, the demands of love express themselves in deeds that are not necessarily based upon proximity, kindred, or affection. If love is simply a matter of loving those who love you, then, what is the point? It is the very point that Jesus makes in the Sermon on the Mount, when he asks: "For if you love those who love you, what reward have you? Do not even the tax collectors do the same? And if you salute only your brethren, what more are you doing than others? Do not even the Gentiles do the same?" (Matthew 5:46–47). Demanding that his followers adhere to a higher standard of love, Jesus makes this uncompromising requirement: "You, therefore, must be perfect, as your heavenly Father is perfect" (Matthew 5:48).

It is to this "perfect" love that Kierkegaard in 1847 addresses himself in *Works of Love*, his ambitious exposition of Paul's discussion of love in 1 Corinthians 13. He called what he wrote "Christian deliberations," and he insisted that they were "not about love but about works of love." Love, he says, like every tree, is known by its fruits. Therefore, although we may not be able to define love in the most precise of philosophical terms, we can see and therefore evaluate what it produces, its fruits and its works. Love in this sense may be like Mr. Justice Stewart's definition of pornography, which, roughly paraphrased, went: "I may not be able to define it, but I know it when I see it."

To help us to appreciate what Kierkegaard is trying to do, a task not out of sympathy with the earlier efforts of Augustine and Aquinas to explicate Paul, we should think of love not in terms of what it is, but in terms of what it does, and why it does it. For Kierkegaard, love is, in some sense, hidden: we see only its outward manifestation. The metaphor of the tree and the fruit is a biblical one and has the advantage of familiarity, but one can see the tree, although one may not know what it is until it produces a recognizable fruit. For Kierkegaard, the matter is a little more subtle than that. He likens love to a placid pond or lake, which we know is doubtless fed by some deep and powerfully moving spring, a source invisible to the eye, yet all we see is the result, the pond. Although we can't see its source, we know the pond had to have come from somewhere. We do not simply posit the existence of the spring, the source; we know it is there, and there can be no other explanation for the existence of the pond save for the existence of the spring. One we see, the other we do not, but both are equally real. For

Kierkegaard, what he calls "love's hidden life" is made known to us by its fruits that we recognize.

Words and platitudes may seem to be the fruits by which love is recognized. We should let the mouth speak out of the abundance of the heart, Kierkegaard says, but we make a serious mistake in confusing words about love for love itself:

> But one should not love in words and platitudes, and neither should one recognize love by them. Instead, one should know by such fruits, or by the fact that there are only leaves, that love has not reached its full growth. . . . Thus immature and deceitful love is known by this, that words and platitudes are its only fruit.[7]

The point of his first discourse is that we must believe in love, just as we believe in the hidden source of the lake. If we are to know anything about love and are to be able to recognize its fruits, we must first believe in it.

This may all seem very metaphysical, which is precisely what it is not supposed to be. Love, for Kierkegaard, becomes real when he discusses love in connection with the love of neighbor, for the love of the neighbor is one of the recognizable fruits of love, for him. First, he argues that the kind of love of which he is speaking, and also the kind of love of which St. Paul and Jesus speak, is neither a fraternal nor an erotic love, nor the love of friendship, of marriage, or, in our day, of a relationship. That kind of love he calls "preferential" love. Preferential love is extended to those whom we choose to love, and thereby excludes as well as includes. Christian love, he argues, is self-denying love. That means we are obliged to love even those whom we would rather not. We cannot simply love those whom we would prefer to love, because that is too easy although it is difficult enough, and its problem is that it is only partial. Christian love is supposed to reflect the wholeness of God's love, God who loves everybody. Not only is it the case that we are to love everybody because God does, but only by loving God above all else, with everything we've got, "heart, soul, strength, and mind" as the commandment puts it, can we love the neighbor in the other human being.

"Love for the neighbor is therefore the eternal quality in loving";[8] but, as Jesus was once famously asked in the colloquy that led to his parable of the good Samaritan, such a distinction hangs entirely on the definition of who, or what, is a neighbor. Here Kierkegaard makes it both clear and difficult as to the duties and fruits of love. The neighbor, he argues, is one who is equal, and that means one's fellow human being. He does not put it this way, but I think it amplifies his thought of equality: whoever is born, lives, and is destined to die is our equal, and hence our neighbor. "The neighbor is neither the beloved, for whom you have passion's preference, nor your friend, for whom you have passion's preference. Nor is your neighbor, if you are a cultured person, the cultured individual with whom you have a similarity of culture—since with your neighbor you have the equality of a human being before God." Who then can possibly be our neighbor? After still more specification as to who is not, finally he says: "The neighbor is every person. . . . He is your neighbor on the basis of equality with you before God, but unconditionally every person has this equality and has it unconditionally."[9]

Since the neighbor is everyone who stands equally before God, and we are obliged to love our neighbors, it follows naturally that we are to love our enemies, for despite the fact that we do not like them and they do not like us, they are our neighbors and therefore we are obliged to love them. This has turned a difficulty—loving those who are similar to us—into an impossibility—loving those whom it is natural not to love because they are dissimilar to us and therefore easily defined as enemies. The enemy is by definition the one who is not like us, for the one who is not like us is not likely to like us either, and thus there will be no natural restraint against the expression of our dislike, except fear. Hatred is the fruit of fear, just as perfect love, as the Bible says, casts out fear (1 John 4:18).

In the discussions about the history of lynching, it becomes increasingly clear that the white South behaved as it did not out of hatred, primarily, but out of a fear that led to its expression in hatred. Hate is the fruit of fear. What, however, did those white Southern Christians have to fear from their recently emancipated slaves, most of whom after emancipation were simply content to be left alone to get along? Was it the fear of a just revenge? One can certainly read in the literature of Southern pride the sense that, having lost the Civil War to the superior forces of the Union Army, the entire culture went into a siege mentality for which the greatest fear was always the enemy within. Who might that enemy be? The ones nearest to them, who knew them better than anyone else, and whom they presumed they knew better than anyone else. That enemy within had a grudge, and an all the more fearful grudge because it was justified.

What atonement could be made for three hundred years of chattel slavery? By the scales of ordinary human justice, nothing less than blood revenge would do; and as the best defense, as always, was a good offense, it was the white South that took an unjustified vengeance upon its own black people. It was fear, not hate, that prompted the fierce retribution of lynching. The ostensible crimes were just that: certainly the imagined threat to white womanhood was "real," they thought, and the break-down of the culture of deference was "real," but, as the philosophers say, what was "really real" was the fear that a just God would permit a righteous revolution where justice and not mercy would obtain. So, people of the white Christian South turned the notion of justice and retribution on its head and exacted it first before it could be exacted upon them, and once they had done it, they could not stop: there was no turning back; each atrocity became the justification for the next one. Fear is the agent of hate, and hate begets what we so casually today call the "cycle of violence."

Jesus understood this. That is why he gives two essential points as the "executive summary" of the law: love of God and love of neighbor; and he makes the definition of neighbor so comprehensive that it must include one's enemies, that is, those who are threateningly dissimilar. The most fundamental moral flaw in Christians is this unwillingness to love the neighbor. We will undertake to love the neighbor after our fashion if we can define the neighbor as one who is as like ourselves as possible: the very notion of neighborhood evokes an image of peaceful homogeneity with "our kind of people" on every side. In the stressful days of forced busing in the court-ordered desegregation of the Boston public schools in the late 1960s and early 1970s, when the chairman of the School Committee, Louise Day Hicks, came out in vociferous support of "our neighborhood schools," everybody knew that she meant schools for and with people "like us."

The Nazi ideology of racism fed into centuries of German anti-Semitism that rested on the premise that the Jews were "not like us," but strangely, and therefore dangerously, different. The great cultural tragedy was that the more the German Jews tried to assimilate, the more they wished to be seen simply as "good" Germans, and the more they lent their skills, talents, and loyalties to an ever demanding German identity, that identity was denied them and their efforts to assimilate decried as a plot to infiltrate and destroy from within. The more cultured, successful, and patriotic the German Jews became under the German state, the greater was the perception of them as "other," and dangerously so. Thus again, not first out of hate but certainly out of fear, were they denied the status of neighbor, and as a Christian was required only to love the neighbor, the Jew was outside of the circle of love and thus subject not to love, but to the fruit of fear, which was hate. The person outside of the faith is outside of the protection of the faith: such a person is "out-of-faith," or, in other words now chillingly familiar to us all, an "infidel."

Religion, rather than helping us to cope with the unknown, more often defines the unknown as unclean, evil, and of the Devil. Thus religion often produces anxiety in the face of the unknown rather than confidence or serenity, and, as Richard Holloway points out so clearly in *Doubts and Loves*, "anxiety of this sort always hates the devil more than it loves God."[10]

For Kierkegaard, among the other works of love in addition to the love of the neighbor, is love as the fulfilling of the law. This is not simply an attitude toward the law, of respect for authority, of deference to the powers that be. "Christian love," he says, "is sheer action, and its every work is holy, because it is the fulfilling of the law. This, then, is Christian love."[11]

Once again we are dependent upon a definition: what is the law of which love is the fulfillment? The law of which Kierkegaard speaks is the law of which Paul and Jesus speak. This is the law that reads:

> *Thou shalt love the Lord thy God with all thy heart, and with all thy soul, and with all thy mind. This is the first and great commandment. And the second is like unto it, Thou shalt love thy neighbor as thyself. On these two commandments hang all the law and the prophets.*
>
> MATTHEW 22:37–40, KJV

The law summarized here comprises "all the law and the prophets," that is, everything that one needs to know in order to do what one needs to do. The law is the maintenance of faithful vertical and horizontal relationships. Nothing is to be withheld from God. God is to be loved with the heart, the seat of the emotions and the definition of being; the soul, which is that vital spark of our existence, our most precious element; and the mind, which is our capacity to reason and to distinguish, and the basis upon which we determine our behavior and our belief. In short, in love we are to give God everything. The second part of the summary involves the duty of love toward our neighbor, neighbor as capaciously defined, and a love that is predicated upon a love of self, which is permitted because we are meant to love that which God loves.

God loves us, and therefore we love ourselves. Not only is it that we love God because God first loved us, but it is because God first loved us that we may also love ourselves. Thus, we love our neighbors in the same way that we love ourselves, which is as a child, a reflection of God's creating love. All of the rest of the law is subsumed under this. It may be articulated more extensively, it may consume volumes of codification, but it all comes down to this.

From this, then, Kierkegaard says that the fulfilling of the law is one of the works of love. There are some, he notes, who customarily make a fierce distinction between law and love. Fashionable as such distinctions have been in theological circles, Kierkegaard will not have it. Love is not the opposite of the duties the law imposes: "Only foolishness sets the law and love at loggerheads, thinks, that is, speaks wisely when it relays comments between them or even speaks ill of the one to the other."[12]

Love is doing what the law demands: it is loving God and one's neighbor. How is this manifested? "To love God is to love oneself truly; to help another person to love God is to love another person; to be helped by another person to love God is to be loved."[13]

Perhaps the most compelling of the works of love, the duty that love imposes, is what Kierkegaard calls "our duty to love the people we see." His text here is 1 John 4:20: "If anyone says, 'I love God,' and hates his brother, he is a liar; for how can he who does not love his brother, whom he has seen, love God, whom he has not seen?"

He begins not with a negative, but with a positive: "How *deeply* the need of love is rooted in human nature!"[14] We need to love, for it is our nature to do so, but also we need to be loved, for it is equally our nature to receive love. This is in part what it means to be human. Even Jesus, the man who had everything, Kierkegaard notes, has this need to love and be loved; but having acknowledged the human need to love, the question is formed: Whom shall we love? Kierkegaard answers in a form now familiar to us: it is our duty to love the people we see. This may sound like more of the neighbor love, but he is quick to make an important distinction: it is our duty to love the people we see, but

> not in the sense as if the discourse were about loving all the people we see, since that is love for the neighbor, which was discussed earlier. It means rather that the discourse is about the duty to find in the world of actuality the people we can love in particular and in loving them to love the people we see. When this is the duty, the task is not to find the lovable object, but the task is to find the once given or chosen object lovable, and to be able to continue to find him lovable no matter how he is changed.[15]

Kierkegaard recognized that this is easier said than done. Our natural tendency is to find people we would like to like, and then to try to like them. Worse still, we often choose to love people in principle, but not in fact. Although I have known missionaries whose love for their people was Christlike in its compassion and devotion, not all missionaries fill that bill; I have heard of missionaries who "loved the people" to whom they were sent, but actually found them, person to person, difficult, ignorant, perfidious, greedy, and the like. One can almost hear them saying to themselves, under the difficult conditions of their work: "I must love God all the more because I certainly cannot love you very much."

Kierkegaard has God say, "If you want to love me, then love the people you see; what you do for them, you do for me."[16] We know that in practice we are supposed to do this, but it is very difficult to accomplish. A clergyman friend of mine, rector of a posh suburban parish, very much a man for others and for Christ, and one who took the gospel imperative seriously, once told me how afflicted in the early 1970s his congregation had been with a collection of increasingly eccentric and demanding characters who interrupted the decorum of the place and pressed to the breaking point the liberal sensibilities of the parish. One of them was a particularly obnoxious and persistent man, recently released from a state mental institution and one of the first generation of the homeless. He was easily classified as the deserving poor, and he was too near to be ignored. My colleague, in a moment of confessional candor, asked, "Would you think me terribly wicked if I pray that this man *not* be Jesus?"

Anticipating the anxiety of respectable Christians asked to love the people they see as one of the works of love, Kierkegaard writes:

> When it is a duty to love the people we see, one must first and foremost give up all imaginary and exaggerated ideas about a dreamworld where the object of love should be sought and found—that is, one must become sober, gain actuality and truth by finding and remaining in the world of actuality as the task assigned to one.[17]

As I read this, I thought of all of my friends and contemporaries who went off to eager service in the first years of the Peace Corps. Unencumbered by the theological burdens of missionaries, this first batch left filled with bright expectations of transforming the image of the ugly American. My college roommate went to Fiji in 1965, and I remember his letters, and our conversations on one of his home visits. The work was rewarding, he was learning much, and he felt he was doing some good, which was important; but although he never said it, I had the sense that he felt the natives lacking in gratitude and appreciation. It was not that the natives were taking all of the benefits for granted; it was that my Peace Corps friend was needing more human approbation, and faster than he was getting it. Years later we agreed that he had somewhat idealized the notion of service in the South Sea Islands. In great candor he said that it was the illusion that had made the reality bearable, but that that does not deny the point that in our duty to love those whom we see, we would like to either choose whom we see or choose ideal circumstances in which to see them, circumstances that would make our duty our pleasure.

What is amazing about Kierkegaard is his insistence that love be translated into the real matter of life and not left in some metaphysical purity. Love is to be wide-eyed; love, as it were, with the lights on. A friend of mine once told me of his experience many years ago in working for Dorothy Day in New York City. There was something very earthy and gritty about Dorothy Day, who espoused radical socialist politics and who had a ferocious Roman Catholic faith. She was not given to an easy sentimentality; no female Father Flanagan she! When one of her new young workers complained ever so gently that the poor were very difficult to deal with, Dorothy Day apparently snapped back with something to this effect: "What gives you the right to think that the poor ought to be nice? They aren't, so get over it." I trust I do the memory of a modern saint-in-waiting no violence by this free recall of a conversation about her so many years ago, but it certainly sounds in character.

Creating an imaginary idea of those whom we would love in place of those whom we see is not fulfilling our duty to love the people we see. "The one who does this does not love the person he sees but again something unseen, his own idea or something similar."[18] Kierkegaard illustrates this point by the example of Jesus' love toward his disciple Peter. We all know about Peter, boastful and failing at the same time, for it is Peter who denied the Lord three times, it is he who boasted of his faith and then doubted while walking on the water, and it was Peter, the "Big Fisherman," who always promised more than he could deliver. How does Jesus deal with him?

Christ's love for Peter was boundless in this way: in loving Peter, he accomplished loving the person one sees. He did not say, "Peter must first change and become another person before I can love him again." No, he said exactly the opposite. "Peter is Peter, and I love him. My love, if anything, will help him to become another person."[19]

Jesus did not end his friendship with Peter, and he did not threaten to do so if Peter did not change his ways. "He preserved the friendship unchanged and in that way helped Peter to become another person. Do you think that Peter would have been won again without Christ's faithful friendship?"[20]

As I read Kierkegaard's thoughts on our duty to love the people we see, I thought about what many Christian people saw as the dysfunctional love of Bill and Hillary Clinton at the height of the Lewinsky scandal. I had not read Kierkegaard at that time and so had no theological nail upon which to hang my puzzlement, but I was puzzled, indeed amazed, by the degree of Christian criticism directed toward Hillary Clinton because she would not disavow her straying husband. Much of this criticism came from those Christians who had made a fetish of family values, one of which, presumably, was the keeping of the marriage vow "till death us do part." Everybody but Hillary Clinton, apparently, knew of the errings and strayings of her husband, and thus people were unwilling to believe that she didn't know, for if she did know, surely she would leave him and punish him as he so richly deserved. She was either a victim or a coconspirator. She could be anything, that is, anything but a faithful wife who, in spite of everything, accepted her duty to love the man she, and we, saw. As many people as could easily imagine a man easier to love than Bill Clinton, just as few could imagine why Hillary stayed with him, and decided that it must be insincere. "The Christian point of view, however, is that to love is to love precisely the person one sees":

The emphasis is not on loving the perfections one sees in a person, but the emphasis is on loving the person one sees, whether one see perfections or imperfections in this person, yes, however distressingly this person has changed, inasmuch as he has not ceased to be the same person.[21]

Still, Kierkegaard argues, we may be tempted to think of our love for another as something that soars, that aspires, that reaches up beyond the person where he is, and by that love takes the person to where he ought to be and to where we will him to be. How often have I heard people say their love will transform the objects of their love, it will make them better than they are: "I do not see her faults, only her good points, what she can be, what she means to be." That, in my experience, is a recipe for disaster. The point of faults is to be able to see them, not to ignore them; and a marriage, a friendship, or a relationship that is predicated upon turning a blind eye is one that is likely to stumble badly in the resulting darkness.

Kierkegaard points out that Christian love comes down from heaven, not up from earth. It is the dove descending that brings the good news to Jesus at his baptism, and it is what the old theologians called "Christ's condescension," the opposite of his ascension, that is, the substance of his incarnation or enfleshment on the earth. "Christian love is not supposed to soar up to heaven, since it comes from heaven and with heaven. It comes down and thereby accomplishes loving the same person in all his changes, because it sees the same person in all the changes."[22]

Christian love "grants the beloved all his imperfections and weaknesses and in all his changes remains with him, loving the person it sees." Hillary Clinton was not oblivious to the manifest faults of her husband, for most spouses know all there is to know about the ones they love, and know far more than the rest of us. To many of us looking on, the faults may very well appear egregious and we think direct action should be taken; but often we are taken to task by the spouse in the relationship whom we purport to help, who essentially says, "I am not oblivious, I see what you see and more, but that is who he is, and I love him."

Certainly, as we can learn in any newspaper or periodical or on any Jerry Springer show, there is in this view the basis of significant abuse, and in the worst of cases even death, yet the ideal remains as Kierkegaard puts it: real love consists in loving the people we see, not the people we wish we saw or the ones we wish were there. In fact, love that does not comprehend imperfections cannot be real love, but only partial love, the loving of only that which is lovable, perfect, and acceptable. What reward is there in that? Carmela Soprano could easily love a good suburban husband who didn't cheat on her, who didn't run the mob, and who could pass as an ethnic Ward Cleaver, but what makes *The Sopranos* a cut above nearly everything else on television is not the sex, the violence, or the vulgar language. Among other things, it is the story of the complex notions of fidelity whereby Carmela loves the Tony who is, rather than the Tony she surely must wish him to be. This is not blind love: indeed, the power behind this love is that it sees everything and there are no illusions or mirages, but the genuine love comprehends it all, just as Jesus loved Peter, and Hillary loves Bill. If perfection were the prerequisite of love then we would all be lost, for who would be good enough for our love, and for whom would we be good enough? As Kierkegaard points out, even Christ would have had a problem, and never would he have had a chance to love, for would he have found the perfect person worthy of his love? No! As Archbishop Fulton J. Sheen, television's teaching priest of the 1950s, once said, "God does not love us because we are valuable. We are valuable because God loves us."

Love Defined by Its Absence

One of my happiest and most demanding duties as Minister at Harvard is to bring to the University from time to time the most significant theological minds of the generation. This is a task I share with the entire

Faculty of Divinity, but there is within my special gift the appointment of a public lecturer who, under the auspices of The Memorial Church, will come and hold forth to a large and diverse public, with an emphasis upon undergraduates, as compared with the more specialized audiences of the Divinity School. A history of these William Belden Noble Lectures since their foundation in the 1890s would be a good index of those whom each generation thought to be the leading theological thinkers of the day; even former president Theodore Roosevelt came to Harvard to deliver these lectures and held forth, typically, on the subject of "muscular" Christianity.

Perhaps the most conspicuous public theologian in the world in the 1970s was the Swiss Roman Catholic priest Hans Küng, and in 1976, at the height of his celebrity, I invited him to Harvard. His book *On Being a Christian* had just come out to great critical acclaim and controversy. The acclaim came largely from the Catholic laity and those Protestants who liked Catholics who sounded like Protestants; and the controversy from conservative Catholics, who felt that Küng was giving away the store, and from the hierarchy of the Roman Catholic Church, for whom Küng was a thorn in the flesh. Küng had made a name as an independent thinker when, in 1968, in response to Pope Paul VI's decision not to change the church's condemnation of artificial birth control, a decision that ran contrary to the advice of the pope's own commission on the subject, Küng publicly questioned the doctrine of papal infallibility. His writings on the nature of the church, together with these outspoken views, naturally aroused the interests of those in Rome responsible for maintaining the purity of doctrine and ecclesiastical authority. In 1975 his views on infallibility were formally rejected, and although he was not deprived, he was clearly a man to be watched. His magnum opus, *On Being a Christian*, brought him into a public controversy with the German bishops, who felt that his views on the divinity of Christ were not sufficiently sound. In 1979, after he reiterated his views on infallibility, his license to teach theology under the auspices of the Roman

Catholic Church was officially revoked. This public rebuke, together with a similarly hard line taken by the church against the theologian Edward Schillebeeckx, made something of an intellectual and theological martyr of a scholar whose influence continued to grow perhaps in direct proportion to the church's efforts to suppress it.

His appearances at Harvard in a series of three public lectures in The Memorial Church were widely anticipated, and each evening he spoke to capacity audiences. The front pews were filled with priests and nuns of the archdiocese, not our usual crowd, and after the first evening I mentioned to Father Küng how impressive it was to see so many of his coreligionists present, given that they probably were not supposed to be there. He remarked that doubtless some were curious to see if he was as wicked as the authorities in Rome claimed, and others were perhaps there to give evidence in any future prosecution. He may have been right to have been so wary, but when I asked some Roman Catholic colleagues from Weston, the nearby Jesuit theological seminary, why they had come, they replied quite simply, "For the show: this is the most famous Roman Catholic theologian since Luther!"

Each evening he distributed a set of *thesi*, or propositions, that he intended to discuss, and at the end of each lecture a panel—of theologians assembled from Harvard and other schools—questioned him closely. He heard all of their questions and responded to each at length, and in an extensive period of questions from the floor he gave substantial answers, often in several languages. At the end of each two-and-a-half-hour evening he summarized his positions of that lecture and gave a short précis of that of the next evening. It was a bravura performance, not unlike what must have been normal theological fare in medieval Heidelburg, in Paris, or at Oxford.

Nearly twenty years later, in 1994, he was still at it, publishing in that year what would appear the next year in English as *Christianity: Essence, History, and Future*, another big book. Early on he turns to a familiar question that in large measure it has been his theological mission to answer. The question is "What makes a person a Christian?" He answers that a Christian is one who, in St. Paul's terms, fulfills the law and, like Kierkegaard before him, although a Protestant Dane and not a Swiss Catholic, understands that love is the fulfillment or the work of the law. Thus, a Christian is one who loves God, self, and neighbor. He quotes the famous aphorism of St. Augustine, "Love God and do as you please," which is not an invitation to license but the sure conviction that if you love God properly, what you do will be pleasing to God. Küng says: "Here is no new law, but a new freedom of love. Here love is not understood as a primarily sentimental and emotional inclination" (which it is impossible to have for everyone), "but as a being there for others which shows good will and a readiness to help."[23]

Jesus, for Küng, embodied this new freedom of love, and Jesus' most complete expression of it is found in the Sermon on the Mount. Worried that this "new freedom of love" might seem too abstract, and mindful that the notion of love can be held hostage either to theology or to erotic and emotional sentimentality, Küng proposed to demonstrate the nature of this love as a theological virtue by placing it in relationship to its absence and opposite. He was unable to cite the source of what follows, but used it to great effect:

Duty without love breeds weariness;
duty with love breeds constancy.

Responsibility without love breeds unconcern;
responsibility with love breeds concern.

Righteousness without love breeds hardness;
righteousness with love breeds reliability.

Education without love breeds contrariness;
education with love breeds patience.

Wisdom without love breeds rifts;
wisdom with love breeds understanding.

Friendliness without love breeds hypocrisy;
friendliness with love breeds grace.

Order without love breeds pettiness;
order with love breeds generosity.

Knowledge without love breeds dogmatism;
knowledge with love breeds trustworthiness.

Power without love breeds violence;
power with love breeds readiness to help.

Honour without love breeds arrogance;
honour with love breeds modesty.

Possessions without love breed avarice;
possessions with love breed generosity.

Faith without love breeds fanaticism;
faith with love breeds peacemaking.[24]

Love, in essence, has produced a syllabus of virtues that includes constancy, concern, reliability, patience, understanding, grace, generosity, trustworthiness, helpfulness, modesty, and peacemaking. It was not Küng's purpose to discuss virtue as such; nor was he, after the fashion of Kierkegaard, trying to demonstrate that love is known and defined by its works, although this is indeed a reasonable conclusion to be made at this point. He was trying to demonstrate that a Christian was one who did not simply believe certain things, but who acted in a certain way in fulfillment of the commandment to love God, self, and neighbor. If you want to know what good is, you do good, which is to love in these transforming ways, and you will, by doing, be good. Christians who ask what the good life is and how they might acquire it are supplied with the answer of the New Testament: obey the law of love and follow Jesus. We know that this is easier said than done. We can perhaps attempt the one or the other, but to do both is rather demanding.

That was the dilemma of the famous "rich young man" who comes to Jesus asking what he must do to inherit eternal life. The account is variously found in Matthew 19:16–22, Mark 10:17–22, and Luke 18:18–23. Jesus asks him if knows the law, and he does. Then Jesus tells him to sell his possessions and follow him. This the young man is unwilling to do, and in each text he goes away sorrowful, "for he had great possessions." The conventional reading is that he is prepared to follow the rules, that is, the commandments, but is unwilling to take the risk of discipleship and dispossession. He weeps because he is given an invitation he had sought but now cannot accept. I think he weeps, that is, goes away sorrowful, because he knows that the life he is living, one that is good in everybody's sight, is not really good enough for him: he lacks that "new freedom of love," as Küng puts it, and thus he suffers greatly because he now knows what he is missing. To be ignorant of the way to eternal life is one thing; to know what that way is, to be invited into it, and then to choose not to accept it is the mother of sorrow and misery. Love teaches some of its most powerful lessons by its absence.

The Chief Work of Love: Forgiveness

"To err is human, to forgive divine," said the eighteenth-century English poet Alexander Pope. Is it fair to argue that the chief work of love, that which makes it the greatest of all the virtues, is forgiveness? Twice on the cross Jesus engages in acts of forgiveness. First, he asks forgiveness of those who crucify him: "Father, forgive them; for they know not what they do" (Luke 23:34); and in the second instance, he forgives the so-called penitent thief, who has asked for the assurance of Paradise: "Today thou shalt be with me in Paradise" (Luke 23:43, KJV). What is remarkable about both of these "words from the cross" is that they are words of power coming from one who appears, to all intents and purposes, to be powerless. Here is Jesus, at the moment of his greatest humiliation, exercising the ultimate power to forgive. We do not often associate forgiveness with power, but the power of forgiveness is actually the power to restore life. Those who are forgiven cannot demand it, and cannot forgive themselves. It is literally out of their hands. Only the one who has the power to forgive can exercise it in forgiveness. That is why forgiveness is associated with the divine, the ultimate power source.

Jesus forgives because it is in his nature to do so, and also because he has the power to do so. When Pope said that to forgive is divine he was speaking in the language of power, sovereignty, and authority, for it is only God who can forgive all, for it is only God who knows all and has all authority. Thus, we know who Jesus is on the cross by what he does: he forgives, and he does so not simply because it is the human thing to do, but for precisely the opposite reason—it is the divine thing to do. Medieval theology loved to depict the crucified Jesus as the Sovereign Christ ruling from the cross as mortal monarchs ruled from the throne. The outward and mocking sign of his kingship may well be the crown of thorns, but the true and visible mark of his kingship was the expression of his divine authority to forgive. The point of the uniqueness of Christian forgiveness is made by William Blake, that crazed English seer-poet. He writes:

There is not one moral virtue that Jesus inculcated but Plato and Cicero did inculcate before him. What then did Christ inculcate? Forgiveness of sins. This alone is the gospel, and this is the life and immortality brought to life by Jesus.[25]

The act of forgiveness is indeed an expression of power, but it comes out of love and thus qualifies as a work of love. I will argue that it is the chief work of love.

Pope John Paul II chose to celebrate the two-thousandth anniversary of the birth of Christ with a pilgrimage of forgiveness, and few who saw the photographs will ever forget them, of an ailing pope moving painfully from place to place asking for forgiveness for the sins committed by Catholics over the course of two millennia. He asked forgiveness of Jews and Muslims, and many other constituencies whom Catholics have offended. The Catholic magazine *America* gave the following account:

> Christians have often denied the Gospel, yielding to a mentality of power. . . . They have violated the rights of ethnic groups and peoples, and shown contempt for their culture and religious traditions. Sins against women—"who are too often humiliated and marginalized"—were also mentioned, as were fellow Christians, "minors who are victims of abuse," the poor, the alienated, the disadvantaged and the unborn.[26]

Cardinal Joseph Ratzinger, head of the institution that succeeded the Holy Office of the Inquisition, and not noted as a soft or easy touch, said at the inaugural service of penance on the first Sunday in Lent 2000: "Even men of the church, in the name of faith and morals, have sometimes used methods not in keeping with the Gospel in the solemn duty of defending the truth."[27]

For some, the pope's actions were too symbolic to count for much, for they wanted mention of specific sins and offenses. The fact that he did not mention the Holocaust, or the Inquisition, or certain missionary activities, or certain exclusive theological claims such as "there is no salvation outside of the Catholic Church" offended those who did not in general wish to exercise the power of forgiveness. Catholics such as William F. Buckley objected on the grounds that once you begin a list of apologies, doubtless you will leave someone out, which will create a new offense and perpetuate the cycle. Whether it was too little or too much, the pope's gesture of self-imposed seeking of forgiveness was the biggest boost for forgiveness and reconciliation in the memory of the modern West.

Forgiveness is like a five-act play. Act One is the acknowledgment of guilt. Act Two is the asking of forgiveness. Act Three is the giving of forgiveness. Act Four is the reception of forgiveness, or the experience of the forgiven. Act Five is the reconciliation that results. To this formula one adds acts of contrition, the expression of sincere sorrow, and acts of penance, penalties that must be done as a sign of one's sorrow. What is meant to naturally follow all of this is what the *Book of Common Prayer* calls the "amendment of life," the fundamental change for the better.

For most of us, however, forgiveness is what the injured party extends to the one who has caused the injury, and it is usually from this point of view that we discuss forgiveness: Whom and what shall I forgive? Who or what shall be forgiven at my hands? Since it is divine to forgive, and since the highest example of forgiveness is the forgiveness that God extends to his fallible creatures, all who forgive see themselves in the God role. Although it is true that God both punishes and forgives, God attracts our attention in the forgiveness mode, for it seems contrary to nature. When offended, gods naturally punish, and for them to be offended and then to forgive is unusual; and, as William Blake has pointed out, that is the unique character trait of the God of Jesus, and hence of the followers of Jesus.

Forgiveness involves a sense of understanding. One need not necessarily understand all in order to forgive all: forgiveness can happen without understanding, but understanding all should enable us to forgive much. The reasoning goes like this: "Now that I know why you said such wounding things to me, now that I understand what was behind your strong feelings, I can forgive what you say." Naturally, the harder task is to say that one forgives whether or not one understands. When we ask God to forgive, however, whose property it is to have mercy, we usually ask God to consider who we are, to "remember our frame," and, as with those who crucified Jesus, we really do not know what we are doing, or why. Jesus forgave his captors because he understood that they did not understand what they were doing, and presumably he would have forgiven them even if he knew that they knew what they were doing—and perhaps that would have been an even more powerful homily on forgiveness. If we forgive the Nazis for what they did to the Jews on the grounds that we don't believe they really knew or understood what they were doing, then they are saved, that is, permitted to receive our forgiveness because of their ignorance. They are saved by what they didn't know, or by what we do not know they knew. If we forgive the Nazis for what they did to the Jews, knowing full well that they knew full well what they were doing, then perhaps our forgiveness is more demanding of us but more magnanimous toward them.

When I think of those Southern white Christians who made a habit of lynching black people throughout much of the twentieth century, I find it easier to forgive them because of their own ignorance. The argument goes like this: "Had they known what they were doing, of course they would not have done it, for their moral and Christian sensibilities wouldn't have let them. I must assume they were under the influence of some terrible frenzy that made them take leave of their senses." Yet the accounts of lynch mobs do not show ordinarily decent folk under some perverse spell or victims of a form of social bewitchery; and what is most chilling about the many accounts available to us is the rationality of the crowds which organized themselves into groups to carry out the dreadful tasks. They knew the effect they intended upon the victim, the spectators, and other black people, and they understood their actions as a rational defense of a way of life. After they had done the terrible deed, they distributed souvenirs of the victim's body parts and then resumed their normal activities, often with refreshments. Although it is easier to forgive them because of their undoubted ignorance, it is more magnanimous to forgive them for doing what they knew they were doing, for what the law in its majesty calls "malice afore-thought."

Understanding does ease the undoubted pain of forgiveness. Not long ago, in 1999, I attended a gathering of the Templeton Forgiveness Project. Under the auspices of the Sir John Templeton Foundation, scholars from across the world were collected in Boston's Museum of Science for a conference entitled "Exploring the Unique Role of Forgiveness." Part of its agenda was given over to the consideration of the role of forgiveness in the reconciliation process in South Africa; and as part of it, Dr. George Ellis, former president of the Royal Society of South Africa and a long-standing opponent of apartheid, noted how easy it would have been for both sides in South Africa to capitulate to what he has called "the mutual capacity for darkness." Fear and revenge could have so easily ruled the hearts and minds of South Africa, and it would not have been impossible to imagine the kind of civil violence and mutual destruction in South Africa that has stained Rwanda, a disaster all too familiar in postcolonial African governments in transition. In order to avoid this at any cost, an easy forgiveness, what Ellis calls a "soft forgiveness," would be easily tempting, a sort of policy of "Don't ask, don't tell." "Soft forgiveness," Ellis suggests, "would not be fully satisfactory, for it would not address the root causes of the fears, resentments, and angers at play." Simply to forgive and forget would deprive the culture of the pain necessary to cauterize the wound; to carry on the first-aid analogy, it would be to put a dressing and bandage on an uncleaned wound, which would result in infection rather than in healing.

Many people advised Desmond Tutu and Nelson Mandela to forgo the predictably painful process of the Truth and Reconciliation project, thinking that to hear and to tell the truth would be too painful for all concerned and the memory so affected as to make genuine forgiveness impossible; and therefore what good would be accomplished? The argument was driven by the conventional wisdom, "Let's move on," expressed in the youth argot of the United States as "That was then and this is now." These two leaders understood that the underlying pain and fear on both sides of the racial divide were so deep, so fundamentally a part of the cultural fabric, that what was required was not amnesia, but exorcism, a terrible summoning forth and summing up. No good could be accomplished before this was done.

Gerrit W. Gong, of the Center for Strategic and International Studies, usefully has discussed what he calls the "Strategic Dimension of Remembering and Forgetting" as part of the Templeton Forgiveness Project. In such a process, he argues, understanding is critical. In exasperation with her Irish subjects' inability to maintain the peace of their island, for example, Queen Victoria is said to have uttered, "They learn nothing; they forget nothing": in places of conflict, the conflict itself often seems fueled by the remembrance of past grievances, a painful remembrance that will not go away or subside in intensity. It seems that the farther each generation is removed from the original atrocity or grievance, the more intently it feels obliged not only to remember, but to accelerate that memory in the next generation even more distant. Thus, the equation in such matters is that lack of proximity equals intensity of grievance.

The genocide of Turkey's Armenian population, toward the close of World War I, is kept alive today not by the heinousness of the atrocity, heinous as it was, but by the remembrance of those who remember. While the original Armenians were helpless to defend themselves against the slaughter by the Turks in 1917, their descendants are now empowered by their collective memory to fight against successive Turkish governments that insult memory by refusing to acknowledge a massacre or to remember those who do. Confessions and contrition, not to mention reparations, are essential ingredients in any public acts of apology and forgiveness, and to fail to acknowledge culpability by refusing to remember is the greatest grievance after the offense itself.

Forgiveness is impossible without understanding, and understanding is impossible without the empathy that enables one to enter into the pain and shame of another.

Painful as it has been, the South African Truth and Reconciliation process has probably done more good than harm, since it has made forgiveness not only a national virtue, but also a national necessity. In a small conversation with Nelson Mandela just before he went out onto the Harvard stage to make his speech and accept his honorary degree in 1999, I remember somebody asking him about the relatively peaceful transition from white to black rule: "However did you do it?" was the question. He replied sweetly, "What else could we do?"

Forgiveness is usually taken as the work of the one who does the forgiving. What about the one who is forgiven? Certainly, we can applaud the gracious magnanimity of Jesus on the cross in forgiving the justly condemned criminals, but what must have passed through the mind of that thief when his prayer for Paradise and the pardon that was its precondition were granted and Jesus said to him, "Today you shall be with me in Paradise"? Christians are supposed to forgive because we have been forgiven: we are supposed to exercise the power of forgiveness because we have known the mercy of being forgiven. There is a burden in being forgiven, however, as we are then in the debt of the one who does the forgiving. We are less free, so we think, than when we were unforgiven. We all know those quarrels where one, assuming the moral and tactical high ground, says, in order to bring the argument or dispute to a close: "I forgive you." More often than not, that infuriates the other person, who says, "How dare you forgive me? Who do you think you are? I will not be indebted to you on your terms." Gratitude, as we have said earlier, is a cold emotion.

In *Works of Love*, Kierkegaard has a chapter called "Love Hides a Multitude of Sins," in which he asks the question, "But why is forgiveness so rare?" The answer:

Is it not because faith in the power of forgiveness is so rare? Even a better person, one who is not at all inclined to bear malice or rancor and is far from being irreconcilable, is not infrequently heard to say, "I would like to forgive him, but I do not see how it can help."[28]

Part of what cannot be helped, we imagine, is the person to be forgiven. Doubting the power of forgiveness, we are not sure that the act of forgiveness will not be wasted on the forgiven one. If it is, the person to be forgiven learns no lesson, gains no experience, and remains unaccountable for the offense. The person is incapable of taking the moral benefit of the act of forgiveness, and the forgiveness may serve either to mitigate the questionable action or even to justify it. Perhaps that is why Kierkegaard's questioner thinks it will do no good.

The other reason that many question the helpfulness of forgiveness is what it does or doesn't do to the one who is doing the forgiving. To forgive too quickly or too easily may not be a sufficient balm to the wound and may make the forgiver feel that the forgiven has literally "got away with it," which only builds up additional resentment and complicates the relationship. To forgive, but really never to have forgiven, is one of the most painful of human experiences. We may well say, "I forgive you," as part of the social or moral convention, but the fact of the matter is we haven't forgiven, and perhaps we can't forgive, and thus we feel guilty at our duplicity, frustrated by our lack of satisfaction, and angry at the one we have too quickly and too easily let off the hook.

These speculations, I hasten to say, are mine and not Kierkegaard's, but they are consistent with his statement of the problem raised when he asks the question, "But why is forgiveness so rare?" Premature or insincere forgiveness cannot do much good, all appearances to the contrary. He goes on to say that for forgiveness really to work, the one who forgives must remember what it was like to have been forgiven: "Yet if you yourself have ever needed forgiveness, then you know what forgiveness is capable of—why, then, do you speak so naively and so unlovingly about forgiveness?"[29]

Kierkegaard points out that there are ways of forgiveness that increase rather than reduce the obligations of guilt, and we all know what that kind of forgiveness is like: we want the moral benefit of forgiveness without entirely removing the moral pain from the one whom we forgive. "Only love has sufficient dexterity," Kierkegaard says, "to take away the sin by means of forgiveness":

If I encumber forgiveness (that is, I am reluctant to forgive or make myself important by being able to forgive), no miracle happens. But when love forgives, the miracle of faith happens (and every miracle is then a miracle of faith . . . that what is seen is, by being forgiven, not seen.[30]

In his 1918 Pulitzer Prize–winning play, *The Magnificent Ambersons*, Booth Tarkington created a moral of forgiveness in the painful relationship between the only child of a widow and the man she loves. Out of an irrational adolescent jealousy, nearly Oedipal in its subtle complexity as brought to the screen by Orson Welles, young George Minafer prevents his mother's dying wish to see her old flame, from whom she has been forcibly separated by the son. She dies, and time passes on. Bad things happen to George Minafer, and he gets the comeuppance for which all have been waiting. At the bottom of his experience, sadder and wiser, he realizes what he has done, and he asks forgiveness of the man whom he has defamed and injured for most of his adult life. The man gives it, not because he is a wimp and not because he particularly likes his young nemesis, but, as he says, out of love for the one who loved them both. Forgiveness is an act of love, and love hides a multitude of sins.

Love: The Final Reality

Love is not something we believe, have, keep, or give: it is something we do, and in its doing, love shows forth works. The world is a work of God's love. Children are the work of the love of their parents. Forgiveness is a work of love of one toward another. Love is the supreme virtue, because in comprehending us as we are—and not as we ought to be or would be—it has the capacity to effect in us a transformation, even an exaltation, that will sustain us long after the fresh blush of enthusiasm will have passed. St. Thomas Aquinas defines charity, or love, as "the friendship of man for God." Friendship sounds like an intimate term for so lofty a relationship: a subject of God, yes; an object of God, indeed; but a friend of God? Can it be that love is not exclusively what lovers do, but what friends do? Can it be that the ultimate relationship, friendship, that allows us to overcome our fundamental fear of loneliness and alienation is the one that is most readily available to any and all of us? If the object of love is friendship with God, is not that objective, that friendship, a human as well as a divine enterprise? Often, the Bible asks how we can love God whom we have not seen when we cannot love our brothers and sisters whom we do see, but perhaps there is another way of putting it: if we are able to love our brothers and sisters whom we do see, that is, to literally make friends of God's children as the object of the good life, then surely our friendship with God is made real.

I am convinced that what this generation of young people most desires to know is the love of God and the love of family and friends. I believe that the young are tired of the vulgar ubiquity of the cheap and sensational substitutes for love, and long for the real thing. They know that this culture of "love," as a four-letter word, is, as they say in country and western music, "genuine rhinestone," and that the real thing is capable of sustaining every shock and tribulation known to this tired old planet, including things past, things present, and things to come.

What do our young people want when everything they have turns to dust and ashes? They want something that is patient and kind, not arrogant or rude, not irritable or resentful, but that rejoices in the right. They want something that bears all things, believes all things, hopes all things, endures all things. Now they are growing up, even as collectively we are all growing up, putting away the cultural toys and foolish superficialities of their cultural adolescence, and they don't know everything and they can't do everything, but on them and with them I am willing to bet the future. As was once said of the biblical Queen Esther in a moment of grave transition and opportunity: perhaps our young people, restless, hopeful, and able, have been called to the nation for "just such a time as this."

CONCLUSION

The end is where we start from . . .
T. S. ELIOT, "LITTLE GIDDING"

Over the door to the preacher's room in The Memorial Church, on the eastern wall there is a tablet to one of my predecessors. A handsome thing of bronze, its inscription has caught the imagination of many and provided food for thought for those minds inevitably wandering from the claims of the sermon:

> *Three generations looked to him*
> *As to a Benefactor, a Friend, a Father*
> *His precept was glorified by his example*
> *While for thirty-three years*
> *He moved among the teachers and students*
> *of Harvard College*
> *And wist not that his face shone.*

Andrew Preston Peabody, to whom this tablet was raised by a subscription of his students, died in 1893, having held every office the College had to offer; but it was as "Dear old Peabo," the College pastor and its chief professor of divinity, that he was remembered. Even in his time few spoke of the profundity of his scholarship or the creativity of his theology, even though he published widely and was well regarded as a sturdy, if not inspiring preacher. What appears, rather, to have commended him to the affectionate appreciation of three generations of Harvard students was the impact of his life upon theirs, for when all that has been learned and taught has been forgotten, what remains of an education is the impact of one life upon another. When one life is that of a wise and engaged teacher and the other of a willing and receptive student, then the magic of education begins and can sustain for a lifetime.

The walls of many of our country's older colleges and schools, I suspect, boast plaques erected out of the affectionate gratitude of students for teachers whose precepts were glorified by example and whose influence far exceeded the sum or substance of the subjects taught. Today, however, in most cases the names of those teachers are now forgotten, and their achievements, because they were fashioned from the frail flesh of human beings, have perished with their last memory. The elaborate testimonials now seem sentimental, naive, and out of synch with what the modern college and research university values and celebrates.

Not long ago I was asked to write a piece for *Daedalus*, the journal of the American Academy of Arts and Sciences, in an issue devoted to the problems of the small, elite, residential liberal arts college. My assigned topic was values and ethics, and I was meant to write an essay on the development of these fields in the modern curriculum and their relationship to what is crudely called the "virtue" industry. Having had the benefit of a good education at the very kind of institution under study, I was delighted to participate in the project. The small residential liberal arts colleges felt themselves increasingly caught in a terrible squeeze between the prestigious and much richer major research universities and the ever improving and more cost-effective public universities and community colleges. The question to be addressed in *Daedalus* was this: What are the distinctives of the small, elite, residential liberal arts college in the last years of the twentieth century that can justify their costly tuition and upkeep and, in an increasingly competitive environment, improve their market share? I had not realized until I began work on the project that only about 1 percent of the American college population attends that kind of school.

When we came together in editorial meetings to discuss the drafts of our essays, there was struck early on a defensive tone that suggested that the values of a small academic community committed to teaching and forming the young were simply not being heard, despite the best efforts of recruitment and public relations efforts that had never been more aggressive or sophisticated. "If people only realized what we have to offer," the conversation went, "then all would be well." Would that, however, necessarily be good?

One of the things I discovered in my own research and thinking was the fact that the influence of the research university has had an intimidating, even a perverse, effect upon the small college. The distinctions between the two kinds of institutions were becoming increasingly blurred, with the small college trying to reproduce the environment of the graduate institutions from whom younger faculty are recruited. Certainly, young, freshly minted Ph.D.s are happy to have a job anywhere, and the small liberal arts colleges depend upon them for the periodic renewal of their resources, but in order to keep them happy, the values of their graduate experience are expected to trump the values of the small college. Tenure in most small schools was usually granted on the basis of a combination of scholarship, citizenship, and service: through the ideal of teaching and forming very young scholars as a priority, and a sense of collegiality and institutional loyalty, you would have a formula which until about a generation ago sustained most colleges. I saw these changes over my years of service on two liberal arts college boards of trustees, where, for my sins, I was on the promotion and tenure committees. The professors whose names adorned the tablets in chapels, lecture halls, and libraries could not pass the scrutiny of the new standards. Teaching was increasingly parsed to mean research and publication, and one's standing in one's profession was the defining characteristic. Once upon a time it had been sufficient to say "I teach" at Bates, Brown, Wellesley, or Smith, but now it is "I do sociology," and so on, for the time being at whatever place I am. Forty years ago, at Bates College, professors were expected to live within walking distance of the campus, not simply for their convenience but because it was expected that they would frequently entertain students in their homes. In an era when no one had yet imagined a whole profession of nonacademics devoted to what are called "student services," extra-curricular life was mostly managed by the faculty, who were encouraged to see the field, the rink, and the pool as areas of instruction just as valid and opportunistic as the laboratory or classroom. In such an environment it was understood that the occasion of formal pedagogy was only the beginning of the educational enterprise, an enterprise that claimed as its domain body, mind, and spirit. Over the doors of the gymnasia in such places often would be found the Latin tag from Juvenal, *Mens Sana in Corpore Sano*, a sound mind in a sound body.

It is a different world now, and that is the point of the anxiety on the part of those concerned with the continuing viability of the small liberal arts college. Younger faculty, usually products of a rigorous graduate preparation, wish to get on in their fields and not settle down as so many genial Mr. Chips. They want the books, the grants, the labs, and all of the things that advance their profession and themselves in it, and the colleges that want them want the same thing. "Faculty building," the agenda of every new college president and dean, has to do with attracting and retaining such ambitious people, often at the cost of what are now regarded as disincentives to recruitment: the professor as tutor and moral mentor, the anarchic responsibilities of a faculty-generated democracy, and a priority on the formation of the whole person.

The thought that professors would be expected to live near campus in order to entertain students, or would give up substantial portions of their private time to extracurricular life, is laughable in many places these days. While such research institutions as Harvard, Yale, and Princeton are constantly tinkering with their systems of small residential units designed to replicate the best of the small college environment, they are finding it increasingly difficult to find senior faculty willing to invest time in such enterprises, and junior faculty simply cannot afford to do it, as such work would be considered by the departments a diversion from scholarship. It is an interesting paradox: in order to compete, the small colleges have inadvertently replicated some of the questionable values of the research model, while the research institutions constantly strive to create smaller and more humane units of residence and instruction within their larger structures.

All of this occurs in an environment where the young are constantly asking for the kind of guidance, nurturing, and mentoring that was taken for granted on the college campus of two or three generations ago. At Harvard, as in other large institutions, there is the continual cry for smaller classes, and prospective applicants always want to know the student/faculty ratio. Studies suggest that one can be taught as well in a lecture class of five hundred as in a seminar of five, but what is actually wanted is not better technique but more human contact, and that should be different and better in a seminar of five than in a lecture hall of five hundred.

Our students are demanding a return to the human dimension of teaching. They arrive as freshmen with the glow of expectation on their faces, prepared to be led by great and good teachers into whose hands they willingly commit both themselves and their parents' money. They have suffered through the drudgery of the American high school and the intimidations of college choice, and now, having arrived, they are prepared to be formed and to experience, for example, that nineteenth-century Williams College romantic definition of education: a student at one end of a log and Mark Hopkins at the other. One can almost hear Maggie Smith, as the inimitable Miss Jean Brodie in the movie version of Muriel Spark's 1961 dark novel, *The Prime of Miss Jean Brodie*:

> To me education is a leading out of what is already there in the pupil's soul. To Miss Mackay [the dour Scottish principal of the Marcia Blaine School for Girls in Edinburgh in the 1930s] it is putting in something that is not there, and that is not what I call education, I call it intrusion.

Both James Hilton's Mr. Chips and Muriel Spark's Miss Jean Brodie have been profoundly out of fashion for a very long time now. They are both flawed teachers, and to some—that remote few who even know their names—they have given teaching a bad name. Nobody wants to molder away on a campus, no matter how green and ivy-covered, or to become a figure of fun or of mild contempt, and yet there remains a persistent, gnawing sense that in this enormous educational enterprise, where more teachers and students are in contact than at any other previous moment in the history of the earth, something is not quite right.

I began this book with the conviction that our students have a right to have honored and addressed their high expectations of themselves and of the academy. They actually believe that education ought not to be merely the ingestion of information or the perfection of technique, but an exercise in transformation, "by the renewing of your minds," as St. Paul famously says in Romans 12. The students I have encountered over the years would love to meet in the course of their careers a professor whose "precept was glorified by his example," and I have no doubt that many have had and are having just such encounters. If they do happen, however, it is, alas, against the cultural and institutional grain, and they are the exception and not the rule. I will not argue that college is the only place in which one can contemplate and cultivate the good life, for all of life is for the contemplation and cultivation of the good life, but I will say that one of the original purposes of colleges was to provide a space apart from the world where for a precious moment, as the world counts time, the young and the bright and the old and the wise might engage in the contemplation of the good. For

Aristotle, as we have seen, this was a luxury restricted to a male aristo-cratic class, but the history of education in the West has happily been an ever-broadening of that franchise, on the assumption that the more who are at liberty to contemplate the disciplines and experiences of the good life, the better off they and we will be.

For many, I know, this might sound like a call to retreat to an earlier, simpler age, where the consensus was clear and values shared—a moment frozen in time, as in *The Twilight Zone* or in some idealized gated community where the grass is always green and the people all know one another by name in an exclusive definition of what the good life is. What we yearn for is first an enhanced and inclusive definition of what the good life is, and then the opportunity to both contemplate and pursue it. Our hope for this, while guided and inspired by the expe-riences of the past, is not located there, however, but rather out front and ahead of us, where anything worth pursuing is usually to be found. We must admit that what once held the culture and the civic con-sciousness together, and most particularly so in our older colleges and universities, was a consensus based upon Christian convictions.

Harvard, for example, was founded in large part to complete the work of the Protestant Reformation that had begun in the Continental and English universities in the sixteenth century, and for two hundred years those convictions, constantly evolving and fashioning themselves to the times, continued to serve as basis for community and character. Few of those seventeenth and eighteenth century American colleges that were founded under Christian auspices would claim those aus-pices today: Harvard is positively embarrassed by its Christian inheri-tance and does not quite know what to do with it. The question is asked repeatedly in innumerable campuses across the country: What do we do with the great big chapel in the middle of the quad, a building that was once as important in the formation of institutional and individual identity as is the library that more often than not stands opposite it?

One answer is to privatize the religious and spiritual dimension, that is, to regard it as one of the things that a thoughtful institution provides a needy student. The plethora of college chaplains, spiritual directors, and religious-life staff should not be confused with a revival of vital religion on campus, but should be seen as part of the campus consumer services industry—specialty services to those who request them. The fact that faculty and senior administrators are often far removed from these facilities should suggest something of their marginal role in institutional life.

There is also the so-called Christian college, which in recent years has enjoyed something of a comeback as new constituencies redefine their needs for education consistent with their values. Jerry Falwell's Liberty University and Pat Robertson's Regent College are but the most visible tip of a movement designed to restore the relationship between liberal learning and Christian values; and we hear of Bob Jones University, which lends itself so easily to caricature and stereotype that many to point to it as an example of what bad things happen when you make a shot-gun marriage out of liberal learning and Christian values. Bob Jones may not be its own best advertisement, but it certainly is an indictment of what is not happening successfully elsewhere; it, like so many other colleges, was founded to reclaim learning's intimate relationship to faith and to life. We can dismiss the "small Christian colleges" as artifacts from the past, yet their appeals continue to attract those who realize that some of the fundamental questions of the past continue to require exploration and discovery where a religious ideology has not simply been replaced by the illusions of a secular ideology.

William Sloane Coffin at one point coined the aphorism "small Christian colleges make small Christians." In later years, looking at the abysmal values failure in the culture, and the continuing need for places that build people up rather than tear them down, he revised his opinion. Jud Carlberg, president of Gordon College in Massachusetts, an institution happily defined as a small Christian college with evangelical

convictions, says, "Convictions count." Mindful of the charges against
institutions similar to his own, Carlberg has written:

> We try not to fall into the trap of triumphalism, proclaiming that
> we have found it (truth) and no one else has, but we undertake
> the task (the search for truth) seriously and with humility, not
> assuming before we start that the search will be fruitless. . . . Does
> teaching matter? Yes, but it's not enough. Morality matters.
> Integrity matters. Conviction matters. In short, substance is more
> important than style, and that's why a Christian liberal arts edu-
> cation is worth every penny.[1]

So, we do not turn back but we forge ahead, encouraged by a generation of young people who as never before in modern times are prepared
to lead in the search for noble purpose, the truly good life, if we are prepared to help them to do so. They do not ask us to be their friends or
their pals, for they have plenty of those of their own generation, and
they do not ask us to be their dictators or moral tutors; they want to be
free to make their own choices, and most are prepared to live with the
consequences. They do, however, need us, and they want us to help
them in formulating their choices and in acknowledging a wisdom
greater than their own. They want to take consolation and encouragement from the failures as well as from the achievements of the past, and
to share the benefits of our humanity as well as our wisdom. In short,
they want us to live up to the ideals of collegiate life as sold to them by
the artful prose and pictures of the admissions brochures.

As for those of us who teach and speak where many listen, we have
the task of reconnecting knowledge with wisdom, greatness with goodness, and service with scholarship; and we have to do it through the frail
medium of our own humanity, for precepts must be glorified by
example. A professor is meant to profess, that is, to proclaim not only
the facts and truths of a discipline but as well the connection between

what he does and why he does it. In some sense the passion that once drew so many of us to our subjects, but which has since yielded to the decorous tyranny of "objectivity," must once again be unleashed for all to see, and most especially the young, so that they may begin to understand in their professor's relationship to his work and his students the answer to the perennial question: What's in it for me?

Three of my Harvard colleagues have tried to rekindle this flame of passion for the young in a very popular and unorthodox course called "Talking about Talking." Not a speech course, it is a lively, relatively unstructured public conversation between three of our most distinguished and garrulous teachers: Harvey Cox in theology, Alan Dershowitz in law, and Stephen Jay Gould in geology. Although I have never heard them together, I know each of them individually, and I have heard from students who have taken the course that it was amazing, surprising, and even delightful to hear professors actually talk with passion among themselves about themselves and about the big questions that colleges are usually too busy to answer. In a smaller course, with not one of these superstars, one student said to me about a professor, "I learned so much more from his asides than from his lectures." Naturally; for his lectures were about his subject, while his asides were about his subject and his life.

The temptation in higher education today is to equate big with good, and excellence with rankings, publications and, in some cases, salaries and endowment. As we have seen with the Enron scandal, however, to be big, smart, and rich is not necessarily to create a recipe for goodness, happiness, or success. The collapse of Enron, one of the giants of the American corporate world, and earlier the physical destruction of the twin towers of the World Trade Center — themselves icons to a good life defined by size, wealth, and power — have provided an unavoidable parable for our times. Most people are smart enough to get it: What does it profit a man to gain the whole world, and to lose his soul? What is enduring, and what is ephemeral? When one is under threat and all that is familiar is challenged, how does one cope? What is the relationship between virtue and adversity, success and prosperity? How will we behave, and how will we want our children to behave, when the material things that we most cherish are taken from us?

Once again I suggest that the good life does not depend on good times. The test of the good life, as I have been speaking of it, is in its capacity to get us through and beyond the bad times, the times when things turn sour. Everybody can count themselves good, happy, and virtuous when it takes no effort to be so and there is no consequence; living a good life is what prepares one to endure and overcome when life is not so good. For years at Commencement time I have told my students that the greatest challenge to their education and their faith will be their ability to cope when things don't turn out in the way they had expected, for almost anybody can succeed at success. How do you define success in the context of failure? How do you prepare young people to live wisely and well in a world where they are more likely to encounter failure and defeat rather than success and victory?

I am almost embarrassed to raise such old-fashioned questions that seem to come from an age long passed and dismissed, for they sound preachy, homiletical, and even moralistic, adjectives that the public pundits and intellectual elite have used for generations to castigate thought contrary to the conventional wisdom of the age. Then I remember that I am the Plummer Professor of Christian Morals at Harvard, and that it is my job to preach, to offer homilies, and to moralize. I realize that I have stood at the center of one of the great centers of cultural ambition and, for better or for worse, formation, for now over thirty years, and that I have an enormous body of experience upon which to base my preachy generalizations. In this book I have tried to pursue a middle way, a via media, between the celebrations of a reactionary cultural conservatism and a self-satisfied acceptance of the inevitability of the staus quo, and I write out of the convictions of a convinced Christian who appreciates the classical tradition of Western humanistic scholarship. To do this, I know, in an age that boasts of its post-modernity, is to appear reactive and unoriginal. I do not claim originality as a goal or an ambition, and if what I have discovered may appear original to the young, with whom I daily deal, it is simply a recovery of traditions of learning and discourse of which they are ignorant and have been deprived. Since much of the Western tradition of moral analysis has been consigned to the twilight zone of "dead white males," from which there is no reprieve, and since it is very unlikely that the young will discover much of it on their own, then simply to rehearse the arguments from Aristotle to bell hooks on the question of the good life is to render a revolutionary service.

How well I remember a debate among Harvard students a decade ago, when Alan Bloom had just published his incendiary book *The Closing of the American Mind*. A few students on the Educational Policy Committee of the Faculty of Arts and Sciences asked why Harvard couldn't have a "great books" curriculum, for they knew that at a cocktail party with graduates of Columbia, St. John's, or Chicago, they could not possibly hold their own if the conversation depended upon even a superficial knowledge of the cultural heritage of the West. They were told that "success" in such a setting was hardly worthy of Harvard students. Once upon a time they would have been expected to know, in President Lowell's words, "a lot about a little and a little about a lot;" but now, alas, it was clear that most of them were learning more and more about less and less. The history of their own moral tradition was denied them by those who themselves had enjoyed the benefits of it, and even the right to trash or ignore it.

So, I begin this book with the aspirations to nobility of the current student population, a group of people easily misdiagnosed as conformist, indulgent, and ignorant. From what they seek I then turn to a consideration of the qualities necessary and helpful to make that pursuit of virtue, hence my discussions of failure and success, discipline and freedom. Finally I turn to a reconsideration of the rich tradition of virtue in the

West, first discussing the four cardinal virtues of prudence, justice, temperance, and fortitude; and in the great tradition of Augustine and Aquinas I reserve for last, as the summation of the highest good of the virtuous life, the three theological virtues of faith, hope, and love.

In all cases I have tried to relate the classical formulation of the virtues to the contemporary situation. It seemed neither possible nor good to try to stuff the twenty-first century reader back into a pre-modern universe where the classical formulations may have made more sense, yet if the virtues are what I think they have always been — useful habits to goodness — then they address a human situation and ambition that is fundamentally always the same in attempting to answer the same question, which is: "How can I live a good life?" As a Christian I believe I have an answer, and I am pleased that I did not have to invent the answer but could rely at least in broad outline upon the work of St. Augustine. In his sermon on Psalm 32, Augustine notes that all wish to be happy but none will be but those who wish to be good, This is how he puts it:

> You want to be better off: I know it, we all know it, we all want the same thing. Look for what is better than yourself, so that by that means you may become better off than you are.

How is this to be done? Augustine is not unwilling to tell us quite clearly:

> *Christ is the one who in this life gives us the virtues; and, in place of all the virtues necessary in this valley of tears, he will give us one virtue only, himself.*
>
> AUGUSTINE; *ENARRATIONES,*
> IN PSALM 83, II; PL 33; 1065

Not only is this a good place to end,
but it is a better place to begin.

NOTES

INTRODUCTION

1. *New York Times,* January 20, 2002, sec. 9, p. 2.
2. Alan Wolfe, *Moral Freedom: The Search for Virtue in a World of Choice* (New York: Norton, 2001), p. 183.
3. Wolfe, *Moral Freedom,* p. 184.
4. Wolfe, *Moral Freedom,* p. 200.

CHAPTER ONE

1. Seth Wilbur Moulton, '01, was chosen to give the undergraduate English "part" by the Standing Committee on Commencement Parts, a faculty body with responsibility for the selection of three student speakers to address the gathering at the morning exercises of Harvard Commencement. A University-wide competition is held in early spring, when the final three students are chosen; the "parts" are memorized, and the students deliver them in great style before an audience of some thirty thousand people, thus carrying on a tradition that began in 1642 with the first Harvard Commencement. Moulton has since enrolled in the Officer Corps of the United States Marines. A native of Marblehead, Massachusetts, he is also a graduate of Phillips Academy, Andover, Massachusetts.

2. Neil Howe and William Strauss, *Millennials Rising: The Next Great Generation* (New York: Random House, Vintage Books, 2000), p. 4. The extraordinary and counterintuitive findings of the authors are the result of surveys in the public-school system of Fairfax County, Virginia, which included interviews with two hundred teachers in twelve high schools, middle schools, and elementary schools, and more than six hundred members of the Class of 2000 in four high schools. Among many other things included in their 415-page study, the authors conclude: "Starting very soon, parents and politicians will rivet public attention onto college students—just as they did with these same kids in every earlier age bracket, from the 'Baby-on-Board' of the mid-1980s, to the soccer-mom'd kids of the early 1990s, to the teens of the late 1990s. Campuses will experience a new public spotlight on academic standards, student safety, wholesome community, vigorous political action, and national service." One can only hope that Fairfax County, Virginia, is not too dissimilar from the rest of the country.

3. *Down East: The Magazine of Maine* (December 2001): 81.

CHAPTER TWO

1. *Boston Globe*, May 13, 2001.

2. *Boston Globe*, May 13, 2001.

3. Derek Bok, in Ken Gormley, *Archibald Cox: Conscience of a Nation* (Reading, MA: Addison-Wesley, 1997), p. 413.

4. *Harvard University Gazette* 69, no. 8 (November 2, 1973): 1. Although Mr. Bok never spoke again at the daily service of Morning Prayers, he scrupulously prepared the baccalaureate addresses he gave in The Memorial Church each year to the senior class. Differently stated, they were almost always encouragement to civic virtue and public service.

5. Norman Lamm, "A Moral Mission for Colleges," *New York Times*, October 14, 1986. Subsequent Lamm quotations are taken from this same article.

6. Nathan Marsh Pusey, *The Age of the Scholar: Observations on Education in a Troubled Decade* (Cambridge, MA: Harvard University Press, 1964), p. 145. *The Age of the Scholar* is a collection of Pusey's speeches and sermons over the course of his first decade as Harvard's president. Previous to his Harvard appointment in 1953, he had been president of Lawrence College in Appleton, Wisconsin. A scholar of the classics, he specialized in the field of Athenian democracy. He included many of his baccalaureate sermons in this volume.

7. *Boston Globe*, May 13, 2001.

8. Philip K. Howard, *The Lost Art of Drawing the Line: How Fairness Went Too Far* (New York: Random House, 2001), p. 99.

9. Howard, *The Lost Art of Drawing the Line*, p. 100.

10. Chesterton's aphorisms have long floated in the public domain, and I cannot identify the source of this one. Gilbert Keith Chesterton, in the words of his latest biographer, Gary Wills, described his style "as the representation of familiar things from unsuspected angles, under new lights of the imagination, that we might see them with the innocence of surprise." Gary Wills, *Chesterton*, rev. ed. (New York: Doubleday, Image Books, 2001), p. 8.

CHAPTER THREE

1. Sister Mary Mercedes, O.P., *A Book of Courtesy: The Art of Living with Yourself and Others* (San Francisco: Harper San Francisco, 2001), p. 103.

2. *Boston Globe*, August 22, 1999.

3. *Boston Globe*, August 22, 1999.

4. Jonathan Barnes, ed., *Cambridge Companion to Aristotle* (Cambridge: Cambridge University Press, 1995), p. 196.

5. Aristotle, *Nicomachean Ethics*, ed. Roger Crisp (Cambridge: Cambridge University Press, 2000), bk. 1, chap. 10, p. 18.

CHAPTER FOUR

1. Andy Martin, *London Daily Telegraph*, July 21, 1999.

2. *London Daily Telegraph*, July 21, 1999.

3. William James, "The Sick Soul," from *The Varieties of Religious Experience*, in *Selected Writings* (Book of the Month Club, 1997), p. 158.

4. James, *The Varieties of Religious Experience*, p. 105.

5. James, *The Varieties of Religious Experience*, p. 105.

6. James, *The Varieties of Religious Experience*, p. 185.

7. "The Forgotten Man," *Boston Globe*, May 8, 2001, p. C7.

8. "The Forgotten Man," *Boston Globe*, May 8, 2001, p. C7.

9. Jason Rasky, *Failure Magazine*, 2001.

10. David Levering Lewis, *W. E. B. Du Bois: Biography of a Race 1868–1919* (New York: Holt, 1993), p. 538.

11. Pema Chödrön, *When Things Fall Apart: Heart Advice for Difficult Times* (Boston: Shambhala, 1997), p. 9.

12. Chödrön, *When Things Fall Apart*, p. 9.

13. Chödrön, *When Things Fall Apart*, p. 8.

CHAPTER FIVE

1. Henry Wadsworth Longfellow, "Success," in William J. Bennett, *The Book of Virtues* (New York: Simon & Schuster, 1993), p. 422.

2. William James, *The Letters of William James*, vol. 11 (Boston: The Atlantic Monthy Press, 1920).

3. Andrew Albanese and B. Randon Trissler, eds., *Graduation Day: The Best of America's Commencement Speeches* (New York: Morrow, 1998), p. 215.

4. Albanese and Trissler, eds., *Graduation Day*, p. 217.

5. Albanese and Trissler, eds., *Graduation Day*, p. 217.

6. Patricia O'Toole, *Money and Morals in America* (New York: Clarkson/Potter, 1998), pp. 142–43.

7. O'Toole, *Money and Morals in America*, pp. 142–43.

8. This credo is engraved on the balustrade in front of the ice-skating rink at Rockefeller Plaza, where for the past sixty years millions must have seen it. David Rockefeller Jr. told me that it came from a speech his father, John D. Rockefeller Jr., gave in support of the American entry into World War II. I saw it for the first time upon my first visit to New York City after September 11, 2001.

9. Gary K. Clabaugh, *Thunder on the Right* (Chicago: Nelson-Hall, 1974), p. 180.

10. Bruce Wilkinson, *The Prayer of Jabez* (Sisters, OR: Multnomah, 2000), p. 10.

11. Wilkinson, *The Prayer of Jabez*, p. 24.

12. Wilkinson, *The Prayer of Jabez*, p. 49.

13. Wilkinson, *The Prayer of Jabez*, p. 49.

14. G. S. Galbraith, *Christian Science Monitor*, November 25, 1959, in Theodore Parker Ferris, *The New Life* (Greenwich, CT: Seabury, 1961), p. 120.

15. A. Leonard Griffith, *Illusions of Our Culture* (London: Hodder and Stoughton, 1969), preface.

16. Griffith, *Illusions of Our Culture*, p. 113.

17. Abbott Lawrence Lowell, *Facts and Visions* (Cambridge, MA: Harvard University Press, 1944), p. 35.

18. Lowell, *Facts and Visions*, p. 40.

19. Lowell, *Facts and Visions*, p. 41.

20. Lowell, *Facts and Visions*, p. 41.

21. Lowell, *Facts and Visions*, p. 42.

CHAPTER SIX

1. Vernon J. Bourke, ed., *The Essential Augustine* (New York: Hackett, 1974), p. 165.

2. See James Kugel, *The Bible As It Was* (Cambridge, MA: Harvard University Press, 1997), p. 68. I am much indebted to my colleague, Professor Kugel, for his very useful treatment of these texts. Our readings perhaps differ, but my debt to his good work is considerable.

3. Kugel, *The Bible As It Was*, p. 528.

4. Kugel, *The Bible As It Was*, p. 529.

5. Robert Frost, in *Three Centuries of American Poetry*, ed. Allen Mandelbaum and Robert D. Richardson, Jr. (New York: Bantam, 1999), p. 499.

6. William James, *Varieties of Religious Experience* (New York: Penguin Classics, 1985), p. 508.

7. A covenant was one of the formative documents of New England churches, and Baptists adopted the practice from their Congregational neighbors. This covenant remains in use in the Plymouth First Baptist Church, although modern sensibilities recoil at the rebuke and admonition part of it.

8. Augustine *Confessions* 2.1.1.

9. Bourke, ed., *Essential Augustine*, p. 151.

10. Bourke, ed., *Essential Augustine*, p. 152.

11. Charles William Eliot was president of Harvard from 1869 to 1909. It is interesting that he addressed both men and women, as there were no women in Harvard College at the time, and his relations with Radcliffe College, the "Harvard Annex" for women, were correct but cool.

12. Richard Clark Cabot, *What Men Live By: Work, Play, Love, Worship* (Boston: Houghton Mifflin, 1914), p. xv. For some years I have been a trustee of the Richard C. and Ella Lyman Cabot Trust, and I knew something of the good works of the Cabots. I came across this book, however, by virtue of reading the posthumously published memoirs of an old friend, Mathilde Valenti Pfeiffer. In her account of her early days as a young faculty wife in Cambridge in 1922, she recalled hearing Dr. Cabot speak of his little book that had been inspired by one of Count Leo Tolstoy's stories. See Pfeiffer, *My Americanization: Memoir of a Harvard Wife* (New York: Vantage, 2001), p. 45.

13. Cabot, *What Men Live By*, p. xv.

14. Carl Jung, *Modern Man in Search of a Soul* (New York: Harcourt, Brace, 1931), p. 226.

15. Cabot, *What Men Live By*, p. xix.

16. Cabot, *What Men Live By*, p. xix.

17. Cabot, *What Men Live By*, p. xx.

18. Cabot, *What Men Live By*, p. 335.

19. Willard Learoyd Sperry, "The Desire of Discipline," in *Sermons Preached at Harvard* (New York: Harper, 1953), p. 35.

CHAPTER SEVEN

1. Douglas W. Foard, National Secretary, Phi Beta Kappa, in *The Key Reporter* 66, no. 4 (summer 2001): 1.

2. Walter Earl Fluker and Catherine Tumber, eds., *A Strange Freedom: The Best of*

Howard Thurman on Religious Experience and Public Life (Boston: Beacon Press, 1998), p. 283.

3.   Fluker and Tumber, eds., *A Strange Freedom*, p. viii.

4.   Fluker and Tumber, eds., *A Strange Freedom*, p. vii.

5.   Fluker and Tumber, eds., *A Strange Freedom*, p. vii.

6.   Fluker and Tumber, eds., *A Strange Freedom*, p. vii.

7.   Fluker and Tumber, eds., *A Strange Freedom*, p. 283.

8.   Roger Rosenblatt, *The Economist* (November 24, 200): 90.

9.   Philip Larkin, "Church Going," in *Philip Larkin Collected Poems*, ed. Anthony Thwaite (London: Noonday Press/Farrar, Straus & Giroux; London: Marvell Press, 1993), p. 97.

10.   Paul Tillich, *The Courage to Be* (New Haven, CT: Yale University Press, 2000).

11.   Jedediah Purdy, *For Common Things* (New York: Knopf, 1999), p. 110.

12.   Purdy, *For Common Things*, p. 110.

13.   David G. Myers, *The American Paradox: Spiritual Hunger in an Age of Plenty* (New Haven, CT: Yale University Press, 2001), p. xi.

14.   Myers, *The American Paradox*, p. 258.

15.   Purdy, *For Common Things*, p. 207.

16.   Myers, *American Paradox*, p. 9.

CHAPTER EIGHT

1.   William James, *Varieties of Religious Experience* (New York: Penguin Classics, 1985), p. 508.

2.   Hugh Martin, *The Beatitudes* (New York: Harper & Brothers, 1953), p. 11.

3.   Martin, *The Beatitudes*, p. 11.

4.   Martin, *The Beatitudes*, p. 11.

5.   Martin, *The Beatitudes*, p. 11.

6.   Martin, *The Beatitudes*, p. 11.

7.   William Wordsworth, "The Happy Warrior," in *The Oxford Dictionary of Quotations*, 2d ed. (London: Oxford University Press, 1966), pp. 575ff.

8.   Albert Fried, *FDR and His Enemies* (New York: St. Martin's Press, 1999), p. 222, n. 26.

9.   William A. Ulmer, *The Christian Wordsworth, 1798–1805* (Albany: State University of New York Press, 2001), p. 152.

10.   Allan D. Fitzgerald, ed., *Augustine Through the Ages: An Encyclopedia* (Grand Rapids, MI: Eerdmans, 1999), p. 413.

11.   Thomas Aquinas, *Basic Writings of St. Thomas Aquinas*, vol. 2, ed. Anton C. Pegis (Indianapolis, IN: Hackett, 1997), *Summa*, Q 61, art. 5, p. 473.

12.   Aquinas, *Basic Writings*, Q 61, art. 3, pp. 469–70.

13.   Ward, Hannah and Wild, Jennifer, compilers. *Lion Christian Quotation Collection* (London: BCA, 1997), p. 22.

14.   Martin Luther King Jr., "Letter from Birmingham Jail," http://www.triadntr,net/-rdavid/mlkbirm.htm.

15.   King Jr., "Letter from Birmingham Jail."

16.   King Jr., "Letter from Birmingham Jail."

17. Brian MacArthur, ed., *Penguin Book of Twentieth-Century Speeches* (New York: Viking, 1992), p. 351.

18. Willard Learoyd Sperry, ed., *Prayers for Private Devotions in War-Time*, 2d ed. (Cambridge, MA: Harvard University Press, 1991), p. 3.

19. *Gomillion v. Lightfoot*, 364 U.S. 339, 1960.

CHAPTER NINE

1. Augustine, *The Augustine Catechism: The Enchiridion on Faith, Hope, and Love*, ed. Boniface Ramsey (New York: New York City Press, 1999), p. 30.

2. Phillips Brooks, "The Candle of the Lord," in *The Candle of the Lord* (New York: Dutton, 1910).

3. Daniel Bell, "The Return of the Sacred: The Argument About the Future of Religion," *Zygon, Journal of Religion and Science* 13, no. 3 (1977): 187.

4. Bell, *Zygon, Journal of Religion and Science* 13, no. 3 (1977): 201.

5. Bell, *Zygon, Journal of Religion and Science* 13, no. 3 (1977): 200.

6. Bell, *Zygon, Journal of Religion and Science* 13, no. 3 (1977): 203.

7. Bell, *Zygon, Journal of Religion and Science* 13, no. 3 (1977): 203.

8. Bell, *Zygon, Journal of Religion and Science* 13, no. 3 (1977): 203.

9. Bell, *Zygon, Journal of Religion and Science* 13, no. 3 (1977): 204.

10. Bell, *Zygon, Journal of Religion and Science* 13, no. 3 (1977): 20.

11. T. S. Eliot, *Four Quartets*, in *The Oxford Book of Twentieth Century English Verse* (Oxford: Oxford University Press, 1973), p. 257.

12. Bell, "Return of the Sacred," 207.

13. "Return of the Sacred," 201.

14. David Warsh, *Boston Globe*, May 23, 2000.

15. E. F. Schumacher, in Lucinda Vardey, ed., *God in All Worlds: An Anthology of Contemporary Spiritual Writing* (New York: Pantheon; 1995), p. 728.

16. Helmut Thielicke, *Man in God's World: The Faith and Courage to Live or Die* (London: James Clarke, 1967), p. 8.

17. Thielicke, *Man in God's World*, p. 9.

18. Thielicke, *Man in God's World*, p. 9.

19. Thielicke, *Man in God's World*, p. 166.

20. Thielicke, *Man in God's World*, p. 166.

21. Thielicke, *Man in God's World*, p. 170.

22. David Stout, Obituary of the Reverend Ernest Gordon, *New York Times*, January 20, 2002, p. 31.

23. *Northrop Frye on Religion*, vol. 4, ed. Alvin A. Lee and Jean O'Grady (Toronto: University of Toronto Press, 2000), p. 321.

24. *Northrop Frye on Religion*, p. 322.

25. *Northrop Frye on Religion*, p. 323, emphasis added.

26. *Northrop Frye on Religion*, p. 327.

27. *Northrop Frye on Religion*, p. 324.

CHAPTER TEN

1. Thomas Aquinas, *Basic Writings of St. Thomas Aquinas*, vol. 2, ed. Anton C. Pegis (Indianapolis, IN: Hackett, 1997), *Summa* 2.15, Q 4, art. 7, p. 1105.

2. Julian Bond and Sondra Kathryn Wilson, eds., *Lift Every Voice and Sing: A Celebration of the Negro National Anthem* (New York: Random House, 2000), p. 239.

3. Bond and Wilson, eds., *Lift Every Voice and Sing*, p. 3.

4. G. K. Chesterton, *A Treasury of Christian Wisdom*, ed. Tony Castle (New York: Hodder and Stoughton, 2001), p. 117.

5. Dietrich Bonhoeffer, *Letters and Papers from Prison*, ed. Eberhard Bethge (New York: Simon & Schuster, Touchstone Edition, 1970), pp. 400–401.

6. Bonhoeffer, *Letters and Papers from Prison*, p. 372.

7. Geffrey B. Kelly, *Liberating Faith: Bonhoeffer's Message for Today* (Minneapolis, MN: Augsburg Fortress, 1984), p. 65.

8. Bonhoeffer, *Letters and Papers from Prison*, p. 11.

9. Bonhoeffer, *Letters and Papers from Prison*, pp. 174–75.

CHAPTER ELEVEN

1. Richard Frederick Holloway, *Doubts and Loves: What Is Left of Christianity?* (Edinburgh, Scotland: Canongate, 2001).

2. Philip Dray, *At the Hands of Persons Unknown: The Lynching of Black America* (New York: Random House, 2002), p. 80.

3. Dray, *At the Hands of Persons Unknown*, p. 80.

4. Dray, *At the Hands of Persons Unknown*, p. 276.

5. Andrew Delbanco, *The Death of Satan: How Americans Have Lost the Sense of Evil* (London: Farrar, Straus & Giroux, 1995), p. 191.

6. Søren Kierkegaard, *The Journals: A Kierkegaard Anthology*, ed. Robert Bretall (Princeton, NJ: Princeton University Press, 1946), p. 281.

7. Søren Kierkegaard, *Works of Love, First Series*, ed. Howard V. Hong and Edna H. Hong (Princeton, NJ: Princeton University Press, 1995), p. 12.

8. Kierkegaard, *Works of Love, First Series,*, p. 58.

9. Kierkegaard, *Works of Love, First Series*, p. 60.

10. Holloway, *Doubts and Loves*, p. 240.

11. Kierkegaard, *Works of Love*, p. 99.

12. Kierkegaard, *Works of Love*, p. 106.

13. Kierkegaard, *Works of Love*, p. 107.

14. Kierkegaard, *Works of Love*, p. 154.

15. Kierkegaard, *Works of Love*, p.159.

16. Kierkegaard, *Works of Love*, p. 160.

17. Kierkegaard, *Works of Love*, p. 161.

18. Kierkegaard, *Works of Love*, p. 165.

19. Kierkegaard, *Works of Love*, p. 172.

20. Kierkegaard, *Works of Love*, p. 172.

21. Kierkegaard, *Works of Love*, p. 173.

22. Kierkegaard, *Works of Love*, p. 173.

23. Hans Küng; *Christianity: Essence, History, and Future* (New York: Continuum, 1995), p. 56.

24. Hans Küng; *Christianity*, p. 57.

25. S. Foster Damon, *A Blake Dictionary: The Ideas and Symbols of William Blake, revised edition* (Hanover, NH: University Press of New England, 1988), p. 141. For

Blake, the outstanding example of Jesus was his forgiveness of the woman taken in adultery. He says, "Learn . . . to distinguish the Eternal Human . . . from those States or Worlds in which the Spirit travels. This is the only means to Forgiveness of Enemies" (p. 141).

26. *America*, March 25, 2000.
27. *America*, March 25, 2000.
28. Kierkegaard, *Works of Love*.
29. Kierkegaard, *Works of Love*, p. 295.
30. Kierkegaard, *Works of Love*, p. 295.

CONCLUSION
1. Jud Carlberg, Opinion, Gordon College, May 1999.

INDEX

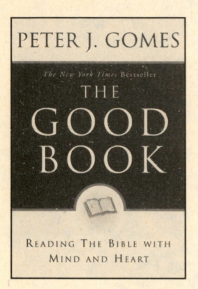
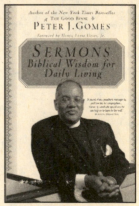